BEYOND
TUESDAY
MORNING

Books by Karen Kingsbury

One Tuesday Morning
Oceans Apart

BEYOND TUESDAY MORNING

KAREN KINGSBURY

ZONDERVAN™

GRAND RAPIDS, MICHIGAN 49530 USA

ZONDERVAN™

Beyond Tuesday Morning
Copyright © 2004 by Karen Kingsbury

This title is also available as a Zondervan audio product.
Visit www.zondervan.com/audiopages for more information.

Requests for information should be addressed to:
Zondervan, *Grand Rapids, Michigan 49530*

Library of Congress Cataloging-in-Publication Data

Kingsbury, Karen.
    Beyond Tuesday morning / Karen Kingsbury.
      p. cm.
    ISBN 0-310-25771-9 (Softcover)
    1. September 11 Terroris Attacks, 2001—Fiction.   2. Terrorism victims'
families—Fiction.   3. New York (N.Y.)—Fiction.   4. Fire fighters—Fiction.
5. Brothers—Fiction.   6. Widows—Fiction.   7. Police—Fiction.   I. Title.
PS3561.I4873B495 2005
813'.54—dc22

                                              2004017038

All Scripture quotations, unless otherwise indicated, are taken from the *Holy Bible: New International Version*®. NIV®. Copyright © 1973, 1978, 1984 by International Bible Society. Used by permission of Zondervan. All rights reserved.

Published in association with the literary agency of Alive Communications, Inc., 7680 Goddard Street, Colorado Springs, Colorado 80920

All rights reserved. No part of this publication may be reproduced, stored in a retrieval system, or transmitted in any form or by any means—electronic, mechanical, photocopy, recording, or any other—except for brief quotations in printed reviews, without the prior permission of the publisher.

Interior design by Michelle Espinoza

Author photo by Shippert Photography

Printed in the United States of America

---

04 05 06 07 08 09 10 /❖ DC/ 10 9 8 7 6 5 4 3 2 1

Beyond Tuesday Morning

(A song)

By Karen Kingsbury

(Chorus)
Let's not move too far beyond Tuesday morning
Let's not forget all the lives that were lost
Let's not move too far beyond Tuesday morning
Remember the heroes remember the cost.

Time has moved on as time always will do
Healing has come both to me and to you.
The towers that stood now stand only at times
A memory that's fading from all of our minds.

The flag on your bumper is yellowed and frayed
It's only on Sundays we take time to pray
For families of folks who did nothing but go
To work Tuesday morning and never came home.

(Bridge)
Still they are crying and still they are trying
To understand all that America lost
Take time to remember, there is no denying
That one Tuesday morning and all that it cost.

Smile at a stranger or do a good deed
Help out a neighbor, love someone in need
Do it to honor the women and men
Who died Tuesday morning and ever since then.

Let's not move too far beyond Tuesday morning
Let's not forget all the lives that were lost
Let's not move too far beyond Tuesday morning
Remember the heroes, remember the cost.

ACKNOWLEDGMENTS

As always, when I bring my heart's thoughts and dreams to the computer keyboard, it's not without the help of a host of people.

In the writing of *Beyond Tuesday Morning*, I must first thank the people of St. Paul's Chapel. It is every bit the mighty mission I tried to make it in the fictional story that plays out on the following pages. The volunteers at St. Paul's continue to play a role in a healing that is far from complete. I learned much from my time at St. Paul's, talking to volunteers and studying the mementos and memorabilia there.

While the rest of us watched in horror that terrible Tuesday morning as the Twin Towers collapsed, we eventually got on with our lives. Not so for many of the people in Manhattan—especially for hundreds of firefighters and their families. Because of that, I am grateful to each of you who still devotes his or her time to the healing process at Ground Zero.

Thanks also to the information office of the fire department of New York. With the cooperation of this office, we were able to send a thousand copies of *One Tuesday Morning*, the first book in this set, to the FDNY—four books per station. The letters I've received from New York City firefighters have often left me in tears.

They tell me they are desperate for light and hope, that the pain lives on every day. And that, in many cases, reading *One Tuesday Morning* gave them a reason to believe again, a reason to turn back to God and their families after being consumed by pain, grief—and even hatred.

I thank each one of you who wrote those letters, because it was your story that I had to complete in this book. Not literally, of course. *Beyond Tuesday Morning* is fictional, and any similarity to real-life people or situations is purely coincidental. But I pray that the hurting people in New York find hope the way Jamie Bryan does in this sequel.

The fact is, with God, the story need not end in grief and despair but with *life*. I pray you'll find that message in this book.

Also thanks to my brilliant editor, Karen Ball, and to marketing expert Sue Brower, and to all my friends at Zondervan Publishing. Thank you for taking my idea about a story of life springing from the ashes of September 11 and helping it become what it is today. Also, a thanks to Cheryl Orefice who listened while I brainstormed the possibilities of *Beyond Tuesday Morning*.

A special thanks to my mother, Anne Kingsbury, who is also my assistant. You have a mind like mine and a heart for the ministry these books have become. Your presence in my life is heaven sent. I love you, Mom. I couldn't do my job without you. And to my father, Ted, who continues to be my greatest cheerleader. Dad, remember when I was writing poetry as a teenager, and you told me I could do anything with God's help? Even becoming an author? Well, I believed you—and look what God has done! I love you more every day.

Thanks also to my agent, Rick Christian. Rick, you pray for me and push me and protect me in ways that go beyond my highest expectations, proving I'm the most blessed writer of all. I stand amazed at your talents—and grateful that beyond anything in the publishing world, you desire God's will for my life, that I serve Him, that I have time for my beloved husband and children, and that I listen to His call. How amazing it is to have found you!

When it comes to crunch time, and I find myself pouring out my heart on deadline, lots of people come together to fill in the gaps. With six kids, it would be impossible otherwise. And so a warm and heartfelt thanks to my husband Donald, my kids—who don't mind having tuna sandwiches for a week on end, my sister Tricia, my parents again, and my good friends Cindy Weil, the Schmidt family, the Chapmans, Thayne Guymon, and Aaron Hisel, all of whom have on occasion caught frogs with Austin in my place.

Thanks also to my special prayer warriors, Ann Hudson, Sylvia Wallgren, Sonya Fitzpatrick, Marcia Bender, Christine Wessel, Teresa Thacker, and so many others who have written to me with promises of prayer. I feel you lifting my ministry up to Jesus time and time again. Sometimes with every breath. I couldn't do this work without your support. Please, please, please keep praying.

And a thanks to my extended family, and to my friends Randy and Vicky and Lila Graves, Bobbi and Tika Terret, John and Melinda Chapman, Mark and Marilyn Atteberry, Kathy Santschi, and my many friends at New Heights Church, Christian Youth Theater, and at the local schools. Your encouragement, love, and support are a constant source of strength.

Also thanks to my retail family across the U.S. and Canada. I've met so many of you—store owners, managers, and frontliners—these past few years, and I still mean what I said back then. You are the other half of what I do. I'm so grateful for the way you've partnered with me. Please know that I continue to send people your way, and that I will always pray for your ministry in books.

Finally, thanks to God Almighty. He is the reason any of this is possible. The words are His, the ideas are His, the gift is His. I pray I might remain obedient to all He is asking of me in this season of writing. Thank You, God . . . thank You.

Dedicated to

Donald, my prince charming, who is forever praying for me, encouraging me, and giving me reasons to laugh. The wings are from God, but you are the wind. Every letter I receive, every life changed by the words God gives me to write, all of it is as much your ministry as mine. That's how much I rely on your love and prayers. You told me when we married that you'd always love God more than me. Ever since then I've been thanking the Lord for that truth, because the love and light you bring to me and our children could only come from heaven above. I love you, Donald. With you, life is always a dance.

Kelsey, my precious daughter, so grown-up. Sometimes I look at you and do a double take. When did that kindergartner with the poofy bangs become the beautiful fifteen-year-old with model good looks? Back then I would say, "Who made you so pretty, Kelsey?" You'd giggle and answer, "Jesus!" It's still so true today, only now, as you grow closer to Him, I see an even greater beauty. The beauty of Christ within you. I'm in awe of your choices, your high standards, your determination to keep God first in your life. High school already, Kelsey? Can you believe it? Your life is everything you dreamed about and the ride gets faster all the time. But in the quiet places of my heart you will always be my little Norm. I love you.

Tyler, my Broadway boy. Once upon a yesterday you would find whoever was home, stop what we were doing, and gather us together. Audience in place, you would sing. Song after song after song. Not regular kid songs, but songs from *Annie, Oklahoma, Les Misérables,* and *Phantom of the Opera.* We always knew you had a gift, but now we gather together in one room *hoping* you'll sing. More people are listening, Tyler, and many more will in years to come. You are only twelve, but the gift God has given you in song and drama and writing leaves me speechless. The mother heart in me is trying to find balance between my excitement for your future and my trepidation, because one day I won't have you and Kelsey singing and dancing in the background of our lives. You are the music of our home, dear Son, and even after you grow up, I will hear your song in my memory forever. I love you, Tyler.

Sean, my sunbeam. You are ten already and I can't believe it's been almost four years since you came from Haiti to live with us. You were the first one to open up about your past, to tell us of the hard times, days when you had to fend for yourself, eating dirt to survive. But today you are the first one with a hug and a smile, looking out for other people as easily as you breathe. You are a talented reader, a devoted son, and a respectful young man. I couldn't be more proud of you. You are gifted in sports, yes, but that's not why you're the first boy picked when they form teams at recess. It's because of who you are on the inside—the kind, loving person God made you to be. I'm forever glad God led you to our family; you belonged here from the beginning. I love you, Sean.

Josh, my rough-and-tumble sweetheart. Since I met you, I've known you had an amazing gift of persuasion. There I was at the Haitian orphanage, meeting Sean and EJ for the first time, but the first one to talk was you. "I love you, Mommy," you told me, using beautiful English. Do you know that the room went silent, Josh? Forty-two children clamoring and laughing and yelling in that tiny orphanage courtyard, and all I could hear was you, a child I'd never met until that day. No question, God wanted you in our home, because you arrived on September 8, 2001. Three days later political tensions might have meant you would never come home. Isn't God amazing? At ten years old, your talents are too numerous to mention, but above all God will use that wonderful charisma to bring people to Him. Save me a seat in the front row, okay, honey? I love you, Josh.

EJ, my wide-eyed overcomer. Like a precious, beautiful flower, you continue to unfold a little more each day, proving to everyone in your world that you are capable of great things, even at eight years old. I'm so proud of the way you hold your head high, the picture of kindness and character you present to the world. In the garden of life, you are becoming a leader, one forged by hanging onto Christ and letting Him pull you to the top. I know God has plans for all of His children, but yours gets a little clearer every day. I cherish our quiet times, when you sit beside me during devotions. Your smile makes our home so much brighter. I love you, EJ.

Austin, my six-year-old Green Beret. When God brought you safely back from infant heart surgery, I knew He had a special reason for letting you live. Now I can only dream of what He has in store. "I don't need to learn piano, Mommy. I told you . . . I'm going to be a Green Beret!" That and a Green Bay Packer. Oh, and the next (blond) Michael Jordan. Or maybe a champion bull rider. All that rough, tough men's town stuff, and you still cry when you think of Jesus on a cross. Talk about a heartbreaking cutie! But for now, the only broken heart is mine, because already our special babyhood days together are over. You are out of kindergarten, into full-day school like the others. But don't be surprised, little first-grader, if one morning you look up and I'm there to take you out for a special date. One more time to share lunch and give-and-go and cuddle time. Whoever said it was harder letting go of your youngest was right. Keep holding onto Jesus, Austin. I love you.

BEYOND TUESDAY MORNING

ONE

She was surviving; the commute proved that much.

Jamie Bryan took her position at the far end of the Staten Island Ferry, pressed her body against the railing, eyes on the place where the Twin Towers once stood. She could face it now, every day if she had to. The terrorist attacks had happened, the World Trade Center had collapsed, and the only man she'd ever loved had gone down with them.

Late fall was warmer than usual, and the breeze across the water washed over Jamie's face. If she could do this—if she could make this journey three times a week while seven-year-old Sierra was at school—then she could get through another long, dark night. She could face the empty place in the bed beside her, face the longing for the man who had been her best friend, the one she'd fallen for when she was only a girl.

If she could do this, she could do anything.

Jamie looked at her watch. Nine-fifteen, right on schedule.

Three times a week the routine was the same. From Staten Island across the harbor on the ferry, up through the park, past the brick walls that after September 11 were plastered with pictures of missing people, into the heart of lower Manhattan's financial district, past the cavernous crater where the Twin Towers had stood, to St. Paul's. The little church was a strangely out-of-place stone chapel with a century-old cemetery just thirty yards from the pit. A chapel that, for months after the attacks, had been a café, a hospital, a meeting place, a counseling office, a refuge, a haven to firefighters and police officers and rescue workers and volunteers, a place to pray and be prayed for. A place that pointed people to God.

All the things a church should be.

Never mind the plans for a new World Trade Center, or the city's designs for an official memorial. Never mind the tourists gathered at the ten-foot chain-link fence around the pit or the throngs gawking at the pictorial timeline pinned along the top of the fence—photos of the Twin Towers' inception and creation and place in history. Souvenir picture books might be sold around the perimeter of the pit, but only one place gave people a true taste of what had happened that awful day.

St. Paul's.

The ferry docked, and Jamie was one of the first off. When it was raining or snowing she took a cab, but today she walked. Streets in lower Manhattan teemed as they always had, but there was something different about the people. It didn't matter how many years passed, how many anniversaries of the attacks came and went.

The people of New York City would never be the same.

Yes, they were busy, still driven to climb the ladders or make a name for themselves in New York City. But for the most part they were more likely to make eye contact, and when they did, they were more likely to smile or nod or give some sort of sign that the bond was still there, that a city couldn't go through something like New Yorkers went through September 11 and not be changed forever.

Jamie breathed in hard through her nose and savored the sweet mix of seawater and city air. Jake would've liked this, the way she was facing the situation, allowing her pain to work for good in the lives of others. She had lived in paralyzing fear for so long, but now—now that she'd lost Jake—she could face anything. Not in her own strength, but because Jake's faith lived deep within her.

Funny how she'd come to be a volunteer at St. Paul's.

It was Captain Hisel's idea. He'd been Jake's boss, his mentor. He'd found Jake—or the man he *thought* was Jake—in the aftermath of the collapse of the towers. Of course the man hadn't been Jake at all but Eric Michaels, a Los Angeles businessman who came into Jamie's life by mistake. A man she believed was her husband for three agonizing months.

A man who'd gone home to his family three years ago without looking back. And rightfully so. Jamie had told only a few people the details of that tender, tragic time. Captain Hisel was one of them.

The captain became a special friend in the months and years since the terrorist attacks. At first they shared an occasional Sunday dinner, but since shortly after the first anniversary of the attacks they were together at least twice a week, volunteering at St. Paul's and sharing lunch or dinner. He was *Aaron* to her now, and the two of them had everything in common.

Or at least it seemed that way.

Jamie turned a corner and saw the old cemetery. It was clean now, free of the ash and debris that had gathered around the tombstones and remained there for months after the attacks. The island of Manhattan was a different place since that terrible Tuesday morning, more vulnerable, less cocksure. But warmer too. Stronger. For most of America, time might've dimmed the horror of what happened to New York City when the Twin Towers fell. But those who were there would always remember. The connection it gave Manhattan residents was undeniable.

A few feet in front of her, a street vendor nodded. "Nice day."

"Yes, it is." Jamie smiled and kept walking.

See. There it was again. Before September 11, a vendor wouldn't have made eye contact unless he wanted to push a hot dog or a bag of caramelized almonds. Now? Now the man was familiar. She saw him every time she volunteered at St. Paul's; he probably knew where she was headed, what she was doing.

Everyone in lower Manhattan knew about St. Paul's.

Jamie crossed the street, stopped, and turned—same as she did every day. Before she could enter St. Paul's Chapel, before she could open her heart to the picture-taking tourists and the quietly grieving regulars who couldn't stay away, she had to see for herself that the towers were really gone. It was part of the ritual. She had to look across the street at the grotesque gargantuan hole where the buildings once stood, had to remind herself why she was here and what she was doing, that terrorists really had flown airplanes into the World Trade Center and obliterated the buildings—and two thousand lives.

Because Jake had been one of those people, coming to St. Paul's kept him alive in some ways. Being at Ground Zero, helping out . . .

that was something Jake would've done. It was the very thing he'd been doing when he died.

Jamie let her gaze wander up into the empty sky, searching unseen floors and windows. Had he been on the way up—he and his best schoolboy buddy, Larry—trying to reach victims at the top? Or had he been partway down? She narrowed her eyes. If only God would give her a sign, so she would know exactly where to look.

She blinked and the invisible towers faded. Tears welled in her heart, and she closed her eyes. *Breathe, Jamie. You can do this. God, help me do this.*

A deep breath in through her nose. Exhale . . . slow and steady. *God . . . help me.*

My strength is sufficient for you, daughter.

She often prayed at this stage of the routine, and almost as often she felt God whispering to her, coaxing her, helping her along as a father might help his little girl. The way Jake had helped Sierra.

The quiet murmurs in the most hurting part of her soul were enough. Enough to give her strength and desire and determination to move ahead, to go through the doors of St. Paul's and do her part to keep the vigil for all she lost more than three years ago.

She turned her back to the pit and took determined steps beside the black wrought iron fence bordering the cemetery, around the corner to the small courtyard at the front of the chapel. The hallowed feeling always hit her here, on the cobbled steps of the little church. How many firefighters had entered here in the months after the attacks, firemen looking for food or comfort or a shoulder to cry on? How many had passed through it since the building had reopened, looking for hope or answers or a reason to grieve the tragedy even if it had never touched them personally?

Just inside the doors, Jamie turned to the left and stopped. There, scattered over a corner table, was a ragtag display of hundreds of items: yellowed photos, keepsakes, and letters written to victims of the attacks. She scanned the table, saving his picture for last. Beneath the photo of a balding man holding a newborn baby, the grin on his face ear to ear: *Joe, we're still waiting for you to come home . . .* Scribbled atop a wedding photo: *You were everything to me, Cecile; you still are . . .* Tacked to the side of a wallet-sized picture of a young FDNY guy:

Your ladder boys still take the field every now and then but it's not the same without you. Yesterday Saul hit a homer and every one of us looked up. Are you there?

Every time Jamie did this, her eyes found different letters, different snippets of pain and aching loss scattered across the display. But always she ended in the same place. At Jake's picture and the letter written by their daughter, Sierra.

Jake was so handsome, his eyes brilliant blue even in the poorly lit corner. *Jake . . . I'm here, Jake.* When there weren't too many people working their way into the building, she could stand there longer than usual. This was one of those days. Her eyes locked on her husband's, and for a moment he was there again, standing before her, smiling at her, holding his arms out to her.

Her fingers moved toward the picture, brushing the feathery photo paper as if it were Jake's face, his skin.

"Jake . . ."

For the briefest moment she was sure she could hear him. *Jamie, I'm not gone, I'm here. Come see for yourself.*

She drew her hand back and wrapped her arms around her waist. People had caught her touching his picture before; it made the volunteer coordinators nervous. As if maybe she wasn't ready to comfort others when she was still so far from healed herself.

She didn't mean to touch the photo; it just happened. Something about his eyes in the picture made him seem larger than life, the way he'd been before . . .

Before.

That was it, wasn't it? Life before September 11, and life after it. Two completely different lives. There were times when she thought she could hear Jake. His voice still rang in the corridors of her heart, the way it always would. Tears blurred her eyes and she gritted her teeth. She wouldn't break down here, not now. On his birthday or their anniversary, maybe. On the anniversary of September 11, of course. But if she was going to keep Jake's memory alive, she couldn't break down every time she volunteered.

She glanced at the letter, the one Sierra had written a few weeks ago on the third anniversary of the attack. Her daughter's other letters were safe in a scrapbook, a keepsake for Sierra so she wouldn't forget the closeness she'd shared with Jake. Every few months Sierra wrote a new note, and that one would replace the old one on the display table. The letter showed that Sierra still didn't know how her father had died. As far as she knew, her daddy didn't die on September 11 but three months later. In a fire, trying to save people trapped inside. It was a half-truth; the best Jamie could do under the circumstances.

She just hadn't known how to tell Sierra that the man who'd been living with them for three months wasn't really her father but a stranger. In the three years since Eric Michaels left them, Jamie had yet to figure out a way to talk about the subject. For that matter, Sierra still had a picture of herself standing next to Eric. Once, a little more than a year ago, Jamie had tried to take it down. She could still see the look on her daughter's face when she came running down the stairs into the kitchen, her eyes red with tears.

"My picture of me and Daddy is gone!"

Jamie felt awful about that one. She'd gone up with Sierra and pretended to look for it. That night while her daughter slept, Jamie took it from the closet where she'd hidden it and placed it on Sierra's dresser again. Right next to Jake's fire helmet.

Two other times she'd tried to replace it with other photos, pictures that actually were of Sierra and Jake.

"The one after Daddy got hurt is too sad," she'd tell Sierra. "Let's put it away, okay?"

But Sierra would move the other photos to her bookshelves, keeping the one of her and Eric on her dresser. "That's the last picture of me and Daddy. I want it there forever. Please, Mommy, don't make me move it."

The memory lifted.

Sierra had never even been to St. Paul's; she didn't know that's where her mother volunteered her time. The whole story about Eric and his time with them was getting harder to stand by. Deception wasn't Jamie's style, and lately she'd been feeling that one day soon she'd have to tell Sierra the truth. Her daughter deserved that much.

Jamie worked her gaze along her daughter's neat handwriting and read the letter for the hundredth time.

Dear Daddy, how are you doing up in heven? I'm doing good down here; I'm in second grade, and Mommy says I'm smartst in my class. But I'm not that smart cuz I have some things I don't know. Like how come you had to go to heven when I need you so much rite here? How come you had to help those peple in that fire? Why culdnt they wok out by themselfs. Somtimes I clos my eys and I remember how you lookd. Somtimes I remember budrfly kisses. But somtimes I forget. I love you. Sierra.

Sometimes she forgets.

That was the hardest part of all lately. The chapel entrance was empty, and Jamie closed her eyes. *God, don't let either of us forget Jake. He's with You, still alive somewhere in Paradise with You. But until we can all be together again, help Sierra remember him, God. Please. Help her—*

Someone tapped her shoulder, and she spun around, her breath in her throat. "Aaron!" She stepped back from the display table and forced a smile. "Hi."

"Hey." He backed up toward the wooden pews that filled the center of the chapel. "Someone wants to—"

Aaron looked past her at the picture of Jake, as if he'd only just realized the reason why she was standing there. For a long while he said nothing, then he looked at her, his eyes filled with a familiar depth. "I'm sorry. I didn't realize you were—"

"No, it's okay." She slipped her hands in the pockets of her sweater. "I was reading Sierra's letter. It's been three years; she's forgetting Jake."

Aaron bit his lip and let his gaze fall to the floor.

"It was bound to happen." She gave a slight shrug. The corners of her mouth lifted some, but the smile stopped there. "She was only four when he died."

"I know." A respectful quiet fell between them. "Still hard to believe he's gone."

"Yes." Once more she glanced at Jake's picture. "Still hard to believe."

She felt strangely awkward, the way she had back in high school when some boy other than Jake smiled at her or flirted with her. But

Aaron wasn't flirting with her, and she wasn't in high school . . . and Jake was dead.

But not really; not when he lived in her memory as fully as he'd once lived in her home.

No wonder the strange feeling, the hint of guilt at being caught looking at the picture of her husband. She'd felt this way before on occasion, though only when she was with Aaron. Even so, she refused to make too much of her emotions. They were bound to be all over the board, even if she and Aaron were only friends.

He nodded his head toward the center of the chapel. "There's a lady in the front pew; she could use your help. Husband was a cop, died in the collapse." His eyes met hers and held. Concern shone through, and the awkward feeling disappeared. "You ready?"

"Ready." Jamie fell in beside him and headed down one of the pews toward the other side of the chapel. She wanted to glance once more at Jake's picture, but she didn't.

He pointed to a blonde woman in the front row. "You got it?"

Jamie nodded. "What about you?"

"Over there." He glanced toward the back of the chapel. The memorial tables framed the perimeter of the room. A couple in their seventies stood near the back wall. "Tourists. Lots of questions."

They shared a knowing look—this was what they did at St. Paul's: being there for the people who came through the doors, whatever their reason—then they turned and went their separate ways.

With slow, hushed steps, Jamie came alongside the blonde woman. Many of the widows who visited St. Paul's had been there before, but this one wasn't familiar. Jamie sat down and waited until the woman looked at her.

"Hi, I'm Jamie Bryan; I'm a volunteer."

The woman's eyes were red and swollen, and though she opened her mouth, no words came. She lowered her head into her hands, and a few quiet sobs worked their way through her body.

Jamie put her hand on the woman's back. The woman was in her late forties, Jamie guessed, heavyset with an ocean of pain welling within her. When the woman's tears subsided, she sniffed and found Jamie's eyes. "Does . . . the pain ever go away?"

This was the hard part. Jamie was here at St. Paul's for one reason: to offer hope to those devastated by the losses of September 11. The problem was just what Martha White, the volunteer coordinator, had warned her from the beginning. She couldn't work through her own pain by giving advice to people about theirs.

"I'm fine," she'd told Martha. "I'm working through it, but I'm fine at St. Paul's."

Martha looked doubtful. "You tell me if it's too much." She wagged a motherly finger at Jamie. "You're a victim same as everyone else."

The coordinator's words came back to Jamie now, and she swallowed hard. What had the weeping woman just asked her? Did the pain ever go away?

Jamie looked from the woman to the front of the church, the place where the old ornate cross stood like an anchor. Without taking her eyes from it, Jamie gave a slow shake of her head. "No. The pain doesn't go away." She turned back to the woman. "But God helps us learn how to live with it."

Another wave of tears hit the woman. Her face contorted, and she pinched the bridge of her nose. "It still . . . feels like September 12. Sometimes I think it always will."

A strength rose from within Jamie. Every time she'd been needed in a situation like this one, God had delivered. Every time. She turned so she could see the woman better. "Tell me about your husband."

"He was a cop." She lifted one shoulder and ran the back of her hands beneath her eyes. "Everyone's always talking about the firemen, but the cops took a hit too."

Jamie had heard this before from the wives of other police officers. "Have you been around the chapel yet?"

"I just started when . . ." She held her breath, probably stifling another wave of sobs.

"It's okay to cry."

"Thank you." The woman's shoulders shook again. "This chapel . . . That's why I'm crying." She searched Jamie's eyes. "I didn't think anyone cared until I came here, and now . . ."

"Now you know the truth."

"Yes." The woman grabbed a quick breath and stared at a poster on a wall overhead. *Oklahoma Cares.* Beneath the banner title were hundreds of handprints from children who had experienced the bombing of the Murrow Building in Oklahoma City. One line read, *We love our police!* "I didn't come before because I didn't want to be angry at anyone. But this is where I need to be; I should've come a hundred times by now."

"I'm Jamie." She held out her hand, and the woman across from her took it. "What's your name?"

"Cindy Grammar." The woman allowed the hint of a smile. "Is it just me, or do you feel something here?"

"I feel it. Everyone who comes inside feels it."

"It's the only place where the memory of all those people still lives. You know, as a group."

"Exactly." Jamie folded her hands in her lap and looked around the chapel at the banners, then at the memorabilia lining the walls— items collected from the edge of the pit or left near the chapel steps. One day the city would have an official memorial to the victims of September 11. But for now, those two thousand people were remembered with grace and love at St. Paul's.

"This city loved my Bill. I could sense that the minute I walked in here."

"You're right." Jamie gave Cindy's hand a gentle squeeze. "And no one will forget what he did that day. He was a hero, Cindy. Same as the firefighters."

The conversation continued for nearly an hour before the woman felt ready to finish making her way around the inside of the building. By then her eyes were dry and she had shared the story of how she'd met her husband, how much they'd loved each other. Jamie knew the names of the woman's two sons, and the fact that they both played high school football.

"Thanks, Jamie." The woman's expression was still filled with sorrow, but now it was also tinged with gratitude and peace. "I haven't felt this good in months."

Jamie's heart soared. Her job was to bring hope to the hopeless, and to do it in Jake's name. Again and again and again. She took Cindy's hands again. "Let's pray, okay?"

The woman squirmed. "I'm . . . I'm not sure about God, Jamie."

"That's okay." Jamie's smile came from her heart, from the place that understood God the way Jake had always wanted her to understand. "God's sure about you."

"Really?" Doubt colored Cindy's eyes.

"Really. We don't have to pray; just let me know." Jamie bit her lip, waiting.

"I want to." The woman knit her brow together. "I don't know what to say."

Jamie gave the woman's hand a gentle squeeze. "I'll say it." She bowed her head and began, the way she had dozens of times over the past two years. "God, we come to You because You know all things. You are sovereign and mighty and You care about us deeply. Help Cindy believe in You, Lord. Help her to understand that You hold a flashlight as we walk through the valley of the shadow of death. And let her find new life in You. In Jesus' name, amen."

Jamie opened her eyes.

A fresh sort of peace filled Cindy's face. She leaned closer and hugged Jamie. "I'll be back."

Jamie smiled. "I know."

The woman stood and headed for the outer rim of the chapel with a promise to return some day so that maybe the two could talk—and even pray again.

When she was finally alone, Jamie's hands trembled. Her legs were stiff from sitting for so long. Meetings like that were emotionally draining, and Jamie wanted water before she talked to anyone else.

But before she could reach the stairs, another woman approached her, four young teenage girls in tow, each holding a notebook. "Hi, maybe you could help us."

"Of course." Jamie gave the group her full attention. "What would you like to know?"

"We're a homeschool group and—" she looked at the girls— "each of the students has a list of questions for you. They want to know how St. Paul's was instrumental in serving the people who cleaned up the pile of debris after the towers collapsed."

"Okay." Jamie smiled, but something grated against her heart. The pile of debris? Jake had been in that pile. It was okay for *her* to call it that, but these people were . . . they were on a quest for details, like so many reporters. She ignored her irritation and directed the group to the nearest pew. "Let's sit here and we can talk."

School groups were common, and always needed help from volunteers. They wanted to know how many hundreds of gallons of water were given out—more than four thousand; how many different types of services were offered free to the work crew—podiatry, massage therapy, counseling, chiropractic care, nursing care, and optometry among others; and what sort of impact did St. Paul's and its volunteers have on the work crew—a dramatic one.

The questions continued, but they weren't out of line. By the time Jamie was finished talking with the group, she regretted her first impression. The girls were well-mannered, the parent sensitive to the information Jamie shared. It was nearly noon when the group went on their way. Jamie scanned the pews first, and then the perimeter of the chapel. She was thirsty, but the visitors came first. The week she trained as a volunteer Martha had made that clear.

"Look for fires to put out." A tiny woman with a big mouth and a heart as vast as the Grand Canyon, Martha was particularly serious about this detail. "Look for the people breaking down and weeping, the ones sitting by themselves in a pew. Those are the ones you should approach. Just so they know you're there."

No fires at the moment.

Aaron was across the room, talking to another pair of tourists. At least his conversations looked less intense than the one she'd had with Cindy. She trudged up the stairs to the volunteers' break room. An open case of water bottles sat on the table; she took one and twisted off the lid. Chairs lined the area, but she was tired of sitting. She leaned against the stone wall and looked up at the aged stained glass.

Funny, the way Martha had said it. *Fires to put out.* It was one more way Jamie was keeping Jake's memory alive. No, she didn't deal with flames and fire hoses. But she was putting out fires all the same. He would've been proud of her.

In fact, if he'd survived, he'd be right here at St. Paul's with her. All the more reason to volunteer as long as the chapel was open. It gave her purpose, and in that sense it wasn't only a way to keep Jake's memory, his sacrifice, alive.

It was a way to keep herself alive too.

TWO

From the moment Clay Michaels started his shift, he felt strange about the day, as if God was trying to tell him something—to warn him. The unsettling sensation churned in his gut and worked through his spine and neck and brain. A knowing, almost, that things weren't right. Or maybe worse. Maybe something awful was about to happen.

Clay wasn't sure exactly what the feeling was, but it bothered him.

All day, while he hunted down the usual speeders on the Ventura Freeway corridor between the San Fernando Valley and the beach exits, the feeling weighed on him. Each time he approached a car his senses went on heightened alert. A college kid late for his classes at Pepperdine; a business guy making time to his office in Camarillo; a carload of tourists unaware of the speed limits. The stops had been routine, nothing more.

Still the feeling stayed with him.

At lunchtime he picked up a McDonald's salad, drove to one of his lookout spots near the westbound Las Virgenes exit, and settled back into his seat.

Maybe the feeling meant it was time to move on.

He'd been to Eric and Laura's house the night before, and the scene had been the same as always. Or the same as it had been since Eric returned home from New York City. Eric and Laura holding hands; Eric and Laura stealing a kiss or two in the kitchen; Eric and Laura sharing a private glance or a joke or an embrace when they thought no one was looking.

Clay tried not to notice. He was happy for them, grateful that the horrific events of September 11 had wrought only good for two people he loved so dearly. Still, he couldn't help but wonder . . .

He took a bite of his salad and watched a car speed past. *Lucky day, buddy.* Only something dangerous would pull Clay away during a break. Especially when the strange feeling was still gnawing at him. It must've stemmed from his regrets about Laura, about the fact that their closeness had dissolved—as it had to—the minute Eric walked back through the door. The thing was, too often Clay caught himself watching Laura, remembering the way things were when Eric was gone, when they thought he was dead.

Clay had gone to college in the Midwest and he'd only been back in Los Angeles a few months when the terrorist attacks occurred. After September 11, while they grieved Eric's loss, he and Laura grew closer every day. They even traveled to New York City together to search for him.

When it was finally obvious that he had died in the collapsed towers, they went home, and the bond they shared grew even stronger. Clay had been convinced that he and Laura would wind up together. After all, they'd known each other since high school. Laura had been his first crush.

Josh—Eric and Laura's son—connected with Clay immediately, barely missing his father. And Laura had relied on him for everything. But that was not a surprise. Back then, Eric was a sorry excuse for a husband and father. He'd been obsessed with climbing the corporate ladder, making another deal, traveling to Manhattan as often as the company's president demanded. All at Laura and Josh's expense.

Clay took another bite of his salad and rolled down his window. The air smelled of late summer and fresh-cut grass.

Yes, he'd been shocked to discover Eric was a lousy husband and father. While he was away at school, he assumed things were great between Eric and Laura. Laura was golden, a beautiful woman with a tenderness and compassion that worked its way through everything she said or did. She was worth more than any job, and Clay intended to tell Eric so.

He never got the chance.

Instead his brother headed for New York City and disappeared from their lives for three months. When he returned, he was a changed man, the victim of amnesia and mistaken identity.

Clay stared at the rolling hills in the distance and watched a hawk land on a lone oak tree. God was here; he could feel it. Never mind the strange certainty that something bad was about to happen, God was here. That was all that mattered.

God . . . what You did with Eric . . . it was all part of Your plan, wasn't it?

Even now, after three years, he could hardly believe what had happened to his big brother. The story was as strange as it was miraculous. Mistaken for an FDNY guy, a man who apparently loved God and his family in a way that should have earned him honors, Eric was taken to the man's home and family. For weeks he'd done nothing but read the man's Bible, his journal, his notes on loving his wife and their daughter.

When Eric finally remembered who he really was, the other man's wife helped Eric find his way home. He didn't talk about the woman much, but she must have been something, first surviving the shock that Eric wasn't her husband, and then helping him return to Laura and Josh. And though Eric never spoke about his time with the woman, one thing was certain: he was a changed man. Because of that, Laura was the happiest woman in the world, and Josh the happiest eleven-year-old boy.

And Clay?

He dated now and then, but no one ever worked their way into his heart the way Laura had. Though his feelings for her weren't right, they were there. And that made it hard to find someone else, someone he could fall in love with and marry and start a family with. The way he dreamed every day of doing.

Clay exhaled hard and tossed the empty plastic salad container into the backseat. He was about to take a swig from his iced tea when his radio crackled to life.

"Urgent! Calling all cars!" The code that followed told Clay the unthinkable had happened. A carjacking and fatal shooting at the gas station at Las Virgenes exit and Ventura Freeway. Suspect a twenty-five-year-old Hispanic male, five-ten, muscular, driving the victim's blue 2002 Chevy Tahoe. "Suspect is headed west on 101. Suspect is armed and highly dangerous. Repeat, suspect is armed and dangerous."

Clay straightened as a rush of adrenaline shot through him. He started his car as he grabbed the radio receiver. He identified himself and confirmed that he was at the location and headed toward the suspect.

Other officers gave their location and stated their intent to begin pursuit immediately and provide backup. But none of them were within ten minutes of Clay's location. He would be first on the scene.

"God, go with me."

He whispered that prayer every time he took a call, but this time there was urgency in his voice. He'd known, hadn't he? That something would go down today? He flipped his siren on, spun his car around, and darted across the overpass and down the on-ramp onto the westbound lanes of the freeway. The dispatcher's words screamed at him again. *Armed and highly dangerous.* He leaned toward the windshield, both hands on the steering wheel.

Chases were fairly common on California freeways. Chases involving a crazy man who'd already killed one person were not. It took three minutes for Clay to spot the blue Chevy tearing down the freeway, weaving in and out of traffic. This was their guy. But without backup . . .

He spoke into the receiver again. "This is Officer Michaels; I've got the suspect in sight. How close is backup?"

Another series of crackling noises filled the car. "We've got CHP officers fifteen minutes away. LAPD detectives ten minutes behind you and catching up. Wait if you can."

If he could?

Too late. The suspect must have seen the red lights and heard the siren. He was picking up speed, darting in and out of all three lanes, jeopardizing everyone on the road. That meant Clay had two choices. Pursue him a few feet from his bumper to help warn drivers he was approaching, or back off until he had assistance. But backing off didn't guarantee the man would slow down or drive more responsibly. He'd just killed a person; he wouldn't mind if someone else died.

Clay decided to pursue. It was his job, and he wouldn't back off just because he was alone.

He maneuvered his patrol car through the traffic until he was a few yards from the suspect's bumper. He could see the man looking over his shoulder, but he couldn't make out his face. Then the man waved his weapon out the window. It wasn't any ordinary handgun; it was an AK-47. The man aimed it at the sky and fired—clear warning that he intended to kill whoever tried to stop him. Clay tightened his grip on the steering wheel, his palms sweaty. Still no backup in sight.

Come on, guys ... hurry.

His foot pushed harder at the gas pedal, moving his patrol car even closer to the suspect. He was in firing range, for sure. If the man were able to fire the machine gun at him while still maintaining his high speeds, Clay would already be dead.

Cars were pulling over now, the way he'd wanted them to do. Amazing what the sound of a siren or the sight of a flashing light could accomplish. Clay glanced at his speedometer. Nearly a hundred miles per hour.

At that instant, the suspect darted across all three lanes of traffic, sped up the hill at the Kanan Road off-ramp, and made a sharp, squealing left turn. He bumped two cars traveling in the right lane, but kept going.

Clay pressed the button on his radio receiver. "Suspect has exited the freeway at Kanan Road, heading west."

"Copy. Backup is closing in, a few minutes away."

Clay gritted his teeth. *Please, God ... I need help. Hurry them up.* He heard no holy whispers or answers. But the strange feeling grew stronger. Whatever was up ahead, he had to be ready. *God, be with me, whatever happens.*

They sped past a series of condos and buildings as other cars pulled to the side or darted out of their way. Again the suspect waved his gun out the window, and Clay checked his rearview mirror. Nothing.

They neared the twisting turns of the canyon, turns that would force Clay to slow down or risk flying over the edge. Suddenly the suspect jerked his car onto the gravelly shoulder, kicking up a cloud of rocks and dust. Clay was still close behind him, and for a moment he couldn't see anything. He heard the debris hit his windshield as he slammed on his brakes.

The cloud settled, and he saw the man was out of his car, the assault weapon trained on Clay's vehicle. He was going to fire before Clay had a chance to get out of his car, let alone grab his revolver. The cloud of dust and rocks had been the suspect's cover, and now Clay was trapped.

Here he sat, the barrel of an AK-47 pointed straight at him, and he could only think of one thing: *I knew this was coming.*

He ducked just as the man braced himself and fired.

A spray of bullets peppered Clay's windshield, shattering the glass and piercing where he'd been sitting just seconds ago. Clay cocked his revolver, glanced over the dash and fired. He dropped back down as the suspect sprayed another round of bullets. This time they came at closer range, louder, more fierce. The man's footsteps were closing in. Clay gritted his teeth. What could he do? At this close range, he couldn't fire without making himself a target. He raised his hand above the dash and fired blindly. Again the man let loose a burst of gunfire. He was closer now. It was only a matter of time.

How could God let it end this way? Death before he'd ever really found life—the sort of life he'd wanted, with a wife and a family. Senseless death because of a crazy man with an assault weapon. Clay's breathing came in short bursts. *God . . . no! Help me, please!*

At that instant he heard two things: sirens and footsteps, both coming closer. Backup was almost here. A few more seconds and everything would be okay. The man shouted something in Spanish, something about having a bad life.

Anger welled up in Clay. He wasn't going to sit there and wait to be shot at; if he was going down, he'd go down fighting. *God . . . be with me.* He peered over the dash and spotted the man, ten yards away and closing. The suspect saw Clay too. The man pulled the trigger just as Clay fired once—straight at the man's chest—then ducked to the floorboard area.

Even as another spray of bullets ripped through his car, Clay heard the sirens getting louder. His heart pounded. He listened, but he couldn't hear the man coming closer. Had he shot him? Had he actually killed a man? The sirens were right behind him now, and he heard two cars pull onto the shoulder, then the sound of doors slamming. A voice yelled, "Police, don't move!"

Someone was running up from behind, along the passenger side of Clay's car. It could be the suspect, but not likely. Still, Clay aimed his revolver at the opposite door just as Detective Joe Reynolds flung it open and looked inside. "Michaels, you okay?"

"The suspect?"

"He's dead." The officer was a black man, a former attorney who'd grown tired of the corporate world and took up police work. He was a detective now, one of the best. He worked the west end and had an office down the hall from the lunchroom. Clay considered him his closest friend in the department.

"I . . . I killed him?"

"You did everyone a favor."

Clay's body shook as relief worked its way through him. "A few more seconds and . . ."

"What'd he do, pull over and come after you?"

"Yeah." Clay set his gun on the seat and pushed himself up. "The guy . . . he was crazy."

"Must've been flying over a hundred."

"He was."

Reynolds was still out of breath. "We got here fast as we could. He was dying on the ground, still reaching for his weapon when we pulled up." He ran his fingers over the bullet holes scattered across the front seat. "Someone must be looking out for you, Michaels. AK-47s don't usually miss."

It was true. Even though he'd ducked into the floorboard, he should've been hit. Weapons like the assault rifle spray their bullets, and one easily could have ripped through the dash and killed him. "I was praying the whole time."

Reynolds cocked his head. "I'd say the Big Guy heard you."

Clay glanced around and saw another officer, one he didn't know as well, in his patrol car on the radio. Probably calling for someone to come get the body.

Clay looked at the covered figure lying a few yards from his car. Nausea rushed up in his belly. "First time I ever shot a suspect."

"They'll want you to take some time, a paid leave." Reynolds studied him. "Part of the investigation."

"Right." He'd had no choice, of course. The man would have killed him if he hadn't shot. In a situation like that—with a crazed suspect running at you, firing a gun—Clay had been taught there was just one way to do it: shoot to kill.

"You okay?" Reynolds brushed the glass off the passenger seat and sat down beside Clay, his feet hanging out of the car.

"Yeah, I guess." He couldn't take his eyes off the covered body. "I don't like how I feel."

"Look, Michaels—" Reynolds stared straight ahead, as though remembering something far away—"I've been on the other side of this game." He looked at Clay. "Let's say you miss. Let's say ol' crazy man takes you down instead of the other way around. He could be out on the streets shooting again in twenty, fifteen if the circumstances were right."

"Fifteen years?"

"I saw it all the time when I wore a suit and tie. All the time." Reynolds glared at the place where the body lay. "No cop likes to shoot his gun. But in this case it was your life or his and, well, let's just say things worked out right today. You handled him better than the courts could've." He gave Clay a halfhearted shove in the shoulder. "Of course, you didn't hear me say that."

Reynolds climbed out of the car and shut the door. Clay wasn't shaking anymore, but the ache in his stomach hadn't gone away. A man was dead because he'd fired his gun. The thought sank in. He'd killed a man on the job; the possibility that always exists for an officer had actually happened.

Clay looked down. He still had shattered glass on his pants. He climbed out of the car, dusted off the crumbly pieces, and leaned against his door. Reynolds was right. It was his life or the suspect's. And if he was honest with himself, in a small way it felt good to fire the gun at a man who'd already killed someone, who'd put every driver they'd passed on the freeway at risk. Yes, things had worked out for the best, and if he were faced with the situation again, he'd respond the same way.

But a man lay dead on the ground because of him. No matter how good and right his actions were, he still felt sick.

It took an hour for investigators to arrive and collect data, and for the body to be removed and taken to the morgue where an autopsy would be performed. During that time, Clay learned more information about the man. He'd crossed the border south of San Diego two days earlier, killing two border patrolmen in the process. Witnesses said they saw him heading south, and when police dogs lost his trail, the search was called off.

No one knew how he'd gotten from San Diego to the San Fernando Valley, but he stayed beneath police radar until the carjacking.

An investigating officer took a statement from Clay and assured him the process was routine. "Your car's shattered with bullets, Michaels. Don't sweat this for a minute."

When Clay got back to the office, Reynolds spotted him and nodded. "They want to see you in the office." He paused, his eyes full of concern. "After that, come see me. I have an idea."

The meeting with the brass was what Clay expected. He was being placed on paid leave until an investigation could be completed. Probably two to three weeks. He was already heading out of the office when his boss stopped him.

"Michaels."

"Yes, sir." Clay felt better than before, but he still didn't have an appetite.

The man tapped a pencil on his desk. "We all hate when this type of thing happens."

"Yes, sir."

"But in this case, I'm glad your aim was on." He leaned forward, eyes intense. "It would've killed me to lose you, Michaels. You're one of the best. Take the break and when you get back, if I have anything to do with it, you'll get a promotion."

A promotion? He'd wanted that since he started with the department. He should be celebrating with a victory fist or a shout. Something. But in light of the day's events, Clay managed only a sad smile. "Thanks, sir. I appreciate that."

The man's eyes clouded. "Don't beat yourself up, Michaels. You did the right thing."

"Okay." Clay held the man's gaze a few seconds more and then turned and headed through the door to Reynolds's office. He shut the door behind him.

"Paid leave?"

"Two or three weeks." Clay shrugged. "When I get back my office might be across from yours."

A grin played out across his friend's face. "I *knew* it. They asked me last week who I thought was ready."

"You told 'em me?" Clay sat down and planted his elbows on his knees.

"Nope, I told 'em Hardy down the hall." Reynolds chuckled. "Of course I told 'em you."

Clay stared out the window behind Reynolds and wondered. On a day like today, what would it be like to have someone to go home to? Someone to share the details of the chase and the gun battle, someone to hug him and hold him and spend three weeks' paid leave with. Someone to congratulate him for getting promoted.

Someone to comfort him for what he'd had to do.

"Michaels, you daydreaming again?" His friend raised one eyebrow and slid back from his desk. He kicked his feet up. "I asked you a question, and you just stare out the window like you're daffy or something."

"Sorry." Clay understood. Reynolds was trying to keep things light, helping take the focus off the shooting. "Ask again."

"I was saying I think I know where we can go for a vacation."

"Vacation?"

Reynolds pushed a file across the desk. "Take a look."

Clay opened it and read the flyer inside: *Detective Training Offered by New York's Finest.* Starting in late November and running through the second week of December, the NYPD was offering a series of workshops and on-the-job training for officers from anywhere in the United States.

"You can't take three weeks, can you?"

Reynolds smiled. "I can when it's part of my ongoing training."

"Hmmm." There was no one waiting at home for Reynolds, same as Clay. It wasn't something the man ever talked about, and Clay didn't ask. But on the man's desk was a small photograph of a pretty brown-skinned woman and a little boy with eyes like Reynolds's. Clay had the feeling the man had some hidden pain, a story he shared with no one.

"I already talked to the chief. He says he could count three weeks for your leave. Three weeks in the Big Apple, Michaels. Whaddaya say?"

The idea sounded better with every passing second. He'd wanted to get back to New York ever since the terrorist attacks—same as every police officer and firefighter he knew. But he hadn't had time. Besides, he knew it would be hard—looking at the crater, imagining the lives lost in a single morning. When he had time off, he usually went hunting with guys from the department or boating up at one of the northern California lakes. A trip to New York hadn't figured into his plans.

"Well?" Reynolds crossed his arms, looking proud of himself. "Can I call and sign us up?"

Clay stared at the flyer again. The department had a block of rooms in a hotel on Staten Island. An effort at saving money, no doubt. If the department picked up his bill, it would be a fantastic opportunity. He would come back ready to step into his new role, the sickening memories from earlier that day at least a little dimmer.

He looked at Reynolds. "The two of us, huh?"

"That's right." Reynolds dropped his feet to the floor. "Showing the New York boys how to get it done."

Clay closed the folder and tossed it back on the desk. "Let's do it."

That night when he was back home Clay didn't turn on the television, didn't take a swim in the community pool down the street, didn't do anything except run a mental tape of what happened that day. Every time guilt tried to say something, he stopped it with the truths others spoke to him all day long.

Reynolds telling him he'd done everyone a favor; his captain assuring him he was glad the outcome hadn't been different. The news that the suspect had killed two border patrol officers.

It was his life or the suspect's. Plain and simple.

By the time he turned in for the night, God had replaced his nausea with a certainty that he'd done the right thing. The only thing he could've done. He should be at peace with the situation and how it had played out.

But he wasn't.

Three weeks away would do him good—less because of his gun battle than because he needed a change of scenery. His last thoughts before he fell asleep were proof of that because they were even more wrong than the earlier ones involving the shooting. They were thoughts of his brother's wife. Wrong thoughts. Thoughts that had him wondering what would've happened if Eric had never come home, if he'd never found his way back.

And whether Laura ever wondered the same thing.

THREE

Jamie was back at St. Paul's, her second time that week.

Aaron worked the night shift, and on the days she was at the chapel, he wound up there too. It was just a few blocks from the station, so he would go home and catch some sleep when their shift ended after lunch.

It was still early. Aaron hadn't arrived yet, but a young woman sat in the center of the pews, crying. Jamie drew a deep breath. *God ... give me the strength.* She kept her eyes on the woman and took soft, respectful steps toward her.

"Hello, I'm Jamie Bryan, a volunteer here." The woman was actually a teenage girl. In her hands was a picture of a middle-aged man in a suit and tie. The girl's father, no doubt. "Would you like to talk?"

The girl looked up, her eyes swollen and bloodshot. "It's his birthday." She held up the photo. "My father."

A pang of guilt stabbed at Jamie. At least this girl had somewhere to go, a place where her father's memory was honored. Sierra had the right to come here too. If the timing was right, if God gave her the words, she would tell her daughter soon. Maybe before Christmas.

Jamie sat beside the girl. She'd been trained to keep her questions minimal. That way the visitor would steer the conversation the direction they wanted to go. Her heart ached for the girl, who looked a little like Sierra might look in ten years. Long blonde hair, pretty face—and a hole in her heart where her daddy had been.

The girl sniffed and looked at the picture. "He wasn't supposed to go in that day. He was on vacation, but someone called and said they needed him." Her eyes lifted to Jamie's. "I told him I needed him more, but he ..." She hung her head. "He thought I was teasing him. 'You have school,' he told me. He kissed ... me on the forehead and said he'd see me that afternoon. After I got home from school. Our family was supposed to go away the next morning for a family reunion." She shook her head. "But it never ..."

Jamie slipped her arm around the girl. "I'm sorry." So much pain, so many wounded and battered hearts still wandering the streets of New York, searching for hope. Sometimes she wasn't sure she could take another day at St. Paul's, and yet moments like this, she knew. She was exactly where she was supposed to be, no matter how much it hurt. If she came to St. Paul's, she would never forget what Jake had done that awful Tuesday.

He might have been helping this girl's father, for all she knew.

Jamie gave the girl a light squeeze, a half hug that told her she wasn't alone, that anyone who stayed long at St. Paul's could understand the hurt she was feeling. Then she took her arm from the girl's shoulders and faced her. "Are you ... I guess I didn't get your name."

The girl looked at Jamie again. "Sami. Sami Taylor."

"Hi, Sami." Jamie's tone was soft. "Do you believe in Jesus, Sami?"

"I used to."

Jamie could almost hear herself telling Jake the same thing, back when he'd wanted nothing more than to share a Sunday morning church service with her. If she could have anything in the world it would be to tell him yes, just once. To go with him to church and sit beside him and pray to the God he'd always believed in. Her only comfort was that somehow, up in heaven, he had to know the truth, had to see that his prayers for her had been answered. She held her breath for a moment. *God ... she's just like I used to be. Give me the words.*

The girl spoke before Jamie had a chance. "When my dad was alive, we'd go to church every Sunday. My mom too. He was a rock, I guess. Sort of the anchor for our family."

She could've been describing Jake. "My husband was that way too."

"Your husband?"

"Yes." Jamie swallowed back the lump in her throat. "He was a firefighter." The past tense still got to her. Her eyes felt the sting of tears, but she blinked them away. "He was in the South Tower helping people when it collapsed."

"That's awful!" The girl's mouth hung open. "Were you . . . were you married for very long?"

"Not long enough." Jamie tried to smile, tried to keep the conversation from going to the deep places where she would break down and cry. Not that it hadn't happened before, but it couldn't happen every day. And she didn't want it to happen now. "We have a daughter. She's seven now—in second grade."

"How can you . . . how can you be here?" Sami waved her hand toward the memorabilia lining the walls. "I would never stop crying."

This time Jamie's smile was sad but easy. "I come because God gives me the strength."

"God let the towers fall." Her answer was quick, sharp.

"No, Sami." Jamie took the girl's hands in her own. "God is good. He has nothing to do with evil."

Fresh tears filled the girl's eyes and spilled onto her cheeks. She looked at the picture of her father again. "But He could've stopped it."

"There are some things we won't ever fully understand this side of heaven." Jamie squeezed the girl's hands. "What happened September 11 is one of them. But I know this . . ." Jamie's voice lowered. She waited until Sami was looking at her. "I couldn't have survived it without faith in God. Faith that I found after my husband died, even though he prayed for me to find it every day while he was alive."

Sami's eyes widened. "So you didn't always believe?"

"No." Jamie released the girl's hands and leaned her shoulder against the hard back of the pew. "My parents died in a car accident when I was about your age. I stopped believing in God that day and didn't talk to Him again until three years ago."

The girl shifted and set the photo on her knee. She ran her fingers beneath her eyes. "We were very close." She looked at Jamie and stifled another sob. "My mom's a wonderful person, but my daddy knew me best." Her gaze fell to the picture again. "I miss him so much."

"Tell me something, Sami."

She looked up. "What?"

"Would your dad want you angry at God?" It was more than she would usually say, but that didn't matter. It was what Jake would've said. And since she did this in his honor, she would gently prod and push people back toward God as often as she had a chance.

The girl picked up the photo and held it tight against her chest. She hung her head and uttered a gut-wrenching whisper. "No."

"If your father loved God, then he's in heaven now. Probably grateful that you wound up here today."

Sami nodded. "I think I've missed God almost as much as I missed my dad. I had to . . . had to work at being mad at Him."

"I know." And she did. Jamie remembered a conversation she'd had with Jake not long before he died. He'd found out that she'd been asking Sierra about Sunday school. He wanted to know if maybe she'd changed her mind, if maybe she wanted to come one Sunday just to see what it was like. Just to find out if she still wanted to hold a grudge against God.

At the time she'd had to work to tell him no. It was her pride, really. The fact that she didn't want to need God, didn't want to love Him. But it wasn't that she didn't believe. No matter what she told herself about God not existing and about the Bible being made up of fine-sounding fairy tales, she always knew the truth. God was alive and waiting for her. Hounding her relentlessly until finally He used Jake's Bible and journal to catch her, to break down the walls and allow her the chance to run to His arms.

"It's just . . ." Sami lowered the photo so she could see it again. "I want to be with him on his birthday. And when I get married one day, I want him to walk down the aisle with me. I want it so bad."

"But you can't blame God that you won't have it, okay, Sami? God loves you very much. He loves your dad too." Jamie took the girl's hands again. "Let's pray, okay?"

"Okay."

They bowed their heads and Jamie prayed. "Suffering is a part of life, God. You showed us that on September 11. We almost never understand why." She hesitated, trying to keep her composure. "But we know this: You love us. You loved us so much You gave us Jesus. And no matter how much Sami's suffering right now, You're here holding her, speaking peace into her heart and soul." A Scripture came to mind. "Jeremiah 29:11 tells us that You know the plans You have for us. Help Sami remember that, God. Give her Your hope as she leaves this place, Your certainty that You haven't forgotten her, and that one day she'll see her father again."

There was a silence while Jamie waited. She was about to finish up when Sami cleared her throat. "I'm sorry, God. I hate trying to get through this without You. Plus . . ." She sniffed once more. "Plus You've got my dad with You. So please, Lord, tell him happy birthday for me. Please."

When they finished praying, Jamie hugged the girl and promised to keep praying for her. Before she left, Sami gave Jamie a lopsided grin. "I came here because it was something I could do for my father. But instead . . . my heavenly Father did something for me." She stood and touched Jamie's shoulder. "I wasn't expecting that."

After Sami left, Jamie looked across the chapel at Jake's picture. She could make it out from any spot in the building—maybe not the details of his handsome face, the strength in his jaw, or the sparkle in his eyes, but she could find it all the same.

Sami was right. St. Paul's was a place where the unexpected happened. It had been that way for three years, ever since the towers collapsed, leaving the old church completely unharmed. It was an unexpected rescue mission back then and, because of conversations like the one she'd just had, it was an unexpected rescue mission now.

She noticed Aaron talking with another volunteer near the television at the back of the chapel. But before she had a chance to tell him hello, two women approached her. They were FDNY widows, women who had been in before.

"Hi, Jamie." The first one smiled.

She couldn't remember their names, but she didn't want to say so. Instead she exhaled and rose to greet them. "Back again?"

The women looked tentatively at each other. Then the first one crossed her arms. "We want to see about becoming volunteers."

"Like you," the other woman said.

"Like me?"

Jamie could hear Martha's words of warning. "Most FDNY widows won't ever be ready to take on a job like volunteering at St. Paul's. Discourage women who want to be like you as much as possible, for their sakes."

Jamie had bristled at the coordinator's comment. "It's good for me; why wouldn't it be good for them?"

"You're the exception, Jamie. Trust me. For most people volunteering at St. Paul's wouldn't work them through the stages of grief, it would stall them."

"What if someone asks about it and I'm not sure?"

Martha had given her a wry sort of smile. "You'll know. Ask them a few questions. If they break down, they're not ready."

Jamie blinked at the women, hating what she was about to do. The questions she had to ask were like poking a pin at an open wound to see if it was healing. But if Martha was right, it was the only way to make sure the women were able to move past their own grief long enough to help strangers with theirs.

"Why don't you come this way and we'll talk about it." Jamie led the women back to the pews, to the same place where she'd been sitting with Sami a few moments earlier. She started with the more outspoken of the two. "I'm on your side, ladies, but sometimes people only think they're ready for volunteer work here." Her voice was low, discreet. "Can you each tell me what you've done to work through your losses?"

The first woman nodded. "I've been in counseling at my church for a year. Sometimes I take my children with me—so they can talk about their feelings."

"Do they remember their father?"

"Yes." The woman's eyes flooded. She folded her hand and stared at her lap for a moment. "The youngest doesn't, but the other three remember him."

"If someone sat across from you and told you they'd stopped believing in God because of what happened September 11, would you feel comfortable helping them find their faith again?"

This time the woman looked up, and a strength filled her eyes. "Absolutely. That's why I'm here. I believe God wants me to share His truth with people who come here hurting." She looked at her friend, and then back at Jamie. "The way you shared it with us the first time we came in."

Jamie patted the woman's shoulders. She was passing with flying colors. Usually by now widows who weren't ready would be breaking down, asking questions of their own. Questions they had a right to ask, but that proved they weren't ready to work at St. Paul's. Not this woman.

"I understand there's an application we have to fill out?" The strength in the woman's eyes was softened by a compassion that only came from knowing pain personally.

"Yes." Jamie hesitated. "I'm sorry. I remember you, of course, but I've forgotten your names. A lot of people come through here."

"I'm Janice." She nodded to her friend. "This is Beth."

"And Beth, what about you? Tell me about your husband."

She lifted a dainty shoulder. "I don't know; he was my hero, I guess."

"You were married a long time?" Just because Jamie was ready for work at the chapel didn't mean Beth was.

"We'd only been married three years. I was—" Her voice broke. She looked up at the cross and bit her lip. "I was expecting our first baby, our son, when he died."

"I'm sorry." Jamie leaned forward. "Would you feel comfortable talking about that with strangers?"

For a moment Beth said nothing, only kept her eyes glued to the cross. Then, as tears streamed down her cheeks, she gave a slow shake of her head. "No, his memory is too precious for that."

Jamie waited.

Beth looked at Janice and then at Jamie. "I guess I'm not ready for this. I'm sorry. I thought I was. I wanted to be ready."

"There are lots of things you can do, Beth, even if this isn't one of them." Jamie's heart ached for the woman. Next to her, Janice gave her friend a hug.

After a moment, Jamie handed Beth a tissue. When she was more composed she looked at Jamie. "What can I do? Everywhere I go, people have forgotten about September 11. It's as if it bothers them to remember that it ever happened at all. But I want to do something."

"You can go home and love that little boy. He's three years old, Beth. He needs you. And you can keep alive every single memory you ever shared with your husband. You can write them in a journal so that when your son is old enough he'll feel as if he knew his daddy personally."

Beth's eyes filled with another layer of tears, but there was something else there. A light, a ray of hope the woman hadn't had before. "I never thought of that."

Jamie kept her tone compassionate. "If you don't do that for your son, who will?"

When the women left late that morning, Janice had an application, and Beth had a plan, a purpose. Proof again that Jamie's work at St. Paul's was important, that it did indeed carry on Jake's legacy— offering people hope in the name of Jesus Christ.

And that morning, the results were so strong, so eternally important, Jamie could almost feel Jake working beside her.

FOUR

Some volunteers stayed on at St. Paul's indefinitely—people like Jamie and Aaron Hisel. But most worked for a season and then moved on. Which meant the little chapel always needed new volunteers.

As Jamie headed for the stairs that morning, she thought about Janice. From what she could tell, the woman would be a wonderful addition to the staff. Close enough to share the pain of visitors who needed comforting; strong enough to offer them the spiritual hope they needed.

But as wonderful as the morning's outcome had been, Jamie was exhausted, emotionally drained. More so than usual. She headed for the break room and grabbed a blueberry muffin from the table. People were always bringing in cases of water or trays of baked goods for the volunteers. A way of encouraging them to continue the work they did at St. Paul's.

Jamie peeled back the wrapper and took a bite. The issue with Sierra was weighing on her. How was she supposed to tell her daughter the truth? Should it happen in stages? Maybe start by telling her that her father was killed in the Twin Towers with hundreds of other firefighters, and then see if she remembered having someone who looked and acted like her daddy living with them after that?

Footsteps sounded on the stairs and Jamie looked up to see Aaron step into the break area. "How'd it go?" He took a bottle of water and dropped to the nearest seat. "That first one looked tough."

"It was."

"A couple of volunteers from the weekend showed up." He crossed his arms and gave a slight tilt of his head. "Let's leave early. We can grab a bite to eat and take it to the park."

"Battery Park?"

"Right." He grinned, something she couldn't remember seeing him do until well after the second anniversary of the attacks. "Central Park might make you late for Sierra."

"True." She pulled herself to her feet, finished her water, and waited for him. There was something different in his eyes, something she couldn't quite make out. She didn't say anything. She'd ask him later, on the way to the park.

He finished his drink, stood, and led the way down the stairs. They bid the other volunteers good-bye and left. The sun was overhead now, warming the early October afternoon. Jamie pulled a pair of sunglasses from her small bag and slipped them on. She and Aaron were comfortable together. Every moment between them didn't need to be filled with conversation, and they stayed silent as they passed the crater where the towers had stood.

Jamie waited a few more blocks, then she shaded her eyes and looked at him. "What's on your mind?"

"Hmmm?" Aaron raised his eyebrows. "Nothing, why?"

"Yes, something." She looked straight ahead again. "I saw it in your eyes back at the chapel."

The captain shoved his hands into his FDNY windbreaker and kept his tone even. "What'd you see?"

"I don't know." Their conversation had a casual pace. "Something I haven't seen before. I'm not sure."

"Hmmm." The corners of Aaron's lips raised just a notch. He turned into a café and looked at her over his shoulder. "Let's get lunch."

They ordered turkey sandwiches, chips, and two cans of pop, which the deli man packed in one bag. Aaron carried it, and ten minutes later they reached Battery Park and found a bench with a view of the harbor.

Aaron pulled out her lunch first, and then his. He was about to take a bite, when she bowed her head and started praying. "Thank You, God, for our food. Thank You that we can find meaning and purpose helping the people at St. Paul's. You're a good God, Lord, and You know the plans You have for us. Amen."

A chuckle came from Aaron. "You insist on doing that, don't you? Praying for me?"

Jamie smiled. "If I don't do it, who will?"

She and the captain didn't exactly see eye to eye on matters of faith, but she would never preach at him or force him to see things her way. It hadn't worked for her when she was the one on Aaron's side of the fence. It wouldn't work for him, either.

"No one, and I'm fine with that." He took a bite of his sandwich.

"I know, Aaron." Her tone was mixed humor and mock boredom. "God doesn't exist. Same drivel I used to drive Jake crazy with."

He opened his mouth to say something, then changed his mind. Instead he took another bite. "Good sandwich."

"Okay, fine." She held up her turkey roll. "Good sandwich."

"Brat." He gave her a light nudge in the ribs with his elbow. "I'm not that stubborn. You could try a little harder."

She felt her eyes dance in light of the easy banter. "Would it work?"

"No." He set his sandwich down and laughed again. "But you could at least try."

They finished their sandwiches, their arms occasionally brushing against each other. Two people had stepped up and become her support system since Jake died. Sue, who'd been married to Jake's friend, Larry—another FDNY man lost on September 11—and Aaron.

She appreciated Aaron most at times like this, when she couldn't rattle off another statistic about the terrorist attacks, couldn't give another hug without running to the picture of Jake and falling in a heap on the floor. Times when the chance to smile or laugh gave her one more piece of tangible proof that yes, she would survive. Somehow she would keep waking up, keep breathing, keep raising Sierra the best she knew how, and the world wouldn't come to an end.

Aaron finished his sandwich, tossed the wrapper in the bag, and set it on the ground. He turned to her and the look was back, the one she'd seen earlier in St. Paul's break room.

"There it is again." She had her sandwich in her hands, but she let them fall to her lap. "That look, the one I was telling you about earlier."

"You don't let up, do you?"

"No. You can't hide anything from me." Jamie stuffed what was left of her sandwich into the bag and pushed the wrapper in after it. "You shouldn't even try."

"Is that right?"

"Yes." She crossed her ankles and stared out at the harbor. Aaron would tell her what was on his mind. He always did. He was a man of few words, the type who communicated more through glances and nuances. And because of that, he was nothing like Jake. Certainly he lacked Jake's way of lighting up a room, the charisma that came so naturally for Jake. No, Aaron's appeal was subtler, but after sharing her grief with him over the past years, they were close enough that she was right.

Jamie could read him perfectly.

They were quiet again, watching a triple-decker boat of tourists sail past on their way to the Statue of Liberty.

Finally he cleared his throat and looked at her. "Can I throw something out there?"

"Of course."

His eyes grew deeper than before. "How long, Jamie?"

"How long?" For the first time in a long while, Aaron had her stumped. "How long what?"

Aaron squinted at the sun's reflection on the water. "How long before you're ready to move on with life?"

"Move on?" Fear kicked Jamie in the gut and left her breathless. "I am moving on. Working at St. Paul's is moving on."

"Not that way." He leaned over and dug his elbows into his knees. His eyes found hers. "Jamie, I have feelings for you." His tone was heavy and certain. A long sigh sifted between his lips, and he looked out at the water again. "I've wanted to tell you for a long time."

Jamie felt her eyes grow wide, frightened. She wasn't sure what to do next. Had she read Aaron wrong from the beginning? He'd wanted friendship, right? So where had this . . . this change of heart come from? Or had it been there all along and she just hadn't wanted to see it? Part of her wanted to back up slowly, turn around, and run for her life. But still another part needed to hear him out. Not because she was ready for what he was saying, or because she could even manage the thought of Aaron being anything more than her friend. But because deep in her soul she'd known he was going to say this.

She'd known it and been so afraid she hadn't been able to admit it even to herself.

Her fingers shook. She laced them together to keep them from catching Aaron's attention.

He looked at her again. "Don't leave me hanging here, Jamie." He forced a laugh. "I cough up the hardest words I've ever said and you're speechless."

"I don't . . ." She raked her fingers through her hair and leaned hard against the back of the bench. "You're one of my best friends, Aaron. I haven't . . . I can't . . ."

Aaron shifted his position so he faced her squarely. Then, while his eyes never left hers, he took her hands. His voice fell and mixed with the breeze coming off the water. "You can, Jamie. We're together all the time, anyway. We've been through more than most people ever go through before having a first date."

First date?

The words hit her like fingernails on a chalkboard. She could feel the blood draining from her face. What if Jake could somehow see her from heaven? What if he could see her sitting on a bench beside Aaron Hisel talking about a first date? The idea made her shudder.

"Look, Jamie." Aaron straightened and his expression eased. "I know it's going to take time, but I've been thinking about it." He stood and pulled her to her feet. "We belong together. I'll take it as slow as you want to go. Just give it some thought, okay?"

Everything in her wanted to scream at him. No, it wasn't okay. No, she wouldn't think, even for a split second, about dating or loving or mar—

She couldn't bring herself to finish the thought. She wanted to turn around and see Jake standing there laughing, wanted to hear him telling her it was all a bad joke, that Captain Hisel certainly wasn't suggesting they find their way into a relationship when Jake Bryan was the only man she'd ever love.

But she couldn't do any of those things, because Jake was gone. He'd been gone three years and he wasn't coming back. And the truth was, if she didn't want to be alone for the rest of her life, it was only logical that she might wind up with someone like Aaron, someone who shared September 11 with her, who could relate to the losses she'd suffered because in some ways they were his losses too.

Aaron wasn't quite six feet tall, but he had her beat by a few inches. He looked down at her, his eyes a sea of patience. "Just think about it, Jamie. Okay?"

"Okay." She felt all disconnected, as if her mouth was operating separate from her heart and mind and soul. "I'll think about it."

A smile played in Aaron's eyes. "Good." He pulled her close and gave her an easy hug, then walked with her toward the ferry. It was earlier than she usually left, but she needed some alone time, time to process what he'd just told her.

All afternoon while she was waiting for Sierra to come home from school, and even while she helped her daughter with homework, Jamie tried to consider the idea of dating Aaron Hisel.

By the time she tucked Sierra in for the night and gave her butterfly kisses the way Jake used to do, she had willed herself to consider the idea without feeling sick with betrayal. He was handsome, a great guy who knew her pain better than any other man except Eric Michaels—and she'd never see him again.

She and Aaron shared an event that would forever color their pasts, forever shape their futures. Maybe he was right; maybe it was a logical idea, a way to ensure that she and Sierra wouldn't be alone.

It wasn't until she was falling asleep that she remembered something from earlier that day. They'd been eating lunch and Aaron's arm had brushed up against hers. She'd made a note of it, but only in the most comfortable sense. Because Aaron was her friend.

But when her arm had brushed up against Jake's arm—even the last week of his life, when they were jet skiing together—she felt the sensation throughout her body. Jake's touch was electrifying; it had always been that way. But Aaron? Aaron's was comfortable, nothing more.

So maybe that wasn't a bad thing. Maybe there'd never be anyone who electrified her heart and soul the way Jake did, but maybe that was okay. It was still possible she and Aaron could build a relationship. After all, Jake was gone, and she was more lonely than she wanted to admit.

There was one problem.

She'd always been honest with Aaron. She could tell him she'd think about the possibility of the two of them; she could promise he would always be her friend no matter what, even if that meant a comfortable friendly out-together-sometimes relationship. That would be the truth. But if she told him she was open to the possibility of finding their way together, to the chance of falling in love with him, she'd be doing something she'd never done to him before.

She'd be lying.

The place in her heart for electricity and sparks and fireworks, the place that still went weak at the knees at his memory, would always belong to one man and one alone: Jake Bryan.

Even if she had to wait a lifetime to see him again.

FIVE

Sue Henning was walking past a picture of Larry, hurrying from one room to another trying to clean the house for Jamie's visit, when it hit her. Larry had been dead for three years. Three long years.

The anniversary of September 11 didn't allow her time for private reflection, but sometimes—without warning—she would hear Larry's hearty laugh, or smell a faint whiff of his cologne from the bathroom where it stood to this day, untouched. Something would trigger his memory, the image of his sweet freckled face—and the enormity of his loss would hit her all over again.

It happened less often these days, and that, in and of itself, was painful. How dare her mind and heart and soul move on without him, without the life they'd known and loved? They had two children, and once in a while something seven-year-old Katy said or the way little Larry—not quite four—waved at her with one finger, the same way her Larry had always waved at her, triggered the loss.

This time it was the photograph.

The look in Larry's eyes reached out and stopped her in her tracks, demanded that here, now, she remember all he was and all she'd lost. Sue sucked in a fast breath and grabbed the edge of the countertop where the photo stood.

Larry ... I haven't forgotten.

She looked at the edges of his face, the way his eyes twinkled, and she tried to remember those same lines in motion, smiling and talking and loving her late at night. The memory of them was dimmer now, and there was nothing she could do about it. Time stole a little more of it every day.

The doorbell rang, and just as quickly the moment passed.

Jamie hadn't been by in a week, and Sue missed her terribly. The two were closer than sisters since September 11. They talked about their kids—Katy and Sierra were still best friends—and the ways they spent their time. But mostly they talked about the past, about happy moments and memories that had no chance of surviving if they weren't unfolded and held up for display every now and then.

Her friendship with Jamie was God's gift, no doubt. A safe harbor, a place where they could each be completely vulnerable, no matter if the world thought it was time they moved on. And in the midst of that harbor, Sue had found in Jamie the best girlfriend she'd spent a lifetime wishing for.

She gave a last look at Larry's picture and called out over her shoulder. "Just a minute . . ."

It was four o'clock in the afternoon, so Sierra would be with Jamie. The girls could hardly wait to play together and days like this—when the sun was still shining and winter seemed a month away—they could go out back and play the way they'd played since they were toddlers.

Her house was on Staten Island, same as Jamie's. It gave them more room to spread out than they'd have had with a house in the city, and a way to feel disconnected from the hustle of Manhattan. She opened the door and grinned at Jamie. "I miss you, girl. You have to come more than once a week!"

Jamie hugged her. "I know. I was having withdrawals."

Sierra stepped in, her blonde hair falling like a silk curtain over her shoulders. "Hi, Mrs. Henning. Is Katy upstairs?"

"Yes, honey." Sue hugged Sierra. "She's waiting for you."

"Thanks." Sierra ran off and stopped only a moment to brush her fingers through little Larry's hair. "Hi, buddy. Whatcha doing?"

The boy was wearing a miniature Nets jersey, and he had a basketball under one arm. "Shooting hoops."

Larry's small plastic basketball hoop stood on one side of the living room, surrounded by a sofa and a loveseat. Sue didn't mind the boy shooting baskets in the house. The child was practically fanatical about the sport; as long as he had a ball in his hands he was happy. And if he was happy, she and Jamie could hold a conversation without interruption.

Sierra ran off, and Sue motioned to a quieter alcove, a place where they could sit and still see little Larry, but not be hit by loose balls. Sue had made iced tea, and two tall glasses stood on a table surrounded on two sides by comfy chairs.

Jamie was quieter than usual. She dropped into one of the over-stuffed chairs, planted her elbows on the arms, and covered her face. After a moment she let her hands fall to her lap and she looked at Sue. "I wanted to come earlier, but Sierra begged me to wait until she was out of school." Jamie's tone was serious, the corners of her eyes tight with the small lines of worry. She pursed her lips, her eyes locked on Sue's. "You aren't going to believe this."

Sue took the seat closest to her friend and tried to seem interested. "Something at St. Paul's?" Jamie almost always started their conversations with a story from St. Paul's. There was a time when Sue wanted nothing more than to be at the quaint little chapel. For months she would've gladly gotten up every day and gone to St. Paul's, walked the walls of memories and mementos, and pretended even for an hour that the souls lost that day were still vibrant and alive.

But never once had she considered volunteering there.

She was worried about Jamie. It was one thing to help out for a while. But Jamie had been working three days a week, sometimes four, ever since the first anniversary, the day they reopened the chapel to the public.

Jamie shook her head; her face was tight and pale. "Not St. Paul's. Captain Hisel."

"Captain Hisel?" Sue wrinkled her nose. Jamie and the captain were friends; everyone knew that. Now Sue felt her heart skip a beat as she waited for the news. "He's okay, isn't he?"

"Yes." She gave a quick nod. "Nothing like that."

Sue felt her heart skitter back into a normal rhythm. That was one thing about September 11. Before that day, Sue was vaguely aware of tragedy; now in some morbid sort of way, she expected it. As if by expecting it, the eventual blows life dealt would somehow be easier to take. "Okay. Then what am I not going to believe?"

"I wanted to call you yesterday, but I had to work through it."

Sue was even more confused. "Work through something with the captain?"

"Aaron."

"Okay, Aaron." Sue took a sip of her tea. "It's still weird to think of him that way, I guess."

"Yeah." Jamie sat back in her chair and gripped the arms. "Wait till you hear this."

Sue waited. The quieter she was, the better chance Jamie would get to the point. At that moment the girls came barreling down the stairs.

Katy skipped into the room, breathless and happy. Sierra was close on her heels. "Can we go outside and play?"

Sue looked at Jamie and caught her look of approval. She smiled at Katy and pointed to the closet. "Get your coat. It's almost dark and the nights are getting colder now."

"Yes, Mommy."

Sierra raised her eyebrows at Jamie. "Me too?"

"Yes, silly. You too." Jamie was clearly trying to keep her tone light.

When the girls were gone, Sue looked at Jamie. "So . . . ?"

"Okay." She breathed in slow through her nose. "Here's what happened." Jamie's fingers came together. The tips of her knuckles were white. "Yesterday after working at St. Paul's, Aaron and I went to Battery Park with our lunch. I didn't think anything of it, I mean, at the time I didn't, anyway. We eat out together all the time, especially after working at the chapel."

Sue nodded. "All the time."

"But yesterday there was something different in his eyes. I couldn't put my finger on it while we were at St. Paul's, but when we were sitting on a bench at the park, watching the tourist boats in the harbor, I asked him about it." Jamie paused. Her shoulders sank a notch, and the lines on her forehead grew more pronounced. "He told me he has feelings for me, Sue. That he could picture the two of us together some day, and that . . . that I should at least think about it."

Relief flooded Sue's veins. Relief and sorrow all at the same time. Her question to her friend was both kind and pointed. "Can you blame him, Jamie?"

Jamie leaned forward. Her eyes held an angst Sue had never seen there before. "Can I blame him?" She uttered a sound that fell short of a laugh. "I wasn't sure whether to kick him or run for my life."

Sue tried to picture her feisty friend having that reaction to Captain Hisel's admission. "Jamie, you didn't kick him!"

"No." She bit the inside of her lip. "But I didn't run, either."

"Because . . ."

"Because maybe I didn't want to run." Her voice cracked. "And maybe that's worse."

Sue set her tea down. Her heart hurt for her friend. Moving on was going to be painful for both of them, but it was bound to come. Time would see to that. She reached out and took hold of Jamie's knee. Her voice was just loud enough to hear. "Because maybe deep down you've considered the possibility yourself? Is that it?"

"I don't know." Jamie's lower lip and chin quivered. "I don't know, Sue. I only know that I feel this terrible guilt, as if I'm betraying Jake by even talking about this."

For a long while, Sue said nothing. There were no rule books or guidelines about how to start living again. Some FDNY widows had already remarried, some not much more than a year after the attacks. Neither Sue nor Jamie could imagine moving on so quickly, but everyone handled grief differently.

And not everyone had a husband like Larry or Jake.

Sue tucked her feet beneath her up onto the chair and stared out the window. The girls were swinging, pushing their toes toward the sky and giggling all the while. She looked back at Jamie. "I've wondered about this, about whether I could ever even find another man attractive after Larry."

Jamie massaged her temples. "You never told me."

"It's like you said, just mentioning the idea feels like a crime."

"But when you do . . ." Jamie looked at the floor for a moment, and then back up at Sue. "When you do think about it, how do you usually end up feeling?"

Peace hugged Sue's shoulders and settled in beside her. She spread her hands out before her and nodded toward little Larry and the girls in the backyard. "Like this is enough. My children, my memories. They're all I need. At least for now, until God shows me something different."

"What if that's what He's showing me?"

"Well . . ." Sue took hold of her tea again. She ran her fingers along the dewy moisture that had built up on the glass. "Do you, you know, do you feel anything when you're with Capt—" She caught herself. "When you're with Aaron?"

Jamie closed her eyes and scrunched her face. When she opened them she looked more bewildered than before. "Not really." She lifted her hands from her lap and dropped them again. "But the idea of being more than friends isn't altogether horrible, either."

"Hmmm."

"Yeah, I know." She stood and paced across the room. For a few moments she watched little Larry make three baskets in a row. Then she came back and sat in her chair again. "No one ever teaches you how to do this."

"No."

"I've been thinking what would Jake want, and even there I'm not sure." Jamie ran her finger around the rim of her iced tea glass, her eyes distant. "He wouldn't want me alone, not for the rest of my life." She looked up. "But how could he want me with another man?"

"I've thought about that too." Sue's stomach turned. The conversation was as difficult for her as it was for Jamie. They hadn't wanted their marriages to end; they'd simply been cut short. And in their place was a void that even the best memories couldn't fill completely. "Of course Jake wouldn't want you to fall in love with someone else, not if he were here. But he isn't. He's gone, and so is Larry."

"But it feels so wrong, like they aren't really dead unless . . . until we move on with life, find someone new." Jamie's voice was thick with emotion. "You know?"

"Yes." Sue thought of something. "There is something else."

"What?"

"What's Aaron think of your faith?"

Jamie hesitated, but only for a minute. "He . . . he teases me about it, especially when I say I'm praying for him. He tells me there's no point."

"Hmmm. I didn't know that."

"Some of the guys at the department struggle with faith, at least that's what Aaron tells me. I hadn't thought much about that." She took a sip from her glass and looked at Sue over the rim. "Too busy trying to sort through my feelings, I guess."

Quiet came over them again. Sue wasn't sure what to say. She was certain a relationship with Aaron should never materialize as long as he didn't share Jamie's faith. But it was probably too soon to say anything. Still, she couldn't stay silent; her faith wouldn't allow it. She bit her tongue and tried to pick the right words.

After another minute, Jamie said, "I know what you're thinking."

"What?" Sue crossed her legs.

"You're thinking Aaron isn't a believer. Right?"

Sue pursed her lips. "Was it written on my forehead?"

"No." Jamie sank back into her chair. She sounded defeated. "In your eyes."

"I'm not saying I'm right, Jamie, but if I were you I'd keep his friendship and consider anything more a closed subject."

"Except for one thing."

"What?"

"Jake didn't do that to me. He loved me despite my lack of faith . . . and look what happened."

"You were kids when you met, that's different." Sue could've said more, but she didn't want to push, not now. "God will make it all clear to you—however things work out."

"Yes." The lines on Jamie's forehead eased completely and her eyes looked more peaceful. "I'll keep you posted. I guess the whole discussion has made me wonder if it's time to move on, to think of myself as single, not widowed."

Sue smiled, the first time either of them had done so since they sat down. "Since you brought it up . . ."

"Brought what up?"

"Moving on." Sue uncrossed her legs and slid to the edge of her chair. "Jamie, maybe it's time you stopped working at St. Paul's."

Jamie's eyes grew wide and her mouth hung open. "Quit St. Paul's?" Jamie uttered a hard exhale and raked her fingers through her dark hair. "St. Paul's and Sierra—that's all that drives me, Sue. God's given me those two as a reason to get up every morning, to keep existing even when I feel like I'm already dead."

Sue put her hand on Jamie's knee again. "But maybe that feeling is because of St. Paul's, because you're reminded of September 11 over and over again."

"No." Jamie gave a hard shake of her head. "It's not because of St. Paul's. That chapel gives me a way to keep Jake's legacy alive, a way to help other people have faith and hope, the way Jake would've helped them if he were still alive. Every day I go there I feel a little better about myself, my purpose in life. Even when I leave there exhausted."

Sue didn't say anything; she didn't have to. If Jamie was leaving St. Paul's feeling emotionally drained, then maybe she would see it was time for a break. She'd said as much before, but Jamie was determined to stay at St. Paul's. The place made her feel closer to Jake. Only Jamie could make the decision about leaving. "Okay." Sue looked at the girls again. "I'll ask you the same thing Aaron did." She caught Jamie's eyes again. "Just think about it."

They were too close to argue, and even now Jamie didn't seem frustrated by Sue's request. Just certain. "The day it doesn't feel like Jake's up there smiling at me, I'll turn in my notice, deal?"

"Deal."

The conversation shifted to the girls, and Jamie admitted she was thinking of telling Sierra the truth about Jake's death, and the fact that the man who had lived with them after September 11 hadn't been Jake at all.

Before their conversation ended, they joined hands and prayed that God might give Jamie wisdom about how and what and when to tell Sierra. After dinner and a game of Uno with the kids, Jamie and Sierra headed home.

Sue tucked in Larry and then Katy. They had their own rooms, but most nights Katy liked sleeping on Larry's top bunk.

"He likes company, Mommy," Katy had told her. But the truth was something different. Since losing her father, Katy hated being alone. It was one more reminder that nothing would ever be the same again.

This time when Sue passed the photo of Larry, she didn't feel any sharp reminders or rushes of sorrow. Instead she smiled back, and as she did she remembered something Jamie had said earlier that evening. The day it didn't feel like Jake was up there smiling was the day she'd turn in her notice.

Jake was always smiling. He and Larry could've been brothers that way, even if they looked nothing alike. Sue could picture Jake smiling at Jamie out on the water, flying over the harbor on her jet ski, or while taking Sierra to dance classes, even helping out at church.

But talking about what happened that Tuesday morning, over and over and over again?

No matter how hard she tried, Sue couldn't picture Jake Bryan smiling about that.

Sierra was trying to get to sleep, but she couldn't. Something Katy said while they were swinging made her stomach feel bouncy. Like the curls on Cinda May in her second-grade class. She did a big breath and rolled onto her side. "C'mere, Wrinkles. Where are you, boy?"

Wrinkles was her big gray cat. Sierra named him *Wrinkles* because when he was a little baby he had a wrinkly face. He slept in Sierra's room, but not always on her bed. Mommy said that was 'cause Wrinkles had an attitude. Most cats had attitudes, actually.

"Wrinkles . . ." Sierra made her voice a loud whisper. Mommy thought she was sleeping, so she couldn't be loud. But she needed to talk to someone. Wrinkles was the only other person in the room.

Sierra heard a little meowing sound, and Wrinkles jumped onto the bed. He padded over with his soft cat feet and looked straight at her.

"Hi, Wrinkles." Sierra patted the cat's back. "Lay down."

Wrinkles pushed at the covers three times and then curled his legs beneath him. As soon as he was down, he started purring. Purring was when cats were happy; that was something else Mommy had told her.

"I'm glad you're happy, Wrinkles." Sierra rubbed her nose against the cat's tiny pink one. It was cold and wet like the morning grass. "Wrinkles, I'm feeling a little sick." She studied the cat. "You know, in my tummy. That kind."

Wrinkles leaned his head back and yawned. He yawned so big she could see the little prickly things on his tongue. When people yawned it meant they were bored, but not Wrinkles. When he yawned it meant he wanted her to keep talking. That's what he always did when she talked to him at night.

"I'm gonna talk to Jesus about it before I go to sleep, but I thought I'd tell you first." Sierra sat up and folded her legs crisscross applesauce. "Wanna know what Katy said?" She waited. "She said it was weird that Daddy died in a building fire saving people because he was with her daddy in the Twin Towers and they never stayed apart." Her nose itched. She gave it a little scratch. "Doesn't that make you feel kind of sick, Wrinkles? Because if my daddy and Katy's daddy were together in the Twin Towers, how come they didn't die at the same time, actually? How come my daddy came home for a little while and then he died, huh?"

Wrinkles looked at her, but only for a few seconds. Then he began licking his skinny legs. Sierra liked when he did that. The way his tongue was all bristly, licking his fur was kind of like combing it. But the trouble with Wrinkles was, he didn't have a lot to say. He didn't have anything to say, really.

And this was the sort of problem that needed words on the other side. Words from someone who could help her understand. Otherwise Katy was right; it was weird.

Sierra did a yawn, almost as big as the one Wrinkles did. She lay back down, careful not to wake up her cat. Then she pulled the covers up to her chin, closed her eyes, and thought about it again. If her daddy and Katy's daddy were together, why didn't they die together? She squeezed her eyes shut very hard and tried to remember.

Daddy was hurt, because she remembered him in the hospital. Then he came home and he slept downstairs. Sierra remembered that too. At first he didn't know things—like where he was or who people were, actually. But then he started 'membering and doing all the things Daddy always did. Like curl her hair and make her blueberry pancakes and watch *Little Mermaid* with her.

Then one day he was gone.

Mommy said he was helping people in a fire when Jesus called him home to heaven. And that made pretty much sense, except for now Katy thought it was weird.

Sleep was coming to get her; she could feel it. She did another yawn and thought about Jesus. She liked talking to Him out loud, because you talked to real people that way. And Jesus was very real.

"Hi, Jesus, it's me, Sierra."

Wrinkles snuggled a little closer to her.

"I'm up late tonight because my tummy hurts. Well—" she opened her eyes and saw the room was shadowy dark—"it doesn't really hurt, it just feels bouncy, actually. And it's all because of what Katy said. First it was weird that my daddy didn't die at the same time as her daddy because they were both in the Twin Towers together." She scratched the tip of her nose again. "But something else, too. She said they found our two daddies' helmets at the same time. At the very same time, Jesus. Isn't that weird?"

Sierra's tummy started to feel a little less bouncy. That always happened when she talked to Jesus. One time Katy asked her if she was mad at Jesus for taking their daddies home too soon. Sierra had to think about that for a long time, but she decided no. She wasn't mad. Sometimes people die—that's what Mommy said. She couldn't be mad at Jesus for that because guess what? Jesus was taking care of Daddy right now. So how could she be mad?

She closed her eyes again. "Jesus, I think I'll talk to Mommy about it, okay? She'll know what to tell Katy, plus she can tell me about the helmets. If it's even true." Sleep was coming faster now. "Good night, Jesus. Tell my daddy I love him."

SIX

Clay was at the wheel of his Ford pickup, heading for Eric and Laura's house. They wanted to have him over for dinner before he left. He stopped at a light and leaned back, adjusting his sunglasses. Now that he'd made up his mind to go, he couldn't wait to get out of Los Angeles.

Eric teased him that he'd freeze to death. Southern California winters rarely dipped below seventy degrees, whereas Manhattan would most likely be buried in snow by mid-December. Clay didn't care. In three days, he and Reynolds would be on the flight bound for LaGuardia and a three-week stay in New York City. Three weeks. It felt like an eternity, and that was a good thing.

New scenery, new people, new challenges. All of it would take his mind off the bucket of things that had been bothering him. The light turned green, and he took a quick lead away from the pack of cars. He was five minutes late and he didn't want to hold up dinner.

But he didn't exactly want to go, either.

The whole thing with Laura was ridiculous, really. She'd never been more than a friend, and the fact that she was happily married to his brother was nothing but good. At least, that's how he wanted to feel. If only he could meet the right person, someone who would fill that yearning in his heart for love and companionship. Someone to laugh with and pray with, someone to walk alongside in faith, one who he could play tennis with and watch ESPN with late at night.

Did people pity him when they saw him out by himself? Eating out alone, shopping alone, seeing a movie by himself. He hated the looks from strangers. Often they came from women—attractive women, even—who let their look linger awhile. The questions were written on their faces. What was a guy like him doing alone, first of all, and was he interested in company?

Another red light. Clay came to a hurried stop and gritted his teeth. He wasn't interested. Not at all. He'd tried that route and nothing but awkward meetings had come from it. Guys from the station tried to set him up more times than he could remember, either with a sister or a friend of their own wife or girlfriend.

"You're a good-looking guy, Michaels," Reynolds told him once. "But you'd think you had three eyes and horns growing out of your head the way you can't keep a girl."

Clay had laughed. "Thanks, buddy. I needed that."

The trouble wasn't with him or the girls. They were generally young and beautiful and fun to be with. Los Angeles had no shortage of pretty women. The shortage was in women of faith. Women who believed the way he did, who saw faith in Christ not as a religion but as a relationship with the Creator.

He'd be out on a blind date, or at a barbecue where one of the guys was trying to set him up, and he'd say something about his job being a blessing or how he was sure God had a plan for people, and the girl would go slack-faced.

"Do you . . . go to church anywhere?"

Blank stare. "Church? You mean, like religion." The girl would offer a polite smile. "I'm not very religious."

Of course not. After three years of such exchanges, Clay wondered if there was even one single woman in Los Angeles who cared about the things he did. They were out there, of course. But he worked so many nights and weekends, he had a hard time connecting with a church group. When he could, he attended Sunday services at a growing church not far from his home—West Valley Christian. But he hadn't had time for any of the weekly groups, and so far he hadn't met single women his age.

The light turned green. He worked his way into the right lane and turned at the first street. Eric and Laura lived in a beautiful subdivision a few minutes up the hill and past a gated entry. He used to love seeing them, visiting with Eric and Laura, and spending time with Josh. But lately when he visited he couldn't wait to leave.

That's why the trip to New York would be so good for him.

He pulled into the driveway, made his way up the sidewalk, and knocked once before letting himself in. Josh saw him first, through the foyer from the kitchen table where he was sitting, working over a textbook.

"Uncle Clay, hey, guess what?" The boy was tall like his father, sandy hair, with the same blue eyes. He had Laura's fine bone structure, but little else.

"Hey, buddy." Clay set his keys on a table near the door and headed toward him. "What's up?"

Josh pushed back from the table and grinned. "I made the A team!"

"Your first year at middle school?" Clay gave the boy a high five. "You'll be playing at UCLA before you know it!"

"You think so?" His eyes grew wider, excitement sparkling. "The Bruins are the best."

"Just wait till they've got you on the team. Then they'll really be something."

Clay took a few steps closer and looked at the textbook. The page was a smattering of geometrical shapes. "Math, huh?"

Josh's tone fell. "Yeah, the worst."

"Need some help?"

"No." Josh nodded his head toward the back door. "Dad helped me when I got home from school. I get it." He gave Clay a crooked grin. "I just hate it, that's all."

There it was again. The reminder that this family was perfectly fine without him. Josh no longer needed him for homework or playing catch or an hour of jump shots outside. Eric took care of all that now.

And Laura . . . obviously she didn't need him. He was her friend, but they spent no time alone together, nor did they have any reason to do so. This was the new way of things. After three years, it wasn't even all that new anymore.

Eric worked from home. He maintained the same type of job, the same income, the same membership to the country club, while spending ten times as many hours with Laura and Josh. It was the type of miracle setup only God could've worked out.

The sliding door opened, and Clay turned to see Eric walk in with an empty platter. "Barbecue's on." He smiled first at Clay, then at Josh. "How's it coming?"

"Okay." Josh made a face. "I wish I was done."

"Why don't you take a break?" Eric set the platter on the vast granite island at the center of the kitchen. "You can help me cook the steaks."

"You mean turn 'em and everything?"

"Yep." Eric chuckled. "Mom's out there finding zucchini. You can help her till I get back out."

Josh didn't hesitate. He pushed his chair away from the table and ran out the door, gangly legs flying beneath him. Clay leaned against the counter and watched, amazed. How much happier and at peace with the world Josh was now that things were different at home. Further proof of what he already knew—the unequaled power of a good father in a boy's life.

Their own father had checked out long before Clay and Eric were teenagers. The man didn't divorce their mother until they were in high school, but by then they barely knew him. Neither he nor his brother had been in touch with him in the years since.

Clay shifted his lower jaw. *That's why I want to be a dad, God . . . so I can be the kind of father a child wants. The way Eric is with Josh.* He gritted his teeth. *Why's it taking so long?*

Eric popped open a Sprite and slid it across the counter to Clay. "You okay?"

"Huh?" Clay straightened himself. "Yeah. Fine."

"You look a little pensive."

"Nah, I'm fine." He wasn't, but Eric didn't need to know that. His older brother wasn't to blame for any of the feelings that had been poking at him lately. "Need help with dinner?"

"No, it's under control." Eric took a pop for himself and came up alongside Clay. "So . . ." He put the can down and crossed his arms. "How did it feel?"

How did it feel? Then it hit him. Of course . . . Eric was talking about the shooting. That's why all the questions. Clay shrugged. "Like target practice, I guess."

"Really?" Eric narrowed his eyes. "No difference?"

"Of course it was different." Clay uttered a sharp laugh and gave a sideways shake of his head. "The guy was spraying an AK-47 at me, and I was shooting from the floor of my patrol car. And instead of ripping some paper target, I killed a guy."

Eric's tone grew softer. "It was self-defense, Clay. Obviously."

"I know." He downed half of his pop and set the can back on the counter. "I was sick about it at first, but the truth was, I had no choice. It was me or him."

"How'd you fire at him without getting hit?"

Clay shrugged. "Same way you found your way home after September 11?" Clay loved this, the easy banter with his brother. For all the ways he was tempted to be jealous of him, he couldn't do anything but enjoy their time together.

Eric nodded, but he didn't answer the question; he didn't have to. They both knew the reason they were standing there that October afternoon. God alone got the credit.

"Josh says he made the A team."

"Yeah." Eric chuckled. "He has me playing better hoops than I did when I was a college boy." He shot an invisible ball toward the patio door. "The kid can't get enough."

"I'll have to catch a few games when I get back."

Eric's smile faded. "So what's this I hear about you spending three weeks in New York?"

"The idea came from Reynolds, one of the detectives at the station. I have three weeks paid while they investigate the shooting. I can also count it as training."

"Training?" Eric gave him a knowing look. "You mean you finally got your promotion?"

"Yeah." Clay gripped the countertop behind him. "Funny timing, huh? Kill a suspect in a shootout, come back to the office, and find out they've made you detective."

"Hey!" Eric slapped him on the back. "Way to go, little brother. You've had that coming for a few years at least." He hesitated. "But why New York? Couldn't you get training here?"

"Sure." Clay pulled away from the counter and stretched first to one side, then the other. He'd pulled a few muscles in his back when he jerked his body to the floorboard during the gunfight. He was still sore. "Reynolds wanted New York, for one thing. Not sure why. But I figure, why not? I've wanted to get back there since the terrorist attacks. After all the firefighters and police officers lost, it's sort of a trek, I guess. Something all of us want to do at one time or another."

Eric finished his pop and headed around the counter toward the sink. He ran the platter under water and sprayed it with a squirt of soap. "I don't miss it."

"Don't miss what?" Clay turned around and faced him. "Working there . . . or living there?"

Eric didn't look up. "Actually, I didn't live there. I lived in New Jersey."

Clay waited, but as usual, Eric didn't go into details.

"To answer your question, I don't miss working in Manhattan every month or so. I can't believe that was my life before September 11."

"And the other? Staten Island?"

Eric's eyes met his. "I think about it once in a while."

"You never talk about it."

"Nope." Eric turned off the water and grabbed a dish towel. "My time with her gave me a life I never would've had otherwise. But we promised each other we'd never talk about it. Not to anyone."

"Not even Laura?"

"Once in a while she'll say something about the firefighter, about how she's glad he kept a journal, glad he wrote notes in his Bible."

"That's what changed you, right? Believing you were this great family guy, a man with an unshakable faith?"

"That—" he ran the towel over the platter—"and her."

"The woman?"

Eric nodded. "She was very special. It killed me to leave her."

This was more than Eric had ever shared about that time in his life. Clay wasn't sure what to make of his brother's statement. "Did you . . . were you in love with her?"

"I thought she was my wife; I was *supposed* to love her. And the girl . . . I remembered her name when I woke up. It wasn't until the end that we figured out that part."

"The helmet?" It was one detail Clay did know.

"Yep. I tripped, as close as I can guess." He set the dry platter on the counter. "The fireman bent over to help me up and his helmet fell off. I picked it up, I remember that. Inside was a picture of the little girl and her name." He knit his brow together. "When I woke up, her name was the only thing I remembered."

"She got to you too, didn't she?" Clay cocked his head. "The little girl?"

"They both did." Eric gave a slight shake of his head. "But not like you think. When I left them it was no regrets. I was a different man." He took the platter and headed toward the patio door.

"You said it killed you."

Eric opened the slider and looked at Clay over his shoulder. "It did." He exhaled through pursed lips. "When I realized I wasn't her husband, things changed between us. I was a married man, so loving her went from being the thing I was trying to remember to something I could never do." He leaned against the door frame. "Yes, it killed me to leave her. Not because I was in love with her or her daughter, but because I knew how alone they would be."

"Hmmm." They stepped outside. Smoke curled up from the sides of the barbecue. A hundred feet away Josh was bent over the garden next to Laura. Clay didn't look for too long. "What was her name?"

"Doesn't matter. I don't like talking about her."

"Sorry. I guess I always wondered."

"It's okay. I was kind of mysterious about her when I came home. I figured no one needed to know."

Clay let that sit for a minute. "You ever call her, to see how she's doing?"

"Nope, can't do that either. God had a very clear reason why I wound up in her house. But when I left, both of us knew we wouldn't see each other again. It was how we wanted it." He lifted the barbecue lid. "I have a new life, one I wouldn't trade for the world. I could never love anyone but Laura, so you see, there's no room for looking back." He poked at the steaks. "The good-bye we said that last day at the airport was final."

Clay stared at the steaks, sizzling and deep brown at the edges. Two minutes passed, maybe three. "But you think about her, right? Once in a while?"

"Once in a while." Eric sprinkled salt on the meat. "She was incredible, Clay. More strength than any woman I've ever known. She loved me unconditionally. We helped each other find a friendship with God. Pretty heady stuff."

"Was she pretty?"

"Very." Eric smiled, his eyes distant. "I'm never sure which was the bigger miracle. That I came home completely in love with my wife, anxious to spend time with Josh, a changed man, really." He looked at Clay. "Or that I was able to walk away from Staten Island."

Laura and Josh were approaching them, carrying a big bowl of zucchini and strawberries. Laura smiled first at Eric, then at Clay. "Josh says he gets the strawberries." She stopped and hugged Clay. Her eyes were serious, concerned. Probably because of the gunfight. "How are you?"

"Fine." He cleared his throat. The conversation about Staten Island was over, and he could sense from his brother's body language that Eric was glad. Clay doubted they'd ever talk about it again.

Josh moved in beside Eric and, under Eric's guidance, the boy began turning the steaks. Laura was persistent. "I was so worried about you, Clay."

Of course she was. She still cared about him, the same as always. The fact that they'd crossed a line or two back in the months after the terrorist attacks probably never figured into her thinking.

She took a nearby chair, her brow knit together. "We watched it on TV and they showed your car." Laura put her fingers over her mouth. "Clay, it was awful. I can't believe you didn't get hit."

"I was praying big time." Clay took the chair opposite Laura. The smell of the steaks filled the air. Dinner would be nice, and then he'd be on his way. Until then, this was good; keeping his thoughts on the current day, the matters at hand. "I was on the floorboard and I could hear him coming closer. He'd already fired at me, so I knew he wanted to take me down."

Josh's eyes got wide. "That's crazy."

"It was." Clay worked his fingers into the muscles at the back of his neck. "I was asking God for a way out, and all of a sudden I knew. If I didn't look over the dash and at least try to stop the guy, I'd be dead in a few seconds."

Laura shuddered. "I haven't stopped thanking God ever since I heard."

"Dad says you're a good shot." Josh grinned at him. "All the kids at school thought it was way cool that you are my uncle."

Clay felt himself relax. How could he need a break from this? His family loved him, cared about him. "Thanks, Josh."

"Well—" Eric turned and looked at them—"Josh is doing wonders with the steak. We'll be ready in about five minutes."

Laura popped up and headed for the patio door. "I'll have everything ready inside." She looked at Clay. "Come help me."

He could hardly say no. He followed her into the kitchen as a memory came screaming back at him. After the Twin Towers collapsed, Laura had been frozen with shock. For five days she did little more than stare at the television and wait for Eric's call. From the first day on, the kitchen—this same kitchen—had been his territory. He made all meals, fed Josh, and helped the boy with his homework.

"You're quiet today." Laura led the way and handed him the bowl of zucchini. "Wash and slice. The pan's on the stove." She took up her position beside him and began rinsing the strawberries. "You sure everything's okay?"

Her chatter interrupted his thoughts, pulling him back to the here and now. Where he wanted to stay, no matter how much his heart refused to cooperate with him. The whole thing was ridiculous. He grabbed a zucchini from the bowl. "I'm fine. Just thinking about New York, I guess. I'm anxious to go."

"Eric was saying something about that." She set into a routine, rinsing a berry, pulling the stem from the top, and tossing it into a china bowl next to the sink. "I think it'll be good for you, Clay." Her eyes met his. "You need something different."

Clay held her gaze. Was she talking about having time away from them, time to find a life of his own? He wanted to ask, but he was afraid of where the conversation would go. "Yeah." He looked back at the vegetables. "The change'll do me good." He finished washing and sliced them into a pan already seasoned with oil. "They're making me a detective when I get back. That's the good news."

"Really?" Laura grinned at him over her shoulder. "Congratulations!"

"The time in New York will get me ready." He put the lid on the zucchini. "Funny how things work out."

Laura put the bowl of berries on the table and cleared away Josh's homework. "Could you hand me four plates?"

"Sure."

"They're in the—" Her eyes caught his. "I guess you know where they are." This time something in her expression told him he'd been right earlier. He must've been.

Again the motions were familiar. Reaching for the right cupboard, finding the plates as easily as if they were his own. He decided to take a chance. "It feels funny, working in here again. Brings back a lot of memories."

He felt Laura come a few steps closer, felt her wait until he was looking at her. "I couldn't have gotten through it without you." She tilted her head. "But sometimes I worry about you, Clay."

"Why?" He forced a laugh. He took the stack of plates and passed them to her. He tried not to notice the way their fingers brushed against each other in the transition. "The police work, you mean. The danger?"

"No." Her eyes were softer than before. "I've been praying for you, do you know that?"

"Since the shooting?"

"No." Her voice was clear and quiet and her eyes reached all the way to his soul. "Since Eric came home." She set the plates in a stack on the table. "I want you to find someone, Clay. If . . ."

He took a step closer. "Go ahead. Say it, Laura."

She let out a small sigh and looked at the floor. When she looked up he knew for certain that she understood how he felt—that he had no intention of coming between her and Eric, but somehow that wasn't enough to stop him from caring about her. Sometimes too much.

She took his hand and gave it a gentle squeeze, then released it. "If Eric hadn't come home, I'd be your wife by now. I believe that, Clay. You're a wonderful man, and I was falling hard for you when Eric came home. We both know that."

"Does Eric?"

"Yes." She stared at the ceiling and drew in a slow breath. "My marriage to Eric was a formality, it was all but over when he left for New York that September day. He knew that." She looked at him again. "You know what he told me?"

Clay wasn't sure he wanted to know. "What?"

"He told me if he hadn't survived, he would've wanted you and me together."

Clay had no idea how to react. He searched Laura's eyes for a minute and then walked past her. He grabbed a handful of forks and knives and carried them to the table. Then he turned to her again. "So that's why you think I need a change of scenery?" He wasn't mad. He simply wanted to know her feelings.

"I have Eric. Things are different for me." She took a stack of napkins from the counter and placed them one per setting. When she was finished she found his eyes again. "But if I didn't, if I were in your place, I'd still be in love with you, Clay. That's how strongly I felt for you." She gave him an understanding smile. "Sometimes I catch you looking and I wonder . . . if maybe you still feel that way about me."

"I don't. I—" Clay stopped himself. Her eyes told him instantly that she didn't believe him. "Laura, I wouldn't do anything to come between you and Eric."

"I know that."

"I hate that I think about you at all."

"Thanks."

He sat on the arm of the closest chair. "You know what I mean. I want to forget those three months ever happened."

"Really?" Laura gave him a small grin.

"Come on, Laura, quit kidding." He chuckled. "It isn't good for me to remember it. I'm happy for you and Eric, but sometimes . . . yeah, sometimes I wonder. And when I do, I beat myself up trying to forget you were ever more than my brother's girl."

She lowered her chin. "That's why I'm praying for you. New York's a vibrant place, from what I hear. Why don't you go there and do something crazy? Meet a perfect stranger and ask her for a walk in Central Park. I don't know." Laura ran her hand over her straight blonde hair. "God has a plan for you, Clay. Maybe New York is part of it."

The patio slider opened, and Josh led the way with the platter of steaks. "Dad says I'm ready for Beverly Hills."

"The boy has the touch." Eric breathed on his knuckles and rubbed them on his shoulder. "Chip off the old block."

Clay caught Laura's eyes one more time before they sat down, and that was it. Another conversation that wasn't bound to come up again.

That night, as Clay drove home, he thought about the evening. How was it he'd had such strange talks with both Eric and Laura? Must've been the fact that he'd almost been killed. Or that he was leaving for New York in a few days.

Something had triggered it.

Whatever it had been, it felt good that Laura knew his feelings. Better still, that she understood. Laura was right about New York City. He should talk to strangers, make friends with the guys in the program, find someone to take in a Broadway play. Why not? He'd only be there three weeks. After that he could come home and start life as a detective. When he did, he promised himself something.

He would get more connected at church, if not his church, another one in the Valley. He would look into the church's singles group or join a Bible study. After all, the people there had everything in common with him. Only by walking through the doors of a church would he ever find someone to fall in love with.

Because maybe Laura was right about that too. She'd been praying for him to find someone, and he'd been praying the same thing. And if this was the time in his life when he might meet someone and fall in love, he knew one thing for certain.

It wouldn't be in New York City.

SEVEN

Jamie still had her hair in a towel when the doorbell rang.

She darted down the hall and leaned into Sierra's room. "I've got it, honey. Keep getting ready." Then she took the stairs as fast as she could. "Coming."

It was Aaron, of course. He was meeting them at her house, taking them to lunch, and then to Chelsea Piers. Sierra had been wanting to visit the indoor pool there, and that Saturday morning was the perfect opportunity.

There was just one problem.

Jamie opened the door and glanced back up toward Sierra's room. She hadn't told her daughter that Aaron was coming. She meant to, but time had gotten away from her and now it was too late.

"Oh." She smiled at Aaron. "Sorry, come on in."

"Hi." He was dressed in a denim button-down shirt and jeans a shade lighter. His look took her by surprise. She was used to seeing him in his FDNY uniform—that was what he wore to work at St. Paul's, and what he had on just about every time they'd ever gone out for a meal. "I'm early."

"That's okay." She nodded toward the living room. "Do you mind waiting?"

"Not at all." He smiled at her, but it wasn't the easy smile they'd shared for the past few years. Jamie's skin crawled, and she chided herself. He'd been to her house before. Why couldn't she see this as just another visit, another chance to spend an afternoon with a friend who'd come to mean a great deal to her?

She gave Aaron a quick smile and hurried back up the stairs. She knew the answer. Nothing would ever be light between them again. Not until she either agreed that it was time to think of being more than friends, or until she put the idea to rest.

Even if she did that, she was pretty sure things wouldn't be the same. She would always know his intentions, and that was bound to make things awkward. The towel fell off her head as she rounded the corner into her bedroom. *Their* bedroom. Hers and Jake's. She hated when she slipped and thought of it as only hers. It had been theirs; it would always be theirs.

She tossed the towel in a laundry basket and set about drying her hair. If only he hadn't come early. She needed to finish getting ready and find Sierra. Before Sierra found him.

Five minutes later, she was dressed and on her way to find Sierra when her daughter stepped out of her room and stared down through the entryway toward Aaron. She made a face and looked at Jamie. "What's he doing here?"

"Sierra!" Jamie held a finger to her lips and closed the distance between them. "He's coming with us."

"To Chelsea Piers?" Her voice was loud and whiny; Aaron was bound to hear her. "I thought it was just me and you, Mommy."

"Look." Jamie took her daughter by the hand and led her back into her bedroom. "I'm sorry; I should've told you he was coming. But don't be rude, Sierra. That isn't like you."

She knit her blonde eyebrows together. "But why's he have to come? I wanted it to be just us. You and me."

"Mr. Hisel wants to be our friend; sometimes Mommy needs a friend, okay?" Jamie straightened herself and made an attempt to fix her hair. "Try to understand, okay, honey?"

Sierra's shoulders drooped a notch. "Okay."

They headed down the stairs together. Jamie had to remind herself to smile so Aaron wouldn't think anything was wrong. The plan was for a round of miniature golf followed by an hour in the pool. Jamie had hinted that she might swim too. But with Aaron along, she had no intention of getting into a bathing suit.

Aaron smiled at her, a smile that told her he was in no hurry. Not that morning for their outing, and not when it came to his interest in her. Jamie felt herself relax. There was no need to feel strange and awkward. This was Aaron Hisel, the man she'd counted on and shared her deepest sorrows with. Certainly they could share a day at Chelsea Piers together without her feeling all tied up in knots.

He crossed the old wooden floor and came up to Sierra. "Looks like we've got us a fun day ahead, huh?"

"Yes, sir." Sierra shot Jamie a look, but at least she remembered to keep both her expression and her tone pleasant.

They headed for Jamie's van, and when Aaron climbed into the front seat, Sierra hesitated and looked at Jamie. No words were needed; Jamie could read her daughter's thoughts perfectly.

Small talk filled the ride, and Sierra remained silent. It wasn't until they were finished golfing and Sierra was in the pool that Aaron finally turned to Jamie and frowned. "She doesn't like me, does she?"

Jamie tried to look surprised. "Who? Sierra?" She forced a chuckle. "She's a seven-year-old, Aaron. She imagined our trip one way, and when it wasn't how she pictured it, she got an attitude. It has nothing to do with you."

Aaron put his hand on her knee. "Come on, Jamie, it's okay. I'm not Jake and I never will be. I won't ever try to take his place. I can understand if Sierra feels funny having me around."

Having him around? Jamie felt her head start to spin. He was talking like they'd already made a commitment to each other. She was probably supposed to be reassured by the fact that he didn't want to replace Jake, but what exactly did that mean? That if by some turn of events they wound up together, he wouldn't try to be a father to Sierra? That he'd treat her with kindness and civility but never the passionate love of a daddy?

It was too much for Jamie. She glanced at her knee and felt her breath catch in her throat. It was one thing for them to be together when they worked at St. Paul's or when they ate together at Battery Park. But here? With Sierra swimming nearby?

She stood up and collected her purse. "Want something to drink?"

Aaron lowered his brow. "Weren't we talking?"

"Yes, but . . ." She massaged her throat. "The chlorine in here. I'm dying of thirst."

"Okay." He made a sound that was almost a chuckle. "Get me a Coke, if you don't mind."

Jamie felt anger bubble its way through her veins as she walked away. She *did* mind, in fact. She minded that she wasn't in the pool with her daughter, and that Aaron wanted a relationship with her.

And most of all she minded that Jake had died in the first place. He should be here now, splashing and swimming with Sierra, picking the little girl up and tossing her into the water until she couldn't breathe from laughing so hard.

She minded all of it.

After she paid for the drinks, she stepped into an alcove, where she could see Sierra through a long window. *God . . . what am I doing here with Aaron? I'm not ready for this, I'm not.*

Daughter, be still.

The holy whispers skimmed across the rough waters of her soul, calming the wind and whitecaps, giving her a moment of peace. *Thank You, God . . . even now You're here.* She leaned against the glass. *I'm so confused.*

I'm here. Be still and wait for Me.

Be still and wait? Jamie took a step back. Where had she heard that before? It was a Scripture, wasn't it? Something Jake had written about in his journal. The journal she'd read a hundred times. *Be still and wait on the Lord.* Yes, that was it. Be still and wait. Being still was something Jamie was never good at. Oh, she'd gotten better. Losing Jake had done that for her.

But times like this, she was glad for God's reminders.

Ever since the fateful lunch with Aaron, she'd been going a hundred miles an hour, running from the future the same way she used to run from God. Be still and wait? It was exactly what she needed to hear, what she needed to do.

She folded her arms against her waist and stared at her shoes. Her heart was still racing, still screaming at her to run or tell Aaron the truth—that she simply couldn't make herself feel something that wasn't there yet.

Calm, Jamie . . . be calm. God knows what you need. Bit by bit she felt the waves grow still, felt order restored to her soul. Her heartbeat slowed and she breathed in long and steady. Everything was going to be okay. Somehow the pieces of her future would come together, and the process would be easier if she didn't fight it. If she was still and waited on God.

She'd been gone almost ten minutes, and Aaron was bound to wonder about her. Holding tight to the direction God had given her, she rounded the corner and found a smile. Aaron was watching for her as she walked up.

"Long line?"

Lying would be the easy way out. She shook her head. "Not really." One of the drinks in her hands was his, and she handed it to him. Then she took the spot beside him on the bleachers and looked for Sierra.

"She's over there." Aaron pointed to the shallow end where a group of girls Sierra's age were playing a game.

"Thanks." She glanced at Sierra and saw her stand on the side of the pool, her legs long and skinny. One of the girls in the pool motioned for her to jump, but she looked for Jamie first. Their eyes met, and Jamie waved, just as Sierra did a cannonball into the water and came up laughing.

Jamie set her drink down. "Aaron . . ."

"Uh-oh." His smile didn't hide the regret in his voice. "Here it comes. The part where you tell me you've thought it over and you only want to be friends, right?"

She was about to explain herself but he kept on.

"Look, Jamie." As a fire captain for the FDNY, Aaron had to be one of the toughest leaders in the department. And, from everything Jake had ever said about him, he was. But now his eyes were kinder than she'd ever seen them. "I never meant to pressure you. It's just . . ." He lifted his hands and let them fall again. "I guess I never would've known if I hadn't said something."

The awkwardness from earlier that morning seemed ridiculous now. Her sudden fear of him was a slip back to the old Jamie—who was so often motivated by a paralyzing fear. The new Jamie, who believed in God's plan for her life, hadn't had to deal with fear in nearly three years.

Until Aaron told her he had feelings for her.

"You're not saying anything." Aaron cocked his head. "I can take a lot, Jamie. But I can't take losing your friendship." He reached for her hand, squeezed it once, and let go. "Okay, say something."

"I will." Her heart swelled with feelings—care or concern or friendship. Or something more, Jamie wasn't sure. "You're right, I have thought it over. But I'm not sure I want only a friendship, Aaron.

I don't know *what* I want. I feel crazy saying it's too soon." She allowed a sad laugh. "Three years is a long time, I know that. But in here—" her hand rested on the place above her heart—"I'm not ready to love someone else. At least, I don't think I am."

Aaron sucked in his cheek and narrowed his eyes. He watched Sierra for a minute, splashing near one of the pool's smaller slides. "So . . . you haven't completely written off the idea?"

"No." This time Jamie gave him a sideways hug. The sensation wasn't strange or awkward. In fact, it felt nice. Safe and warm, if not quite electric. She kept her fingers cupped around his shoulder and waited until he looked at her before letting go. "I care a lot about you, Aaron. I love having you there, talking with you—" she gestured toward the pool—"being together on days like this. It feels right, it feels like it could be more serious one day."

Aaron slid closer to her so that their arms were touching. "That's more than enough for me." He looked at Sierra again, and the hint of a smile played in his voice.

Now that the awkward feeling was gone, Jamie realized something. She wasn't only enjoying his company, she was enjoying the feel of his body against her arm.

A handful of emotions raced around in Jamie's heart. How terrible she was to enjoy the physical contact of a man who had been Jake's boss, his mentor; how awful that she could ever find another man's company, his presence, enjoyable. And the most dominant emotion—how good she felt, now that they'd talked things out, with him at her side.

She ignored the pangs of guilt and leaned into him for a few seconds. "Thanks for understanding."

"I know you, Jamie." He glanced at her and pressed a gentle kiss to her forehead. Then, just as quickly, he straightened and shot another look at Sierra. "I knew you'd need time. I just wanted you to know how I felt."

She remembered Sue's warning, that Aaron could never be right for her as long as he didn't share her faith. Never mind his age or the fact that he'd been Jake's boss. If he didn't believe in Christ the way she did, what depth could they ever share together?

This would be the time to say something about it, to ask if he would ever be interested in learning more about God, maybe going to church with her. But somehow the subject didn't seem to fit. Besides, Jake had never pushed her toward God. He'd lived out his faith every day of his life. Maybe it was her turn to do that where Aaron was concerned.

She remembered the holy whispers in her heart a few minutes earlier. God wanted her to be still and wait. Didn't that mean waiting before making faith an issue with Aaron? Besides, she didn't want to upset him, didn't want him to slide back down the bench from her.

"I like this. Sitting with you like this."

"Me too." He gave her an understanding smile. "As long as we don't think about getting serious just yet, right?"

"Right."

In the distance, Sierra climbed out of the pool and grabbed her towel. It was clear by her actions she was about to run toward them—probably needing something to eat or drink. Panic shot through Jamie. It was one thing to sit this way when Sierra wasn't looking, when she was too far away to make out exactly how close Jamie was sitting next to Aaron. But to have her daughter run up and see them . . . that was more than Jamie was ready for.

She nodded in Sierra's direction. "I think I'll get her a drink. Want anything else?"

"I'm fine." The look in Aaron's eyes told her he understood, and better still, he was at peace with her actions.

Before she turned and went to meet Sierra, she smiled once more at him. "Thanks, Aaron. I . . . I feel so much better about things."

"Me too."

The awkwardness and angst and even the guilt lifted as Jamie walked away. Her steps were lighter than they'd been in a long time. And throughout lunch, only one thought about Aaron remained.

How kind and understanding he'd been through this new phase in their friendship, and how maybe—one day not too far off—his kindness might open doors to a place she would never before have considered.

EIGHT

The angry butterflies were back. Sierra was dressed for bed and heading to the bathroom to brush her teeth, but all she could think about was the talk. This was the night she was going to talk to Mommy about the thing Katy said, the thing about their daddies and the helmets.

"Sierra, are you in your nightgown?" Mommy was in her room folding some towels.

"Yes." Sierra did a gulp.

"Did you brush your teeth?"

"That's what I'm doing right now."

"Okay, sweetie, I'll be there in a minute to pray with you." Mommy's voice was happy, the way it sounded ever since the swimming at Chelsea Piers.

Why was she so happy? Was it because of a fun day out with Sierra? Or was it Captain Hisel? Captain Hisel was nice, but Sierra wasn't sure. He wasn't like her daddy at all, and that's another reason why the angry butterflies were in her tummy.

A boy named James in her class at school lost his firefighter daddy. And last summer his mommy got married again, so now James had a new daddy. No, not a new daddy, but a second daddy.

Sierra walked into the bathroom and made a face at the mirror. She didn't want a new daddy. But sometimes she looked at James and thought how lucky he was because now he had a second daddy. And that wouldn't be so bad, but not Captain Hisel. He was old and he didn't talk to her or play with her the way a second daddy should.

"Ready, honey?" More happy voice.

Sierra jumped. "Almost." She took the cap off the toothpaste and set it careful on the counter. Sometimes if she wasn't careful the cap rolled onto the floor and once when that happened she couldn't find it again. Then she squeezed out a pea-sized spot on her pink Barbie toothbrush, because before she used to put a whole caterpillar size on but then it would grow inside her mouth and come out the sides. When that happened it usually got on her nightgown, so Mommy said use a pea size.

Thinking about her teeth made her tummy feel a little better. Her toothbrush was the best kind. It had a little motor on it. She put the bristly end in her mouth and pushed the white button. The toothbrush wiggled and jiggled and cleaned every tooth sparkly clean. Sierra spit out the old toothpaste and rinsed out her brush.

She was just looking for one of her dinosaur flossers when Mommy walked in and leaned by the door. "Hi."

"Hi." Sierra didn't look up. She found a new flosser, opened it up, and pushed it between her teeth. That way she didn't have to start having the talk with Mommy just yet.

When she was finished, she put everything away, and dried the wet spots off her face. "Okay. I'm ready."

"Well." Her mommy lifted her eyebrows high and looked at the sink area. "That's the neatest teeth-brushing job I've ever seen."

"Thank you." Sierra stood perfectly still, feet together, and waited. "Can we go to my room now?"

"Sure." A strange look was in her mommy's eyes. "Everything okay, honey?"

"Yes." Her tummy did a drop. This was the moment she'd been waiting for. She followed her mommy across the hall and into her own pink bedroom. Then she flopped up on her ruffly bed and let her feet hang over the edge. "Can I ask you something?"

"Sure." Her mommy still sounded happy, even though she looked curious. She sat on the bed too, up near the pillows. She pulled her feet up and hugged her legs. "What's up?"

Sierra turned so she could see her mommy better. "Katy said something weird when we were at her house."

Right away Mommy got a funny look on her face. "Something weird?"

"Mmhmm." She nodded. "She told me how come my daddy didn't die in the Twin Towers if he was with her daddy."

Her mommy's mouth opened, but no words came out. Also her face looked a little whitish. Finally she said, "Well, Sierra, that's a good question."

Good question was what Mommy said when she didn't want to give an answer. At least not a quick answer. Sierra made sure her tone was nice. "So what's the answer?"

"That was a very hard time for everyone, honey. Nothing that happened was easy to understand." Her mommy leaned her head back for a minute. When she looked at Sierra again, her eyes were wet. "God knows exactly when each person will come home to heaven. I guess that's my best answer."

Sierra tapped her fingers on her leg. Her mommy's words still didn't feel like an answer, really. "So that's why he didn't die when Katy's daddy died?"

"Sierra, why did Katy start talking about that? What brought it up?"

"The helmets."

This time Mommy looked sickish around her eyes. Her voice got quiet and shocked. "The helmets?"

Her daddy's fire helmet sat on her dresser. It was cleaned off because it got dirty in the fire where Daddy died. It sat right next to the picture of her and Daddy from one of the days after he came home from the hospital. He had bandages on his head, and crutches. The picture was special, just like every picture Sierra had of her daddy. But the helmet was the most specialest thing Sierra owned. Katy had one too.

"That." Sierra pointed to the helmet. "Katy has one on her dresser too."

"Yes." Her mommy made a coughing sound. "That's because Katy's mommy felt the same way I do. That you girls should have the helmets that belonged to your daddies."

"That's not what I mean." Sierra shook her head. Her stomach still hurt a little but she was getting frustration inside her. "Katy says they found their helmets at the same time. When they were cleaning up the Twin Towers."

Her mother looked at her and blinked. Then she leaned close and hugged her for a very long time. When she pulled back, her eyes said very certain that their talk was over. "Sierra, it's too late for this tonight." She kissed her and gave her butterfly kisses, the way Daddy used to do it. "Let's talk about it tomorrow."

"Tomorrow's Halloween. And it's Sunday. I'll see Katy at Sunday school and then what if she says that thing again? What am I supposed to say?"

Her mommy looked down and said the quiet words, "Help me, God," which Sierra did not understand. Why did her mother need God's help to answer one easy question? Next her mommy looked up and said, "Let's have church at the beach tomorrow, Sierra."

"At the beach?"

"Yes." Her mommy's chin was shaking a little bit. "You and me by ourselves. We'll go to the same beach where Daddy and I used to take you jet skiing, okay?"

"Won't it be too cold?"

"Probably." Mommy did a sort-of smile. "We'll wear our sweaters and bring chairs to sit in. Then we can read from the Bible and pray and have a little talk."

"About the helmets?" Sierra wasn't sure she could wait that long, plus she wanted to tell Katy she was wrong. It wasn't weird at all. But the part about the helmets still didn't make sense.

"Yes, about the helmets."

"And then go to Katy's dress-up party for dinner?"

"Yes, that too."

A good feeling came into Sierra's tummy, then. Because even though she had to wait, at least she would know the answer. She wouldn't have any more questions about her daddy or why he didn't die in the Twin Towers or how come Katy said they found his helmet next to her daddy's helmet.

After tomorrow, everything would make sense.

Jamie barely closed the door and made it to her bed before she collapsed to her knees. "God!" The sound was a whisper soaked with anguish and fear and desperation. "I'm not ready for this."

This time there were no holy messages, no still, small voice assuring her that God was there, standing ready.

Always she had known it would come to this, that someday she would have to explain to Sierra how her father had actually been killed in the terrorist attacks. But now it seemed impossible to say the words, impossible to explain that the man she'd brought orange juice to, the man she'd sat with and sang with and read stories with for three months while he got better, hadn't been her father but a stranger.

In the years since then, Jamie had always figured she'd know when the time was right. But that wasn't really what she'd counted on. The truth was, she hoped she wouldn't have to tell Sierra until she was a teenager, eighteen maybe. That way her daughter wouldn't remember anything but a blur of hazy images from the time in her life when Eric Michaels lived with them.

But now? When she still had the picture of the man on her dresser?

She'd probably looked at it a thousand times in the last three years, and now, tomorrow on the beach, she would have to tell Sierra that the man in the picture wasn't her daddy.

I don't want to tell her, God . . . She hung her head. *What's wrong with me? I should've said something a long time ago.*

Her knees hurt. She struggled to her feet and fell onto her bed. Her own questions echoed in her heart until an answer started to form. She didn't want to tell Sierra because a part of her still wanted to believe it herself. That was the problem, wasn't it? Those were the three most difficult months of her life, and having Eric Michaels, believing he was Jake, was the only reason she'd survived.

God knew she would've crumbled much like the towers if she'd learned that week that Jake was one of the dead. So instead he brought her a substitute. A Jake look-alike.

Once she knew he wasn't Jake, she had helped him to figure out his identity. After that he'd gone home to his wife and son, but a part of her still held on to the comfort of knowing that she'd had Jake three months longer than Sue had Larry, than any of the other FDNY widows had had their husbands.

Telling Sierra the truth would change that time, alter the memories so that none of them brought comfort. How could they if the man in the memory wasn't Jake but a stranger? If she was forced to paint the situation with truth, those memories would be shocking, abrasive. How could she have mixed them up? What was *wrong* with her that she could sit and talk and eat and laugh with a stranger and all the while think him Jake?

No matter that a part of her wanted to tell Sierra the truth. It was easier the way she'd chosen to deal with it.

For three months she'd had Jake back, almost the way she'd always had him. And then, overnight, he turned into someone else, someone with a family in Los Angeles. Before he found his wife and son, she wished he never would, that somehow she could keep him. Even after she helped him find his family, even at the airport with his wife about to get off a plane and take him home, Jamie wanted to grab his hand and run away with him.

But that would've been wrong. First, because the man belonged with his family; second, because he wasn't Jake.

Even now, it felt like Jake had been with them. Eric had done such a good job of studying Jake's Bible, his journal, that as the weeks passed he actually sounded like Jake and acted like him. He even learned to curl Sierra's hair the same way Jake would've curled it.

He was *like* Jake in every way. But he wasn't Jake.

When Eric Michaels said good-bye, Jamie felt God's peace like never before. She watched him walk away, kept her eyes on him while he went to his wife and hugged her, then Jamie turned around without ever looking back. She had kept her promise and told only Sue and Aaron. The media called often back then, but she shared the story with no one.

Jamie stared at the ceiling. What had she done? Were her efforts to close the door on Eric Michaels so good, she'd forgotten to work through her emotions? She'd broken down when they had his blood tested, the day they realized he wasn't Jake. But her grieving had been over losing Jake, not about believing a stranger was her husband.

She looked at the clock. Nine-forty-five; Sue would still be up. The cordless phone was a few feet away, off the charging unit as usual. Jamie grabbed it and punched in Sue's number.

Her friend answered on the first ring. "Hello?"

"Sue . . ." Jamie's throat was thick.

"Jamie?"

"Yes, I . . . Sue, could you pray for me?"

"What's wrong?" Concern flooded Sue's voice. "You sound upset."

Jamie's lungs hurt, and she realized she was holding her breath. She exhaled and pushed her fingers into the roots of her hair. "It's been a long day."

"Weren't you out with Aaron and Sierra?"

"Yes." Jamie closed her eyes. "That's not the problem."

Sue waited. "What then?"

"I guess the girls were talking, and Katy told Sierra that rescue workers found both their daddies' helmets at the same time, in the rubble of the Twin Towers."

"What?" Shock rang in Sue's tone. "Where on earth would she have heard that?"

"I don't know. Maybe she overheard us talking one day, or maybe someone else told her. Anyway, that's not the point. Katy's right; I don't blame her for telling Sierra the truth."

"Did Sierra ask about it?"

"Yes." Jamie opened her eyes, sat up, and slipped out of bed. She had nowhere to go so she stood there, unmoving. "She wanted to know why Katy's daddy died in the Twin Towers and her daddy didn't. And then she wanted to know about the helmets."

"Great." Sue sighed. "I'm so sorry, Jamie. You don't need this right now."

"It's okay. I need it sometime and apparently God wants it to be now."

"What are you going to do?"

"Tell her the truth." Jamie took slow steps toward the tall dresser, the one that had been Jake's. His Bible and journal sat on top, where she could easily find them when she needed to get lost in his heart, his mind, his faith.

"Oh, Jamie, no wonder you want me to pray."

Tears stung at Jamie's eyes, but she resisted them. She put one hand on Jake's Bible. Beside her, within her, she could feel the Lord watching, standing guard, even though she hadn't heard Him speak to her that night. He was there and He would see her through the next day. "Yes, that's why."

"I'll be praying the whole day. Call me when you're ready to talk about it, okay?"

"Okay." Jamie ran her fingers over the Bible's worn leather cover. "Thanks. And who knows. Maybe it'll be the best thing for both of us."

They said their good-byes and Jamie clicked the off button. She tossed the phone back onto the bed and took Jake's Bible from the dresser. With her eyes on the cover, on the smudged place where his engraved name had all but worn off, she backed up until she hit the rocking chair that had always been in their room.

She sat down and opened the old book to a section of Scripture she'd read before. Philippians, the fourth chapter, thirteenth verse. Carefully she turned the pages, savoring the yellow highlighted sections and the precious notations Jake had written in the margins until she reached the right spot.

Her eyes found the Scripture immediately.

I can do all things through Christ who gives me strength.

She looked out the window at the old elm tree outside. It was hidden in the shadows, but she could see its leaves rustling in the evening breeze. She'd been sitting outside watching Sierra play the first time she found that verse. Her mind savored the words again. *I can do all things through Christ who gives me strength.*

Once more she looked at the page, wanting to soak in the truth long enough to lean on it come morning. But instead of seeing the Scripture about strength, her eyes landed on verse four. Jake had highlighted the next few lines in blue, and Jamie couldn't remember ever reading them.

She squinted so she could see the words more clearly in the dim light of the room.

Rejoice in the Lord always. I will say it again: Rejoice! Let your gentleness be evident to all. The Lord is near. Do not be anxious about anything, but in everything, by prayer and petition, with thanksgiving, present your requests to God. And the peace of God, which transcends all understanding, will guard your hearts and your minds in Christ Jesus.

It wasn't one verse but four. Four wonderful, hope-filled lines of truth that breathed new life into her. The best part was that the Lord was near. Wasn't that exactly how she'd been feeling while she was talking to Sue? That the Lord was truly near?

And what were His words of advice for troubled hearts? Rejoice! Find a reason to be glad, and then don't get anxious. Instead pray, and God, because He's so good, will provide a peace the world knows nothing about.

A thin dark line was drawn from that section of Scripture to a scribbled notation near the top of the page. This was her favorite part of reading Jake's Bible. The words he'd added gave her an insight she hadn't had when he was alive.

She shifted so the light was better.

God wants everyone to be gentle, even us tough FDNY guys. The reason? He is closer than we think.

Jake was an amazing man, strong and gutsy and gentle in every way. But times like this she wished she could see him one more time, see him face-to-face and tell him how much it meant to her that he'd left a road map for her and Sierra to follow. Yes, Jake was right; God was closer than they thought.

She closed the book and held it to her heart. *Jake . . . if only you knew how much I miss you.* Tears came and this time she didn't stop them. *I know you so much better now.*

For a while she sat there, pretending Jake was beside her, lying in bed sleeping, ready for an early-morning shift. If only she could crawl into the covers and find him there one more time, his sweet breath warm against her face. Nights like this, if she thought hard enough, she could almost feel him stirring in his sleep, putting his arm around her and making her feel like the safest, most loved woman in the world.

She opened her eyes and looked out the window again.

God had pulled her through every day since September 11; He would get her through the talk with Sierra. She set Jake's Bible back on the dresser, brushed her teeth, and climbed into bed. Lying there, she did a quick inventory of the day: the trip to Chelsea Piers, how she had enjoyed sitting by Aaron.

But as she fell asleep it was something else that made her smile.

After tomorrow, Sierra would know the truth about Jake's death; there would be nothing left to hide. She would simply tell their daughter what really happened and be there for her, whatever she needed.

And best of all, God would be with her. Strength would come not only from the truth in the Scriptures but from the truth Jake himself had written. And that was almost like having him there too.

NINE

The beach was cold, just like Sierra thought. But it wasn't rainy, and that was a good thing. Rainy days were better for inside, cuddled up near the fire with Mommy and Wrinkles. She didn't care about the weather; just that Mommy would finally tell her about the weird thing Katy said about her daddy and his helmet. She was dying to make sense of it all.

Mommy was driving. She turned the car into the parking lot, and Sierra sat a little straighter so she could see. Yep, it was their favorite beach. The one they came to last summer with Katy and her mommy. But it looked different with winter on it, not as blue and happy. The water was ice gray and the sand looked wet. "You sure it won't be too cold?"

"If it is, we won't stay long, okay?" Mommy smiled at her. She reached out and took Sierra's hand. "I've always wanted to come out here in the winter, before the snow comes, all by ourselves."

Sierra peered down the beach a ways. "There's two people in chairs there, Mommy. And three over by the water."

Her mommy did a little laugh. "I don't mean all by ourselves, exactly. I mean without the summer crowds."

"Oh." Sierra wiggled her nose. She could already smell the sea-water.

The car stopped and Mommy squeezed her hand. "Okay, let's go." Mommy took the picnic basket and the big Bible, the one that belonged to her daddy before he died in the fire. She also took two chairs from the back of the van and a big, bushy blanket, the warmest kind they had.

Sierra grabbed her pink Bible and pulled her coat tight around her middle. Out on the sand it wasn't as cold as she thought. A medium sort of cold, but that's all. Plus the sky was the bluest blue. The seagulls looked like white kites against that sky.

She pushed her feet over the sand and kept up with Mommy. They already had a plan. Sierra would read something favorite from her Bible, and then Mommy would read something favorite from hers. Well, not really hers, but sort of hers. She always read the Bible that *used* to be Daddy's.

The more they got close to the water, the more Sierra started to remember. This was the place they came a year after Daddy died. They brought a balloon that day. Sierra squinted at the water. She gave butterfly kisses to the balloon and wrote something on it. A message for Daddy. Yep, that was it.

This was the same exact place.

She stopped, and after a few steps, her mommy stopped too.

"Sierra?" Her eyes had sun in them so she made a shade with her hands. "What's wrong, honey? You need a rest?"

It was a long way from the car to their spot near the water. But she wasn't tired. "No."

"Okay, then . . ." Mommy sounded curious and maybe a little confused. "Come on. Let's set up."

"I'm sad."

Her mommy's face got melty. "Sad? Why, honey?"

"Because this is where we sent the balloon to Daddy when I was in kindergarten."

A lonely breath came from her mommy. "Yes. You remember that?"

"Mmhmm." She started walking again. Her mommy did too. "I was just a little kid, but I remember a lot. Even now that I'm grown-up."

"Yes." Her mommy bit her lip. "I remember too. And you're right, honey. It is sad."

A few more steps and her mommy set down the chairs and basket. But not the Bible. Sierra helped her open the chairs. They sat down and Mommy spread the blanket over their legs. With their coats and the blankets, it was actually sort of snuggly warm.

Sierra looked out at the water. "It's kind of happy too."

"What?"

"Being here." She gave her mommy her best smile she could. "I think Daddy can see us in this place, all the way from heaven."

"Yes." Her mommy's eyes got small. She looked out at the water. "Yes, Sierra, I think there must be windows in heaven. And I'll bet you're right; I'll bet Daddy is up there smiling at us right now."

Heaven was a long ways away, but Sierra liked to try to see it. She made a shade over her eyes and stared straight into the blue. For a long time she just looked and didn't say anything. The seagulls and the waves did all the talking.

"Sierra?" Her mommy scooched her chair over closer. Now their arms were touching. "Ready to read your favorite verse?"

"Yes." She pulled her children's storybook Bible out from beneath the snuggly blanket and turned to the story about Peter and his friends in the boat one stormy night. She was an excellent reader. That's what everyone said. She looked at the first words and did a cough so her voice could say them.

"'One day Peter and his friends were in a boat in the middle of the night.'" She used her finger to follow along, but it wasn't hard. This story was one she read to Wrinkles all the time. "'A storm came up and Peter saw a man out on the water. "Who is it?" Peter asked. The man on the water said, "It is me, Peter." Peter was very amazed. The man on the water was Jesus. "If it is you, Lord, tell me to walk on the water . . ."'"

Sierra made a tired sound. She needed a little rest. A seagull landed close by because he wanted to listen to the story. She laughed out loud at the bird.

"What's so funny?" Mommy did a little laugh too.

"That seagull." Sierra pointed at him. "He wants to listen to the story."

"Hmmm." Her mommy raised her eyebrows at her. Raised eyebrows meant Come on sillypants, get back to reading. "I'd like to listen to the story too."

Sierra looked out at the ocean and took a big breath. "I'm doing good, huh, Mommy?"

"Very good. I can't wait to hear the rest."

A big smile came on Sierra's face, because Mommy was funny. "Okay, here it is." She found her place on the page. "'Jesus said,

"Peter, come to me." So, Peter went out of the boat and came to Jesus on top of the water. But when he saw the wind and big waves he began to sink. He held his hand out to Jesus. "Help," he cried. Then Jesus helped Peter out of the water. He said, "Peter, you need to have more faith."'" She closed her pink Bible. "The end."

"Nice job, honey. I like it." Mommy was quiet for a little bit. "What's your favorite part?"

"The part about Jesus helping Peter out of the water."

"Why that part?"

"Because sometimes . . ." Sierra closed her eyes and listened to the waves. She kept them closed, even when she started talking again. "I hate not having a daddy. No one to swing me around or give me horseback rides or curl my hair or anything." She opened her eyes and looked at Mommy. "I hate it so much." She leaned her head back so she could see the sky again. "Sometimes I miss my daddy so much I feel like I'm drowning. Just like Peter. But then I reach for Jesus, and He helps me be okay."

"I'm sorry, Sierra." Her mommy's voice was full of sad.

"About what?" It wasn't Mommy's fault.

"I'm sorry you don't have a daddy. I can only tell you I miss him as much as you do."

"Probably more, 'cause you knew him longer."

"Yes." Her mommy's smile was still very sad. "Probably more." The sound in her voice was like when sometimes she was going to cry. But her eyes were dry when she opened the big Bible and turned some pages. "This is a Scripture your daddy gave me, long before I even knew Jesus."

"You mean when me and Daddy used to go to church by just ourselves?"

"Right." Mommy made a frown. "Back then." She looked at the pages and started to read. "It's from Jeremiah 29:11. It says, "'For I know the plans I have for you,' says the Lord, "plans to prosper you and not to harm you, plans to give you hope and a future.""'"

Sierra nodded. "I've heard that before. I like it."

Her mommy closed the Bible but kept it on her lap. Then she put the blanket back over them. "I wanted to read that because you and I need to have a little talk, Sierra. I want to answer your questions from last night, okay?"

"Okay." Sierra's stomach did a somersault. 'Cause this was the big answer, actually. Mommy's voice was serious, only that didn't make sense. Because Katy didn't know that every person has a time when they die. At least that's what Mommy said. So that meant Katy's daddy had September 11, and her own daddy had another day. That's all. She squiggled her toes in her shoes and waited.

"Whatever we talk about here, I want you to remember that Bible verse, Sierra. God has a plan for you and He has a plan for me. Sometimes strange things happen and God can make them into something good, all right?"

"Yes." Sierra held tight to the arms of her chair. "Can you tell me now?"

Her mommy nodded. "Let's pray first. That way we can end our Bible study."

"Okay."

She took hold of Sierra's hand and looked out where heaven was. "God, we are so glad You're always there for us, that when we fall, You pick us up. Even when it feels like we're drowning." Her voice sounded sad again. "Right now I ask You to be with Sierra, so she can understand what I'm about to tell her. Give me the right words. Be with both of us, Lord. We need You. In Jesus' name, amen."

When she was finished she looked at Sierra. Her eyes were the same as they were last summer when Sierra woke up one morning and Mommy told her some sad news. That their old dog Brownie died in her sleep. Yes, her eyes were the same now. Sierra liked the way her mommy's hand felt around her smaller one. "I'm ready now."

"Okay." Her mother took in a long breath. "Sierra, Katy is right about Daddy. He did die in the Twin Towers, just like her daddy."

Sierra frowned. She stared at her mommy. Why would she say that? The pieces of her heart felt all mixed up.

Mommy looked a long time at her. "After the towers fell down, Captain Hisel was walking around and he saw a man who looked like your daddy." She stopped and looked up. Then she whispered, "God . . . help me. This is harder than I thought."

That was a problem. Whenever Mommy prayed in the middle of talking it was a problem. She swallowed. "It's okay, Mommy. I want to know."

Anyway, they took that man to the hospital, and told me it was your daddy. He was hurt and he had bandages on his face, but he looked . . . he looked exactly like your daddy, Sierra. Exactly. But he wasn't Daddy. He was a man named Eric Michaels. A man who—"

"That's not true!" Sierra pulled her hand away from her mommy and crossed her arms tight. "He was *so* my daddy! He gave me horse-back rides and curled my hair and made me blueberry pancakes." Her tummy hurt very bad now. "He *was* my daddy, Mommy. Maybe you got your story wrong."

"Sierra . . ." She had a strange sound this time, like she was scared. "I *promise* I'm telling you the truth. You *thought* he was Daddy, and I thought he was Daddy. I was shocked when I found out he wasn't Daddy. But, Sierra, Daddy died in the Twin Towers. That man—Eric Michaels—was from California. He only *looked* like Daddy." Tears broke into her voice and made it scratchy. She did a few sobs and covered her face for a long time. When she looked up she was more sad than Sierra had ever seen her. "Can you believe me, honey? Please?"

She had to think about this, actually. Before she could answer her mommy's question, she needed a little time for her brain to work. "I want to walk for a minute, okay?"

"Okay." Her mommy sat back in her chair. New tears were in her eyes, but she didn't sound as sad.

Sierra pushed the blanket off, set her Bible down, and walked down the little hill to the water. It was colder there, but she didn't care. How could it be true? How could Daddy have been someone else for all that time? She scrunched down the way they did in gym class sometimes, sort of sitting but not touching the sand with her bottom. Her head felt all swishy inside, but Sierra knew one thing.

Mommy never lied to her. She might wait a long time to tell the truth, but she never lied.

Never.

So if Mommy wasn't lying then it had to be true. The daddy who came home from the hospital wasn't her daddy. Sierra felt sick, the way she felt when they served tuna casserole for hot lunch. Even if it was true, her head was still all mixed up.

She stood and walked up the hill, careful not to get sand in her tennis shoes. When she got there she put her hands on her hips, because this was very serious business. "The man who lived with us in the downstairs bedroom? He wasn't Daddy?"

Mommy's eyes were still wet and a few tears spilt onto her coat. "No, honey. Your daddy died in the towers right next to Katy's daddy."

"That's why they found the helmets together?"

"Yes, that's why."

"So he gave me horsie rides and curled my hair, but he wasn't my daddy?"

"No, sweetheart. He really wasn't."

Sierra sat back down in her chair, picked up her Bible, and pulled the blanket up around her. All of a sudden she thought of something, something that took away some of the sick feeling in her stomach. She looked at her mommy. "Then that daddy who lived with us is still alive, right?"

"Yes, but he—"

"I know! Let's find him and he can be my second daddy! James in my class—remember James?"

"Sierra, you don't understa—"

"His daddy was a firefighter and he died in the Twin Towers, but now his mommy got married again and he has a second daddy. Isn't that nice for James, Mommy?"

"No, Sierra, it's not like that. The man who—"

"So maybe that man who looked like my daddy could be my second daddy." She made a sad face. "He would never be my special first daddy, because no one could ever be him." Her smile came back, just a little. "But that man was very nice, Mommy. I liked him a lot, even if he wasn't my real daddy. He looked like Daddy and he seemed like Daddy. So now you can go find him and marry him and we can be a family like when he was here." Sierra was out of air so she breathed in real fast. "Could you do that, Mommy? I really like him and plus, he's alive."

Mommy pulled her arms out from under the blanket and put them on her knees. Then she put her head down on them, like maybe she was tired. She stayed that way a long time, and also her shoulders did a little shaking.

"Mommy?"

Her fingers covered her face, and she sat up straight. Then she wiped her tears and let her hands fall back to the blanket. Her cheeks were almost as red as her eyes. "No, Sierra." She looked at her really close. "It can't be like that. It can *never* be like that. The man who lived with us—Mr. Michaels—didn't have his memory because his head got hurt in the towers. Everyone told him he was our daddy, and even he thought so. But then he got better and he found out he wasn't our daddy. That's when he left to find his real family."

Sierra didn't want to hear those words. "His real family?"

"Yes. His real family."

Sierra stared at her lap. Maybe that was why he left, and that was when—

She looked at her mommy. "When he went away . . . that's when you told me about Daddy dying in the fire, right?"

"Right." Her mommy's eyes still had wet in them. "I'm sorry, Sierra. I should've told you a long time ago, but I didn't know how or when." She sniffed and wiped her eyes again. "I'm so sorry, baby. I just didn't know how to say it."

Sierra looked at the sand and made her brain think very fast. When she looked up she had an idea. "Are you sure that other daddy has a different family?"

"Yes, honey. They live in California."

"Oh." Sierra stretched her feet out and thought some more. "Can I see him sometime?"

Her mother's breath came out long and she looked very tired. She shook her head. "No, Sierra. We can't see him."

Sierra didn't like that very much—but she did like that at least she had a second daddy for a little bit of time. That was more than Katy had. She stared out at the water. The daddy she really wanted was her own daddy. She looked to heaven, and little tears came into her eyes. At least Daddy was with Jesus. Plus, one day they'd be together again.

"Are you okay, honey?" Her mommy reached for her hand, and Sierra let her take it.

"I think so." Two seagulls danced around a piece of bread a little bit away from them. She yawned and held tight to her mommy's fingers. "Can I keep his picture in my room?"

"Honey, why?" Mommy's mouth dropped open. A wave came up and smashed onto the sand at the bottom of the hill. Mommy made a huffy sound. "I told you, he wasn't your daddy. Not even for a little while."

"Yes, Mommy. He was my *second* daddy. For that little bit of days he was my second daddy." Sierra rubbed her thumb over her mommy's hand. "So, can I keep the picture?"

Her mommy waited. "I don't know, Sierra . . . "

"Please, Mommy."

"Oh—" her shoulders dropped a little bit—"Okay. I guess so."

"Thank you, Mommy. I can remember him better with the picture." One hand was still in hers. With the other one, she tapped on her Bible. She wasn't sick anymore, but she was still a little bit sad. "Guess what, Mommy?"

"What?"

"I like it better that Daddy died in the Twin Towers. Know why?"

"Why?" Her mommy snuggled close to her and their two heads came together like best friends.

"Because Teacher said the firefighters who died on September 11 were heroes. And Daddy was a hero, that's why."

"Sierra . . ." Her mother made a funny sound. Not really a laugh or a cry. "All people who die in the line of duty—firefighters, police officers, soldiers, missionaries—all of them are heroes."

"But you know what, Mommy?"

"What?"

"Our daddy was a superhero." She stretched her hands out as wide as she could. "The biggest superhero of all. Right?"

She could hear a smile in her mommy's voice. "Yes, honey, he was." She gave Sierra another little hug. "He was the best superhero of all."

TEN

The plane couldn't go fast enough for Clay.

It was Halloween—not that a wasted holiday like that meant much—but it was the last Sunday in October, and Joe Reynolds was beside him. The adventure was underway. On the following afternoon they'd be in orientation for the course. Now that he'd said his good-byes to Eric and Laura and Josh, now that he'd made his mind up that somehow God was doing something in his life, Clay couldn't wait to get to New York.

Reynolds felt the same way. The first hour of the flight they guessed at what the training might include, talked about a kidnapping case from a year ago that Reynolds had worked, and speculated about the outcome of a robbery case that was still open.

Small talk, really.

Clay looked out the window. Funny how a person could go years thinking someone was his friend and never really know him. Reynolds was in the middle, sandwiched between Clay and a big man on the aisle. When they ran out of things to talk about, Reynolds nodded off. He'd been sleeping ever since.

The main thing Clay wanted to ask was, why New York? There were twenty cities where they could've gone for training. San Diego, for instance, where the weather was at least warm, or Phoenix, which would be heaven this time of year. The man didn't make impulsive decisions, as far as Clay could tell, so why New York? And what about the picture on his desk, the one of the pretty woman and the little boy? The one he never talked about?

The flight attendants came through with lunch, and Clay elbowed Reynolds. "Time to eat."

His friend opened one eye and then the other. He stretched as much as he could and pulled his tray down. "Gourmet, no doubt." He grinned at the young woman serving them. "Are you single?"

The woman was a redhead with striking caramel eyes. Clay looked at her left ring finger; it was bare. He could've gladly strangled Reynolds for what he figured he was about to say.

The flight attendant returned the smile, but her cheeks turned red as she gave Reynolds his meal. "Who wants to know?"

Reynolds punched Clay in the shoulder. "My single friend here, that's who." Reynolds looked from the flight attendant to Clay, then back again. "He's handsome, wouldn't you say? The flight won't last forever—it's late and getting later."

Clay held up his hands and gave a shake of his head, as if to tell her he was definitely not the instigator.

"Yes." The woman was still blushing. She made eye contact with Clay, but only for a few seconds. Clay couldn't blame her; he was thirty-five and she looked ten years younger.

Clay gave Reynolds a kick. He caught the flight attendant's attention and gave her a weak smile. "Don't mind my friend. He's delusional when he first wakes up."

The flight attendant laughed and pushed the food cart down a few aisles. Twice she looked back and caught Clay's eyes. When she was busy helping another passenger, Clay turned and stared at his friend. "Reynolds, remind me not to go out in public with you when we're in Manhattan."

Reynolds held up his hands in mock surrender. "Just trying to help. My friend can't seem to connect with the ladies . . . I figured I could make something happen."

"Yeah, well, figure not." Clay looked at his meal. It had the look of lasagna, but it smelled suspiciously of fish. He caught his friend's eyes again. "I'll meet someone soon enough."

Reynolds chuckled. "I'm not sure."

They poked at their meals and took a few bites. "You taste any fish in that stuff?"

"No." Reynolds sniffed close to his plate. "But I smell it." He pointed to a small dish of something white. "Could be the warm cottage cheese."

"Mmmm." Clay put his fork down and wiped his mouth. "I think we were lucky to get a meal at all."

Reynolds pointed to a few passengers across the aisle with Subway sandwich bags. "Those are the lucky people, man, let me tell you."

They ate what they could, and after the flight attendant filed back to clear their trays, they shared a comfortable silence. Clay looked out the window again. It was another hour before they arrived in New York, and night was trying to fall on the East Coast. Several thousand feet below was a layer of puffy white clouds, but otherwise the sky was starting to turn colors—deep blues with streaks of lavender and pink.

God's artwork.

"Beautiful." Reynolds was leaning forward, watching the sunset.

"Yep. Only God can paint a sky."

Reynolds settled back in his seat. "You a believer?"

"Longtime believer." Clay sat back too. Funny, but the two had never talked about God before. "What about you?"

"Pretty much." Reynolds stroked his chin and his eyes grew soft. "Not like I used to be."

Clay let that sit. After a few seconds he leaned against the window and looked at Reynolds. "I got a question for you."

"Shoot."

"Why New York?"

The shadows that fell over his friend's eyes told him he'd hit a nerve. Reynolds looked past Clay to the sunset. Lines appeared at the corners of his eyes. "You wouldn't believe it if I told you."

So there *was* a reason. Clay kept his voice low. "Try me." He thought about his brother, Eric. "I've seen some pretty strange things."

At first it didn't look like Reynolds would talk, but maybe because they were suspended between two cities, thirty thousand feet above the ground, he gave in. Reynolds made his lips into a tight straight line and began to tell his story.

"Her name's Wanda. She's the girl in the picture on my desk." He sucked in a breath and held it before letting it ease through his nose. "I was crazy in love with her from the moment I met her— our senior year of high school."

Clay knew Reynolds tended to spit out details in starts and fits, so he waited.

"After high school, I joined the service so I'd have a way through college." He stroked his chin again. "Wanda went with me, lived with me on the base. A year later she had Jimmy and everything, well—" He let out a little laugh, one that lacked humor. "Everything was great until the Gulf War."

"You fought?" Another surprise.

"Yeah, I fought. I was in the first wave, the ground attack." The muscles in his jaw flexed. "It was crazy." His tone was soft, but intense. "That sissy guy you shot the other day? That was nothing to the Gulf War, man. Nothing."

"How long?"

"I was there the better part of three years." He made a sharp sniff. "Came home and found Wanda and Jimmy having dinner at the cafeteria with one of the commanders." He looked out the window again. "I came unglued. Stormed out of there, straight to our apartment."

"Did she see you?" Clay had no trouble picturing Reynolds angry; that's how he worked. Angry and focused.

"Yeah, she saw me. Flew after me with Jimmy running behind her. I heard her, heard both of 'em. Wanda calling my name, Jimmy shouting for his daddy." Reynolds shook his head. "I was so mad, I wouldn't stop, wouldn't turn around for nothing. Not even my little boy."

Clay felt the tension in his friend's voice. Whatever was coming, it wasn't good.

"A road ran through the base, and I crossed it no trouble. Wanda . . . she was twenty yards behind me, running like crazy. She got to the road just as some crazy drunk came flying up the hill." He looked up at the airplane's vents and shook his head.

"Hey, it's okay, man." Clay's stomach tightened. He never would've asked about New York if he'd thought it would lead to this.

"No." Reynolds looked at him again. "I'll finish." He searched Clay's eyes. "Wanda saw the car and stopped in time, but Jimmy—" His voice broke, and he pinched the bridge of his nose. His words were barely audible over the sound of the jet engines. "He called my name one more time, and that's when I heard the thud." Reynolds dropped his hand back to his lap. Gone was the invincible look that made him a hero at the police department. His eyes were red and full of pain. "He was dead before he hit the ground."

Clay's stomach sank. No wonder there were no updated pictures of the boy on Reynolds's desk.

"Watching that boy hit the ground . . . seeing Wanda kneel next to him, screaming for him to be okay . . . seeing that drunk stumble out of the car . . ." He bit his lip. "I still have nightmares about it."

Clay wanted the rest of the story. What happened to Wanda? And how come they weren't together any more? But he wasn't going to push. He looked at his hands for a minute and then back at Reynolds. "I'm sorry."

"It was an accident, I know that." He crossed his arms. "But it was my fault. And you know what?"

"What?"

"Turns out the commander wasn't seeing Wanda at all. He was asking her if we wanted an upgrade in our living quarters."

Clay dug his elbow into his thigh and let his forehead rest on his knuckles. Reynolds was right; he never would've believed a story like that one, never would've thought a man as bulletproof as Joe Reynolds would've suffered such a loss.

"Guess we all have a story."

The captain's voice came over the speakers then, advising them of weather conditions in LaGuardia. Cold with a storm moving in.

Clay lowered his hands and looked at his friend again. He had to ask. "What happened to Wanda?"

"She couldn't look at me, couldn't talk to me." He hesitated. "I mean, Michaels, she was crazy with grief. Absolutely crazy. Her baby was dead and it was my fault." A sad smile hung on the corners of his mouth. "We had a strong faith back then; everyone at church tried to help us. After the service we got counseling, and the army gave me a paid leave." He knit his mouth together and shook his head. "Wanda wanted none of it. A week later we found out the guy who hit Jimmy, he was a child molester out early for good behavior. Got himself drunk and crashed through the gate at the base." Reynolds fired the words like bullets. "Never shoulda been out of prison in the first place."

"I hate that."

"Yeah." He made a sarcastic sound that wasn't even close to a laugh. "Talk about having an incentive to get to work."

Now Clay understood something else. When Reynolds showed up on the scene, a minute after Clay had shot the carjacker the other day, his words had been something of a surprise. *You did us all a favor.* Wasn't that it? Yes, that was what he'd said. *You did us all a favor.* Reynolds worked by the books, arresting criminals, forming cases against them, testifying in court. But when a killer made a fatal move in a gun battle with a cop, Reynolds wasn't going to lose any sleep over it.

"For three months we kept trying, me and Wanda. She was hurting so bad, and there was—" he gave a sharp shake of his head— "there was nothing I could do to help her. Finally one day I asked her if she wanted me to leave."

Clay already knew what Reynolds was going to say and it made him sick. Two people who loved each other so much, who shared a faith in God, torn apart when they were both hurting the most.

"She said yes. Seeing me every day, remembering what happened, it was too hard for her." Reynolds's eyes were distant again. "I told her I felt the same way; if she wasn't going to let me help her, I wanted out too." He shrugged. "So I finished my service in California and she moved to Queens. Soon as I had the chance I started college classes and I didn't look back until I had my law degree. Figured I'd fight the bad guys in courtrooms, where I could lock 'em up longer than the jerk who killed my boy."

"Didn't work out that way, huh?"

Reynolds chuckled, and the hurt in his eyes dimmed. "Not for a minute. The whole thing was a game, Michaels. Just one big stinking game." He straightened himself and buckled his seat belt. "I like it better in uniform. At least we get 'em off the streets for a while."

A flight attendant came on this time, telling them to prepare for landing. Clay let the details of his friend's story play again in his mind. "You and Wanda? You've kept in touch?"

"For a little while." He looked at Clay. "She married a firefighter, FDNY. Guy wasn't around much, at least that's what Wanda's mother said. She told me Wanda never stopped loving me; she just didn't know how to show me after Jimmy died."

Clay frowned. "Her husband was FDNY?"

"Yeah." Something more serious crossed his expression. "After the terrorist attacks, I had to know if the guy was one of 'em." He paused. "He was. Lost right up there in the South Tower. Every day since then I've wanted to call Wanda, just to tell her I'm sorry. Sorry about doubting her, sorry about running that day when I came home, sorry about Jimmy. Sorry about her husband." His voice was shakier than before, broken. "Sorry about all of it. But I never made the call."

"Instead you're going to see her in person, is that it?"

The plane was coming in for a landing. Reynolds glanced out the window at the skyline of Manhattan. "I'm not sure." He looked at Clay again. "You're a praying man, is that right?"

"I am."

"Then pray for me. So I'll know if I should look her up, or if seeing me again would only make things harder for her."

They didn't say anything else until they touched down and the pilot welcomed them to New York City. That's when the idea hit him. He turned to Reynolds as he pulled his travel bag from the floor beneath the seat in front of him.

"Hey, we're off tomorrow morning, right?"

"Right. Orientation begins at four o'clock. I guess a few of our shifts will be with the night crew."

"Right, so I have an idea for the morning."

"Okay." Reynolds looked like he was back to himself again, with one small change for the better. His guard was down. "What's your idea?"

"Ground Zero."

Reynolds hesitated. "Hmmm." He gave a slow, thoughtful nod. "Might be a good place to pray."

"That's what I was thinking. We could take the ferry over early."

"Hey, I just remembered. One of the guys from the downtown precinct was telling me there's this little chapel there, right across the street from where the towers stood. St. Peter's, something like that. All sorts of letters and pictures from the attacks."

"Now that—" Clay patted his friend's back as they stood to make their way off the plane— "would be a good place to pray."

ELEVEN

Jamie was looking forward to seeing Aaron on Monday.

She boarded the ferry at nine o'clock and took a seat inside. A storm had kicked up the night before and it was still sprinkling. The forecast included snow later in the week, and Jamie thought they might be wrong. With the weather outside, it might snow before lunchtime.

The inside of the ferry had two levels. Jamie took the first, which was practically empty; few tourists were willing to brave a day like this. Jamie settled into a corner seat and held her bag to her waist. Whitecaps covered the harbor, evidence the ride would be rougher than usual.

For the tourists' sake—if there were any—the captain was saying something about the sights, the part about the Statue of Liberty welcoming the masses, and Liberty Island being a symbol of freedom. Funny how she'd never really listened to the spiel before Jake died. When the two of them crossed the harbor, they were too caught up in their own conversation to notice much else.

Now she knew it by heart.

The ferry rocked and rolled, but Jamie wasn't worried. She'd crossed over in far worse conditions.

She looked around at the other people on the first level. Across the way were two guys—one blond, one black. They were good-looking, tall and well built. Jamie wondered if they were coaches, maybe, or tourists meeting up with their wives.

Not far from her, three guys in their early twenties sat in a circle. They might've been college kids, but they looked a little shady. Probably actors. Lots of Broadway dreamers lived in Staten Island and commuted to Manhattan for a shot at a role. Now that she'd noticed them, though, she saw something else. Every now and then, one of them would smile at her or do something to catch her attention, and then whisper to his buddies.

Strange... Did she spill something? Was her zipper undone? She glanced down at her white turtleneck sweater and dark jeans. No, everything looked fine. Just as she was about to look up she felt someone standing near her table.

"Excuse me." The guy couldn't have been even twenty-one. He had a baby face with freckles and a crew cut—but there was something hard about his eyes. "Are you on vacation?"

"Me?" Jamie looked around to make sure he was talking to her. Maybe it was some sort of practical joke.

"Yeah." He glanced back at his buddies. Both of them were smiling at him, egging him on. "We're here with our history class, headed for the Statue of Liberty." He grinned, and two dimples cut into his face. "We, well, we wondered if you were a tourist. You know, by yourself. Maybe you might want to join us."

Jamie resisted the urge to laugh out loud. It wasn't a practical joke at all. This college kid was hitting on her! Her face grow hot. "You're serious?"

"Sure." The guy looked toward the bathrooms. "You're by yourself, right?"

"Yes." Jamie wasn't offended. If anything, it made her feel good.

But before she could say anything else, the guy pushed into the spot beside her and put his arm around her. "Don't say a word, got it?"

At his low, hissed words, Jamie's heart slammed into double time. How could she have been so stupid? She never should have said she was alone. She should've gotten up as soon as he started talking to her.

"I'm armed, but I don't want to hurt you, see?" He kept smiling, but his fingers jabbed into her shoulder.

She winced and tried to jerk free, but the guy's friends stood and came over. One of them took the seat on her other side.

"Hey there, baby doll." This one had dark hair. His eyes were bloodshot, and Jamie's fear increased. *God, help me . . . they've got to be on something.* His sweatshirt said OSU Football.

"Leave me alone." She hissed the words at the newest member of the group. "Go back to your seats or I'll scream."

"Do it, witch, and I'll shoot you straight through the heart." The freckle-faced kid laughed, and the rough sound made Jamie's skin crawl. "We killed two people earlier this morning. We'll kill you if you don't do what we say."

Jamie doubted he was telling the truth, but just then she felt something jab into her ribs.

"We're serious, lady." It was the third guy, the one with the baseball cap. "You're ours for the day, whatever we want to do with you. Got it?"

"Yeah, and don't make a scene, or we'll shoot everyone on board."

"God . . ." Jamie closed her eyes and tried to be still. It wasn't possible. Her mind was racing too fast to make a plan. "Get me out of here, God."

The crew cut laughed hard at that. "Oh yeah, God'll show up here. Sure thing."

His buddies joined in the laughter, and Jamie looked around the first level. Couldn't someone see she was in trouble? Or was the laughter from the three men convincing the other passengers that she was part of their group, a bunch of friends having a great time together?

"Wait till you see what we've got planned for you, baby." The football sweatshirt sneered the words up against her ear.

His breath smelled like marijuana, and she jerked away, repulsed. *God . . . help me out of this.* Her heart raced so fast she couldn't catch her breath. The most logical way out was to scream or make a run for it. But what about the gun?

It was one thing to take her chances on her own. So what if they shot her? Seconds later she'd be in heaven with Jesus, being welcomed home by the husband she missed so badly. But she didn't have only herself to think about.

She had Sierra.

And because of that, she couldn't scream, couldn't make a run for it. Instead she had to think. The only passengers in sight were the two men across the way. If only they'd look at her, she could send some sort of signal with her eyes. Her captors wouldn't notice—two of them were slurring their words; none of them were paying her that much attention now that they had her trapped.

Come on, God. Make one of them look at me. Please . . .

At that moment, the blond man stood and headed toward them. He looked back at his black friend and pointed to the restrooms. This was it, the chance Jamie needed. He had to walk right past her! If only he'd look at her. He was tall with a square chin, and he looked strong enough to handle all three of the punks circled around her.

Jamie stared at him, blinking as hard as she could, willing him to look.

"So whatcha going to do to her when it's your turn?" The crew cut rattled off a string of expletives. He was so loud, he didn't see the blond man coming up along the aisle to his left. "My turn might not leave much. I better go last."

Suddenly the blond man stopped, pulled out a gun, and pointed it at the four of them. "Police, everyone freeze!"

Jamie couldn't believe her eyes. She had to be dreaming, but she wasn't. A second later the black man pulled out another gun and jogged over.

"You punks better get your hands up!" He glared at them. "Which one of you has the gun?"

All three of the young guys instantly put their hands in the air. "Hey, man," the crew cut kid forced a laugh. "We're just havin' a little fun. Come on, nothin' to get riled over."

"Sure." The blond officer pointed the gun straight at the guy and looked at Jamie. "Do you know these men?"

"*No!*" The word was more a cry than an answer. Jamie jerked away and hurried up next to the blond officer. She pointed at the dark-haired kid. "Be careful! He's got a gun!"

"We saw it." Her protector took her hand with his free one and guided her behind him. "Stay there; I'll cover you."

With the blond still aiming his gun at the young men, the black officer moved in and grabbed the gunman. "Give me your weapon. Now!"

"Hey—" He managed a nervous chuckle, his hands still in the air. "It's like my man Jason said, we're just havin' a little—"

"Give me the gun!" The officer's voice left no room for negotiation.

Jamie could barely see the drama unfolding. Was it really happening? Had three guys tried to abduct her in broad daylight? And who were the police officers? Angels?

Her heart was still racing, but she felt safe behind the blond man. He was much bigger than she, and with his body covering hers, she knew she was safe. *Calm, Jamie . . . be calm. God's with you; it's okay.* She pictured Sierra and felt tears sting her eyes. If things had been different . . .

Jamie squeezed her eyes shut until the bad thoughts went away. She opened them and stared at the officer a few feet away. The situation was under control; the kid was going to give up his gun. God had given her a miracle, one that was still playing out in front of her.

"I said, give me the gun!" The black officer was angry now. His voice told all of them he was sick of the charade.

"Whatever." It was the dark-haired kid. He snarled at his friends. "Look, I'm not going down for this." He lowered one of his hands to his pocket.

"Slow!" The blond barked. He still held Jamie's hand.

"Okay, man, okay." The kid pulled the gun from his pocket and reached it out, slowly. His hand shook. "Take it, already."

"Shut up!" The blond officer barked at him and turned to the others. "Any other weapons before we search you?"

A round of muted "No, sirs" came from the trio. All three of them had their hands in the air; none of them were laughing.

"Hold the cover." The black officer glanced at his partner. Then he slipped his own gun back in his pocket, spun the dark-haired kid around and slammed him against the ferry wall. With rough, sharp movements he ran his hands along the kid's sides. "You have the right to remain silent." He jerked his hands up and down the guy's chest. "Anything you say or do can and will be used against you in a court of law . . ."

Jamie's hands and knees were shaking now, probably from the adrenaline. What were the odds that the only two other people on this level of the ferry were police officers? *Thank You, God . . . thank You.* Her heart rate was barely slower, though.

The blond officer leaned his head back, keeping his eyes on the other two kids. "Did they threaten you?"

"Yes." Jamie tried to swallow but her throat was too dry. "They . . . they said they'd kill me if I screamed. They were going to rape me."

The officer turned to his partner. "Did you hear that?"

"Loud and clear." He finished frisking the kid and shoved him onto the bench. "Keep your hands in the air."

He repeated the process with the other two, and found no weapons on either of them. Even so he took his gun out and kept it aimed at the trio. With a glance over his shoulder, he grinned at his partner. "Go tell the captain we've made us some friends down here."

The blond officer laughed. He was still holding her hand, and now he motioned for her to follow him. They were halfway up the steps when he looked back at her. "I'm Officer Clay—"

The horn on the ferry blared, and Jamie strained to hear him.

". . . from Los Angeles."

"Clay Miles?" The wind was whipping on the upper deck and she had to shout to be heard.

"Yes," he stopped at the top of the stairs and faced her. Even then it was hard to hear. "What's your name?"

"Jamie Bryan." She was safe now, and the fact that he still had her hand in his felt . . . actually, Jamie couldn't figure what she felt. The man was tall, obviously strong, and rugged looking. All that and he'd just saved her life. "I don't know what to say."

Officer Miles let go of her hand and pointed to the captain's office. "Let's talk in there."

She nodded and followed him into the glassed-in area at the top of the ferry. He explained that he was a Los Angeles police officer and then told the man what had happened. They were almost at the Manhattan shoreline, but the captain called dispatch and found out the guys were wanted. They'd held up a convenience store at gunpoint before boarding the ferry. Police lost track of them and were about to contact the captain—in case they were aboard.

The captain held out his hand to Officer Miles. "Nice work." He shook his head. "You're on vacation from LA, is that it?"

"No. We're here for detective training in Manhattan. NYPD." He leaned against the glass wall and looked at Jamie. "We saw the suspects approach this woman, and my partner saw the gun."

Jamie wanted to run over and hug him. Instead she steadied her knees and gripped the back of the captain's chair. "They . . ." She looked straight into the officer's eyes. "You saved my life."

He grinned and shrugged one shoulder. "I guess the training started sooner than we expected."

The captain was on the phone, making arrangements to have an NYPD officer at the docks when the boat pulled up. He was saying something about stalling until the unit was on location.

"So, Jamie Bryan—" Officer Miles gazed out at the choppy water—"why're you going into Manhattan by yourself on a day like this?"

"I'm a volunteer. At St. Paul's." She met his eyes again. What was it about him? She'd never seen him before. At least, she didn't think she had. But something in his eyes made her feel as if she'd known him all her life.

The officer raised his eyebrows. "St. Paul's? You won't believe this. That's exactly where we were headed."

"Really?"

"Yep." He angled his head and studied her. His eyes were beyond kind, the perfect compliment to the tough guy she'd seen a few minutes earlier. "We have the morning off. Orientation's this afternoon."

Jamie smiled. "I think you just had it."

"True." He laughed, much more relaxed than he'd been with the bad guys downstairs. A sober look filled his eyes. "The chapel, it's across the street from the pit, right?"

"Right." Their conversation was easy, and Jamie realized she was drawn to him. "You aren't an angel, are you?"

"I'm afraid not." He grinned. "Just a regular guy, warts and all."

Jamie didn't see any warts. "I prayed for help, and a minute later you had your gun out."

"Hmmm." He kept his gaze on hers, unblinking. "I prayed God would use me in New York however He saw fit."

The captain was still on the phone, but he'd put the ferry back into gear. They weren't far from the dock now, and Jamie saw three squad cars, lights flashing. She shuddered; how different things might have been if the officers hadn't been there.

"So . . . you believe in prayer, is that right, Officer—"

"Call me Clay." He slipped his hands in his jeans pockets. His leather jacket looked sharp against his beige oxford. "And yes. To tell you the truth, God's just about everything to me."

Her voice dropped a notch. "Me too."

"Is that why you volunteer at St. Paul's?"

"Sort of." It didn't seem right to talk about Jake. She would probably never see the guy after today. Why trouble him with her personal heartache? "How 'bout you?"

"My partner's got some stuff going on. It's a long story."

A gentle bump told them the ferry had reached the dock. The captain picked up his radio and made an announcement to the passengers: "We are requesting all passengers stay seated; I repeat, all passengers please stay seated. A police matter has arisen and officers will need a few minutes to take care of the situation. Again, please stay seated."

During the captain's announcement, Jamie thought she saw Clay glance at her left hand. But it happened so fast, she wasn't sure. What with the scene downstairs—and the inexplicable connection she felt to a total stranger—she had no doubt her imagination was working overtime.

The captain thanked Clay again and bid them good-bye. "I need to be downstairs when they take the suspects."

"Fine, sir. Glad we could help."

The captain left and they were alone.

"Do you need to go?" She looked again at the police officers scrambling out of their cars and heading for the ferry ramp.

"Nope. This isn't our jurisdiction. We can stop a crime in progress, but after that it belongs to the locals."

"I see." Jamie should've thanked Clay for saving her life and proceeded to make small talk. But the feeling that she'd known him—known him well—wouldn't go away. She studied her hands. "I'm still shaking."

He closed the distance between them and, as naturally as if they'd been friends all their lives, pulled her into a hug. "I didn't want to say anything." He drew back and smiled at her. "You were flushed at first, but now . . . you're white as a ghost."

"I am?" She didn't know why, but she didn't want anything to interrupt the moment. "Even now? I'm still pale?"

"Mmhmm." He put his hands on her shoulders. "Blow out a few times, long and slow, that should help."

She did as she was told, and he studied her. "Do you feel light-headed?"

"Maybe that's it. I have this feeling I can't explain."

He still had his hands on her shoulders, watching her, making sure she was okay. "You're looking a little better now." His tone was polite, the public servant caught in a time of need.

But his eyes held more. Jamie wasn't sure she'd ever get her color back under that blue gaze.

Another announcement came over the loudspeakers: "Thank you for being patient. It's now safe to debark."

Clay pulled back and nodded toward the door. "Can a couple of LA cops escort you to St. Paul's?"

Jamie smiled. "Please."

Clay grinned. "It's late and getting later. Let's go."

They made their way back to Clay's partner, Officer Joe Reynolds, and the three of them grabbed a cab and headed for St. Paul's. They were halfway there when Jamie finally identified what she'd been feeling, the strange sensation that came over her when Clay held her behind his back, sheltering her from the suspects, then again when he pulled her into his arms. It wasn't fear or shock or even light-headedness.

It was electricity.

TWELVE

She was gorgeous, no doubt about that.

Clay wouldn't have noticed she was in trouble if it wasn't for the fact that from the moment he boarded the ferry, he hadn't been able to take his eyes off her. Reynolds had even teased him about it. "Take a picture, pal. She'll think you're a tourist."

Things happened so fast since then. He'd managed to come off as a professional, but taking her in his arms was totally out of character for him. Out of line, really. He could justify it because she looked faint, but he'd seen far worse cases. More than her health, he was concerned about her feelings. She looked scared and shocked and vulnerable; he simply wanted to hold her.

But who was she? And where was she going alone? He was almost certain she was married, why wouldn't she be?

He'd tried to get a look at her left hand, to see if she wore a ring, but he hadn't gotten a clear view.

Now they were in the cab, with Clay in the middle. Reynolds raised an eyebrow at him, but Clay silenced him with a look. This was no time for the flight attendant act he'd pulled earlier. Reynolds seemed to get the point. He gave Clay a halfhearted scowl and made light conversation about the buildings in the area and plans for rebuilding the Twin Towers.

With Jamie talking to Reynolds, Clay tried again to steal a look at her ring finger. This time she had her hands beneath her, probably trying to keep them warm. Clay looked straight ahead out the windshield of the cab. Was he losing his mind? What did it matter if she had a ring or not? He'd known the woman less than an hour.

Reynolds waxed on; the man was brilliant at carrying on empty conversations. Clay didn't pay much attention. Crazy or not, his focus was on the woman beside him. From time to time, he glanced at her and found her looking at him. And he got the sense she'd felt a connection with him, same way he had with her.

The cab pulled up in front of the chapel, and Clay paid the driver. The three of them climbed out, and Reynolds nodded toward the gaping hole, the place where the towers had stood.

"So that's the place."

"Yes." Jamie looked up and squinted, as if picturing the buildings the way they had been. "No matter how many times I look up, it's still hard to believe they're gone."

Reynolds stuffed his hands in his pockets and looked at the others. "Wanna walk over?"

Clay looked at Jamie. "You probably have to get inside, right?"

"It's okay, I'll come with you." She glanced back at the chapel. "There'll be other volunteers on by now."

The three of them crossed the street and moved as close to the chain-link fence as possible. Maybe thirty or forty people stood along the length of the fence, some in small clusters, some alone.

"Most people expect to see flowers or notes stuck in the fence." Jamie kept her voice low, respectful. She stood between the two men and folded her arms. "The city cleans it up every night; some of the stuff gets tossed—flowers, mostly. Teddy bears get donated to the children's hospital, and photos, letters—" she sighed—"they come to us."

"At St. Paul's?" Clay figured he was nearly a foot taller than her. He turned to hear her better.

"Yes." She met his eyes, and again the connection was there, a familiar current, a sense that he knew what she was going to say before she said it. "Wait till you see it."

Reynolds headed up the sidewalk, eyes on the cavernous hole. Clay and Jamie followed, silent. Along the fence, city personnel had posted oversized mounted photos of the history of the Twin Towers. Together the three of them worked their way west, reading the captions, taking in the enormity of both the force it had taken to bring those buildings down and the rebuilding project.

They reached the last photo, and something caught Clay's attention. It was a subway entrance, the stair rail and steps that led down to what at one time must've been one of the busiest subway stations of all. He leaned against the railing and looked down. From the eighth or ninth stair down, the entrance was still filled with debris— jagged cement blocks and twisted steel.

Jamie came up beside him and looked down. Instantly she stiffened and backed away.

"Jamie?"

Her face was pale again. She shook her head. "I . . . I hadn't seen that before."

"It's still full of debris." Clay fell in step beside her, and they moved beyond the stairwell.

"Yes. They should clean it because . . ."

She didn't have to finish her sentence; Clay could see where she was headed with it. The bodies of countless people had never been found. Wasn't it possible a body was trapped in that tunnel?

Of course it was.

She pulled herself away and fell in beside Clay again. Their steps were slow, waiting for Reynolds to catch up. Clay allowed his arm to brush against Jamie's as they walked.

"Are you okay?"

"Yes." Jamie shuddered. She stopped and turned, her back to the chapel. "It was three years ago, after all." She looked up at the bleak gray sky and crossed her arms tight against her chest. "It's freezing out here."

He wanted to put his arm around her and keep her warm; to shelter her from not only the cold weather but whatever had caused her to react so strongly to the damaged subway entrance. Instead he took off his coat and handed it to her. "I'm too warm. Why don't you wear it?"

Though Jamie's teeth chattered, she hesitated—then let him slip it over her shoulders. She reached up to tug it in place.

That's when Clay saw the ring.

On her left hand. No question it was a wedding band. Clay's heart dropped to his knees. So that was that. She was married, probably a bored housewife volunteering at St. Paul's to find purpose in her life—maybe as part of a calling from God.

Either way, she was taken.

Clay jammed his emotional gears. He'd saved her life. She was bound to be friendly, welcoming. Whatever he'd imagined seeing in her eyes was only wishful thinking on his part. He made a subtle move to the side, allowing a gap between them. "You didn't leave your coat on the ferry, did you?"

"No." She gave a slight roll of her eyes. "I'm so scatterbrained. I left it at the chapel last week. Coldest day of the season so far, and I don't have a coat." She wrinkled her nose. "I thought a turtleneck would keep me warm until I got inside."

"Yeah." Clay made a face and grinned. "Then you had to go and meet a couple of tourists, right?"

His jacket was huge on her. She slid her arms in the sleeves and buried her hands in the pockets. Her eyes met his and held. It was as though she looked far beyond the surface, deep into his soul. "You saved my life, Clay. After what you did, I can brave a little cold weather to show you around."

Reynolds met up with them, and they crossed the street again. They were silent as they headed up the sidewalk, along the fenced-in cemetery, and around the corner into the chapel. Jamie turned to the left, toward a display of memorabilia. She hesitated, then turned back to them.

Without moving, Clay let his eyes wander the inside perimeter of the chapel. There must've been thousands of photos and letters and pictures, buttons from firefighter uniforms and badges with NYPD embroidered on them. It was too much to take in without doing what the few other people in the chapel were doing: making their way, with slow steps, around the wall to the other side.

Jamie spread out her hand and gave them a sad smile. "This is St. Paul's."

There was a reverence to the place, a sense that merely by walking through the doors a person was on hallowed ground. No wonder. Clay looked around again, this time noticing the banners that lined the walls, banners from other cities and states offering hope and love and prayers for the people in Manhattan. Between the walls of mementos and the old wooden pews in the center, the place was truly a memorial.

He looked at Jamie. "I can feel God's Spirit here."

"Yes." She smiled. "It's that way every day."

Reynolds was already absorbed in the details, reading notes and inching his way along the displays that lined the first wall. Praying would come later. For now, Clay had a thought: What if Reynolds's wife had been to St. Paul's? Reynolds hadn't been sure where to find her or if she still lived in the area. At breakfast that morning, Reynolds told Clay that Wanda's mother died in 2000, which left him no way to find his wife but to come to New York and look for her.

Did St. Paul's keep a record of visitors? If so, maybe they could figure out if she'd been there, get a name and a city. It was worth asking.

Jamie removed Clay's jacket, gave it back to him, and took a name badge from her purse. She pinned it to her sweater and smiled at him. "Thanks." Her eyes held his. "Are you going to walk around?"

"Well . . ." Clay chewed on his lip. "Could we talk first?" He shot a look at Reynolds. "My friend is looking for someone very special to him. She might've come here."

Jamie was about to answer when an older woman with a volunteer pin like Jamie's came up to them. "Jamie, thanks for coming. The weather's awful."

"No problem." She met Clay's eyes. "I wasn't sure I was going to make it in."

"We're slow." She held up a finger. "That reminds me. Captain Hisel said to tell you he couldn't come today. He's got a meeting at the department."

"Okay." She touched the woman's hand. "Thanks."

The older woman nodded and wandered off, heading for a middle-aged woman in the back pew. It looked like the woman was crying. Clay and Jamie watched the older volunteer make contact, speak quiet words for a moment, and then sit down. Their conversation looked deep from the get-go.

"So this is what you do?" Clay's voice was barely a whisper. He leaned in toward Jamie, but only so she could hear him. "Talk with people who come here?"

"Exactly. Talk, pray, counsel. Listen." The tenderness in her eyes caught at him. "We do a lot of listening." She turned toward a pew in the middle of the chapel and motioned with her head for him to follow.

They sat down, but not too close. Clay made sure their knees didn't touch. Even so, the subtle fragrance of her perfume stirred his senses.

"What's your friend's story?" No pretense, no guarded layers to work through. Jamie simply opened her heart to whatever Clay might have to say, ready to help—just as she must've done countless times here.

"I just found out myself yesterday, on our flight here." Clay looked toward the front of the church. *She's another man's wife.* But the reminder didn't help as much as he'd hoped.

Clay told the story Reynolds had shared with him the day before. When he got to the part about Jimmy getting hit by the paroled felon, Jamie's quiet gasp drew his gaze to her.

"That's awful."

"Yes." He wanted to pull her close, hug away the pain in her eyes, the hurt that surrounded them. A young couple entered the chapel and began moving along the wall, a few yards behind Reynolds. "It gets worse."

Clay shared how Reynolds and his wife tried to make their marriage work, but neither of them could see past their grief. "They were strong believers, but they were blinded by what happened. They divorced a few months later."

Jamie brought her lips together and looked at her lap. She gave a small shake of her head. When she looked up, her eyes were damp. "He hasn't seen her since?"

"Actually, his wife married an FDNY officer stationed somewhere in Manhattan. They lived in Queens, and he commuted in. Like a lot of firefighters, I guess."

She squirmed. "Was her husband killed in the attacks?" A flicker ignited in her eyes.

"Yes. Joe meant to call and see how she was, how she was handling her husband's death, but he couldn't do it; wasn't sure how she'd react after so many years." Clay crossed one leg over the other and braced his arm along the back of the pew. "He heard about the training course out here." Clay spotted Reynolds nearing the end of the first wall. "I think he wants to find her."

Jamie knit her brow together and leaned forward, resting on the pew in front of her. "Something about the story sounds familiar. What was his wife's name?"

"Wanda." Clay thought for a minute. "I can't remember her last name."

"I know a Wanda, at least I've met her. We prayed together here a few months ago. If I remember right, she said something about losing a little boy ten years ago." Jamie sat a little straighter. "What did she look like?"

"Not sure what she looks like now." Reynolds was partway along the back of the wall, still looking at the items collected in the past three years. "Joe has a picture of her on his desk, the last picture taken with her and Jimmy. She was beautiful, a black woman with brown skin and straightened hair. Big, childlike eyes."

Jamie's eyes widened. "That's got to be her." Sadness replaced her excitement. "She's . . . a very troubled woman, Clay. Too many losses."

"Wait—" disbelief worked its way through him—"so you *know* her? You've prayed with her?" He hadn't been in New York twenty-four hours and already amazing things were happening. He didn't wait for Jamie's answer. "Do you have any idea how we could find her?" A realization hit him. "Or if she'd want to be found?"

Jamie put her hand on her forehead. "This is so weird."

"What?"

"I just remembered something we prayed for, Wanda and I." Jamie looked straight at him. "We prayed she might find her first husband. So she could make peace with him."

A chill ran down Clay's spine. He wanted to fall to his knees and look around, in case angels were hovering overhead. "Do you know how to reach her?"

"I think so." She stood, motioning for him to follow her.

They went to the opposite side of the chapel, to a set of stairs that led to a break room. Off to one side was a small office, and inside that, a file cabinet. Clay waited in the doorway while Jamie searched, and after only a few seconds, she pulled out a single sheet of paper. "Here it is!"

"What?" Clay took a step closer and squinted at the paper.

"Wanda thought she might want to volunteer here. She filled out an application, but decided it was too soon. We kept the information on file, in case she changed her mind." Jamie scanned the sheet. "It has everything. Her name's Wanda Johnston, and she lives in Queens. Her phone, her cell phone, it's all here."

Clay couldn't speak. The day was already so full of miracles, he couldn't find the words to sum it up. Finally he managed a question. "What should we do?"

Jamie shrugged. "I'll call and ask her. I can't give the information out unless she agrees."

"Okay." Clay nodded. *God . . . be with Wanda, let her want this meeting. For Joe's sake.*

The phone on the desk was an older model, with a short cord. Jamie sat down, picked up the receiver and began to dial. After a minute she hung up and looked at the application again. "I'll try her cell."

Please, God . . . An answer this soon would ignite Reynolds's faith and bring him the healing he needed.

Jamie dialed again and waited. Her eyes lit up after a few seconds. "Wanda? Hi, this is Jamie Bryan over at St. Paul's. How are you?" Silence. "Well, you won't believe this. Remember how we prayed when you were here, that you would find your first husband so you could make peace with him?" She grinned at Clay, her eyes dancing. "Well, he and a friend just walked into the chapel this morning." Pause. "No, I'm serious. Joe wants your phone number; I told his friend I'd call you to see if it was okay to give it out. Sure. We'll work it out." Jamie hesitated, then laughed out loud. "I know. We serve a mighty God." She gave Clay a pointed look. "That seems to be the message of the day."

The conversation ended, and Jamie held the application in the air. "Yes!" She scribbled some numbers on a piece of paper and ripped it from the pad. "She wants to see him!"

It was the second time in as many hours that Clay wanted to hug her, but he resisted. They walked back downstairs, Clay reminding himself with every step to keep calm. The mood in the chapel was as hushed and somber as before. Reynolds was at the right side of the back wall, still lost in the items on display.

Clay led the way. When he reached his friend, he tapped him on the shoulder.

"Huh?" Joe turned around. His eyes were watery. "Oh, sorry." He looked at his watch. "Guess I got a little carried away. Like you always say, it's late and getting later."

"I'm not worried about the time." The sense of awe still had a grip on Clay. He gave a single shake of his head. "C'mere, buddy. You won't believe this." He took Joe's arm and led him back to the center pew. Jamie followed along, and she and Clay sat with Joe in the middle.

"Joe, listen." Clay gave Jamie a quick look and couldn't keep from grinning. "I told Jamie your story." He hesitated, studying his friend. "She knows Wanda; she had a volunteer application on file."

"What?" Joe's mouth hung open as he looked at Jamie. His chin quivered and he swallowed hard. "You *what?*"

"I know her, Joe. I called her a few minutes ago." Jamie smiled. "She wants to see you." She handed him the piece of paper with Wanda's numbers on it. "I told her you'd be calling."

Joe took the piece of paper and stared at it, as if it might disappear if he looked away. He clenched his jaw, stood, and looked first at Jamie, then at Clay. "If you'll excuse me." His voice was raspy, filled with a decade of fear, regret, and grief—but layered with a joy that rang out. He smiled despite the wetness in his eyes. "I have a phone call to make."

They watched him go, and Jamie looked to the front of the chapel, at the towering white cross. She took in a long, slow breath and turned to Clay. "What a day, huh?"

He leaned back against the hard wood. It was his turn to walk the perimeter, to look at the remembrances and pay homage to the people who had lost their lives in the attacks. But he couldn't pull away, couldn't cut the conversation with this woman short. So she was married. No harm in talking to her, especially after what they'd been through that morning.

"What's your story, Clay?" She had an easy way about her, gentle words and eyes that hit him at his deepest level. "Married? Kids?"

The question wasn't suggestive, just curious. Clay rested his elbow on the back of the pew. "Never married. I've got a brother not far from me in California, so I spend time with his family." He gave a light-hearted laugh. "Lots of girlfriends, but never the right one."

"Hmmm." She smiled, teasing. "A California playboy, huh?"

"Hardly." Clay chuckled. "Work keeps me busy; I don't get out much. When the time's right, I want to get married, have a family. I guess God'll let me know." He crossed his arms. "What about you? What's your husband do?"

The humor faded from her eyes. A stricken look froze her features, and she looked at her hands for a long while.

Clay studied her, wanting to help. What had he said? Was her marriage in trouble? He hadn't meant to hit a nerve. "Jamie? I'm sorry."

She looked up. "It's okay."

"It's just that—" he looked at her left hand—"you're wearing a ring, and I thought . . ."

"Don't be sorry. I haven't taken it off." Her eyes were dry, but somewhere inside it was clear that she was weeping. "Jake was a firefighter. He . . . he died in the attacks."

Of course. Clay hung his head against his forearm and exhaled hard. Why hadn't he figured that out? She was alone on the ferry, trekking in from Staten Island to volunteer at what was basically a memorial site for the Twin Towers. He pulled his head up slowly and looked at her. "I'm sorry, Jamie."

"The department lost more than four hundred men that day. Dozens more from the NYPD." She sniffed and a smile tried to break through the clouds in her eyes. "I'm hardly alone in my loss."

It was a line she must've repeated over and over a hundred times a month, but Clay was struck with how hard it was for her to say it, even after three years. He wanted to know more, but the timing didn't feel right. "Do you have children?"

"A daughter. Sierra." At the mention of the girl, Jamie's eyes came back to life. She sniffed. "The two of us are very close. She's seven now, in second grade."

Reynolds came through the front door, a grin on his face that warmed the whole chapel. As he got closer, he held his cell phone up in the air and beamed at them. "I'm meeting her for lunch."

"Really?" Clay sat straighter. "You ready for that?" The reunion was bound to be emotional, especially if Joe told her all the things he planned to say.

A sober look flashed in his face. "I was ready years ago." He sat down next to Clay. "Talk to the Big Man for me, will you? It's been awhile." He checked his watch again. "It's noon. I told her I'd take a cab to the restaurant." He looked at Clay. "I'll meet you at orientation."

"Oh, sure." Clay grinned at him. "Ditch me in downtown Manhattan our first day."

"I'm off at 12:30." Jamie looked at Clay. "I'll buy lunch." Jamie stood and ran her fingers through her dark hair.

"You don't have to do that." Clay's heart still ached for her. They hadn't gotten to finish their conversation. "I can find something to do."

"Clay—" The sorrow faded a little more from her eyes. "You rescued me. I think I can cough up lunch."

Before Clay could reply, Joe chuckled. "Yeah, that's right. Try to look upset that I'm ditching you, man." Joe winked at him and raised an eyebrow at Jamie. "I think the two of y'all will be just fine without me."

THIRTEEN

Rain was falling hard again, gusting in torrents and pounding on the roof as Joe left St. Paul's.

Jamie looked up at the old ornate ceiling. "Hope it isn't hailing."

"Could be; it's in the forecast." Clay met her eyes. "He's gonna get soaked."

"Somehow—" Jamie smiled—"I don't think he'll mind." Jamie spotted an older man come through the entrance. She stood up. "Well, back to work."

"I'll look around." He pulled his legs beneath the bench so she could get by. Then he stood and headed toward the closest display, the one near the exit. "Maybe I'll start at the end and go against the crowd."

"Suit yourself." She met his eyes once more before she turned around. It wasn't until she was a few steps away that she felt a sense of relief. By starting at the opposite side, he'd miss seeing Jake, and that was just as well. She wasn't ready to talk about him with Clay, not when her heart was whirling around inside her.

A draft whistled through the old building, but Jamie didn't feel the cold. Not with her mind racing out of control. In three years she'd never met anyone like Clay. What was it about him? His strength, or the way he'd so easily protected her on the ferry? Or was it his eyes? The way she felt she'd known him all her life?

Whatever it was, he made her feel something she hadn't felt since Jake.

And that's why her head was spinning. How dare she allow herself to compare a stranger with the man she'd loved since she was twelve years old? She clenched her hands and chided herself. *Get a grip, Jamie . . .*

She could shout it at herself, but there was no denying what was happening inside her. She felt wonderful.

The man looked up as she approached him. He was well dressed, with the air of an executive at one of the financial firms in lower Manhattan. He was still standing near the entrance—not far from Jake's picture and Sierra's letter. His blank expression told her he wanted assistance.

"Hello." She held out her hand, and he took it. "I'm Jamie Bryan, a volunteer here. Can I help you with anything?"

The man took his hat off and tucked it beneath his arm. "I'm Wilbur George." He stared at the collection along the first wall. "My son worked for Cantor-Fitzgerald."

That was all he needed to say.

Cantor-Fitzgerald had been located near the top of the South Tower; the death toll for that firm was the largest for any company hurt by the terrorist attacks. Jamie lowered her voice. "He didn't make it out?"

"No." His mouth made a straight line. "He . . . he had a wife and two children. A boy and a girl. The wife . . . she's getting married again in March."

The idea of people remarrying was coming up more often lately. Not that all of those widowed by the attacks waited this long. Some would wait much longer. But three years seemed a benchmark, of sorts. Jamie let the man set the pace of the conversation.

"I've met the young man; he's very nice. Our daughter-in-law will be happy with him, and so will the kids." He stared at his shoes for a minute and gave a sad shake of his head. When he looked back up, his stoic veneer was cracked down the middle. "I'm here because of my wife." He blinked three times fast. "She's not handling it well."

"I'm sorry." Jamie motioned to the nearest pew. "Can you sit and talk for a minute?"

The man nodded and followed her. He took his overcoat off and laid it across the pew's wooden back. His hat remained clutched in his hands. "We aren't really praying people, you see." His sad laugh floated around her. "My son was. Good Christian boy, his wife too. But my wife and I never really . . . we never believed much in God."

"I see." Jamie studied the man. *Lord, let this be the day he changes his mind.*

The man worked his fingers into the rim of his gray flannel hat. "Lately I've started wondering." He glanced around the chapel. "Look at all the good that's come from people since that terrible day. Look at the beauty of life itself." He looked at her. "One of my partners at work lost a niece in the Twin Towers. His family pulled together and prayed that her death wouldn't be in vain."

Jamie listened, praying.

"That man's a new person today." Wilbur George worked his mouth sideways, the way men sometimes did when they didn't want to cry. "All he talks about is God this and God that, and whether the Lord would be happy with his dealings at work and how he can live some way that would please his Creator." He hesitated. "At first I thought he was wacky. But now . . ."

"It's starting to make sense?"

"Yes." His eyes widened at Jamie's answer. "That's it exactly." His shoulders drooped a notch. "At least for me. For my wife, she says if there was a God, He'd be her enemy after what happened to our boy."

A heaviness weighed on Jamie. It was the same story again and again and again. Different faces, different names, different floors of the Twin Towers, but so often when the walking wounded found their way here it was with one question. How could God let it happen?

"I guess the question, Mr. George, is whether *you* believe." She studied him. *Father, open his heart. Please.* "Do you believe in God and His Son, Jesus?"

"I do." His eyes shone for the first time since he'd walked into the chapel. "I really do."

She wanted to tread lightly, but if she didn't get to the crux of faith she was wasting her time. The real hope was found in the rest of the story. "Do you want Jesus as your Savior?"

The man frowned. "That's where I'm a little confused. I thought . . ." He looked around the chapel. "I thought someone here might be able to help me. That way I could help my wife."

He looked at the wall of artifacts and letters again. "I've done some reading, talked to a few people including my partner at work. All good things are from God—" his eyes found hers again—"right?"

For the next ten minutes Jamie talked with the man about the basics of faith in Christ. All the things she'd learned from Jake's Bible and his journal, from a hundred or so church services since the terrorist attacks and from her training at St. Paul's. At the end of their conversation, the man was nodding, practically desperate to have Jesus as his Savior.

They prayed together, and when they were finished, Jamie gave him ideas that might help his wife find faith in God. When they were done talking, he looked like a mountain had been lifted from his shoulders.

"Thank you, Jamie. I want to take a look around." He patted her hand. "I haven't been here before." He stood and slipped his coat on. Then he stopped and looked at her. "All good things are from God, right?"

"Right. That's what the Bible says."

"Then God didn't make those towers fall. Something evil did, because evil exists in our world."

Jamie gave him a sad smile. "Yes, Mr. George. That's right."

As he walked away, she looked at her watch. Her shift was over; she and Clay could head out for lunch. She stood, grateful for her time with the man. Without that, she would have been consumed by one thought.

Counting down the minutes until she could go someplace and talk to Clay without interrupting the grieving going on all around her.

She found him not quite finished with the exit wall. "Clay?"

He stepped back, his focus still on a child's letter posted near a photo of a police officer. "It's so sad, Jamie. The pictures and letters, even from people who weren't touched by the attacks, at least not personally." He looked at her, his eyes glistening. "The loss was so enormous."

"I know." She resisted the urge to glance across the room at the first display table, the one where Jake's picture was. "Even after working here all this time, it's bigger than I can really grasp."

"I didn't get halfway through." He drew back from the wall and came up alongside her. "Maybe I can finish it another day."

Jamie thought about Jake. "You could." She cast him a sad smile. "It's really just more of the same."

"I guess." He drew in a sharp breath and peered through the closest stained-glass window. "You have an umbrella?"

"You mean you don't?" She was teasing him and it felt better than she could've dreamed. "What, it doesn't rain in California?"

He tossed her a sheepish look. "Not much."

"Don't worry." She held up her finger. "Wait here, I'll get my coat and be right back. And yes—" she started up the stairs toward the break room—"I have an umbrella."

They caught a cab and found a quiet café fifteen blocks north on Broadway. It was busy, but Clay spotted a table near the front window, overlooking the bustling sidewalk. "Good?"

Jamie nodded. "I like people watching."

"Me too." He stared at the parade passing by, businesspeople mostly, some obvious tourists, a random group of kids decked out in black T-shirts and dog collars. Together they carried enough umbrellas to form an overhang along the sidewalk. Clay rested his forearms on the table. "Doesn't it ever slow down?"

"Not much." She smiled. "I can only take Manhattan in small doses."

He looked at the crowds outside. "I can see why." His heart was racing, even faster than it had that morning on the ferry. What was he doing here? He'd been in town a few hours and he was having lunch with a beautiful widow? Clay Michaels, the guy who didn't rush anything?

The whole scene couldn't have been more out of character for him than if he spiked his hair and dyed it pink. At his soft laugh, Jamie looked at him.

"What's so funny?" She lowered her chin.

"Me." He drew invisible circles on the table with his finger. "Joe told me New York would be exciting, but I wasn't sure."

"And then I enter the picture." She eased off her coat and slid it over the back of the chair.

"That's for sure." He laughed out loud this time, a laugh that was brief and full of amazement. "I had no idea anyplace, not even New York, could be that exciting."

The waiter brought them ice water and took their order, chicken sandwiches with tea for her and black coffee for him. When he was gone, Jamie put her elbows on the table, linked her fingers, and rested her chin. "Do you think he would've shot me?"

Clay wanted to drown in her eyes. She was making his head spin and he barely knew her. "I've asked myself that a dozen times today. Usually punky kids like that won't shoot someone in broad daylight. A move like that could wind them up on death row." He brought his knuckles together and took a drink of his water. "But you believed them, otherwise you would've screamed."

"I tried to catch your attention, but I didn't think you saw me."

He felt his eyebrows lift a notch. "Oh, I saw you."

Her shy smile as she pulled her glass closer was pure sweetness. "Is that a good thing?"

"Yes. Very good." He studied her. The conversation was easy, comfortable. The same way it had been in the ferry captain's office and at St. Paul's. It wasn't the rush of the moment with the criminals or the emotion of the chapel. It was Jamie. She was as transparent as a summer breeze.

"So you really think they would've killed me if I got off the ferry with them?"

A chill ran down his spine, and he felt his smile fade. "I don't want to think about what would've happened if you'd done that."

She looked out the window. "At first I was going to scream anyway. I figured, let them shoot me. Someone would save me or I'd wind up in heaven. I'd win either way."

"Why didn't you?"

"Because of Sierra."

"Your little girl." Clay leaned against the window and watched her. Emotions played out on her face. "You just started telling me about her when Joe came back. She's seven?"

"Yes." She looked at him again. "Long golden hair and a heart as big as the ocean. She's very special."

She must be, if she's anything like you. "What does she like to do?"

"She likes cats and horses and movie nights with me. Right now her favorite is *The Lion King*, but for at least two years it was *The Little Mermaid*." Jamie laughed and poked her straw at the ice in her water. "I enjoy her so much."

"I can see that." Clay hesitated. "What was your husband like?" Clay already knew the answer; he must've been a great guy. The haunting look in her eyes at the chapel earlier told him that the loss had all but killed her. Still, he wanted to hear it from her, wanted to give her a chance to talk about him if she wanted to.

For the first time that day, a wall went up in Jamie's eyes. "We were very close." She bit the inside of her lip. "I fell in love with him when I was twelve. We ... we grew up down the street from each other. His dad was a firefighter." She pressed the corners of her lips up, but it was hardly a smile. "That's all Jake ever wanted to be."

Clay didn't want to push, but he needed to know her, to find out what made her cry when she was alone at night, what memories kept her going when she didn't want to take another step. "Did he share your faith?"

A knowing look crossed her face, as if the answer wasn't an easy one. But she only nodded and took a sip of her water. "Yes. He loved the Lord very much."

He must've loved Jamie very much too. After all, she still wore his ring. The feeling was clearly mutual.

"Jake and I shared something rare. There's never been anyone else." Jamie hugged herself and looked straight at him. "It hasn't been easy."

The sense that he should go to her, pull her into his arms, and soothe away the hurt, was so strong this time he almost gave in. Instead, he willed himself to stay seated. "Is that why you help out at St. Paul's?"

"I think so. It's complicated, really. I go for a lot of reasons, but yes." She looked out the window again. "It's what Jake would've done; I guess I do it as a way of remembering him."

Clay studied the woman across from him. The connection he felt to her was something he couldn't explain. The fact that she was still in love with her dead husband didn't bother him. This woman was loyal to the core, and after loving someone since she was twelve? Of course she still had feelings for him. She always would.

The waiter came with their sandwiches and hot drinks. When he left, Clay met her eyes. "Pray?"

She nodded and bowed her head.

"Lord, we thank You for this food, but more than that, we thank You for bringing us together this morning. You answered both our prayers. Mine that I would make a difference, and Jamie's. It's all You, Father, and for that we thank You. Amen."

"Amen." She was smiling when she looked up, and he sensed she didn't want to talk about her dead husband anymore; not now, anyway. She used her knife to cut her sandwich into smaller pieces. "Okay, Clay. What about you? Isn't three weeks a long time to be away from work?"

"Actually it's four." He took the top slices of bread off his sandwich and shook salt over the meat inside. His body was a priority, one he took care of, but salt was one of his few vices. He used it liberally.

"You're here four weeks?" She looked surprised. "I thought Joe said it was three weeks of training."

"It is." He put the top pieces of bread back on his sandwich, then looked at her for a few seconds. If he told her the reason, would she think differently of him? He took a slow breath. It didn't matter; he couldn't be anything less than honest with her. "I had one week off before I left."

"Vacation?" She held her sandwich, but she held it in midair waiting for his answer.

"I was in a gunfight. A man was coming at me, firing an AK-47." Clay searched her eyes looking for her reaction. "I had to kill him."

Jamie's eyes widened. "So they fired you?"

"No." He smiled. She wasn't repulsed at the shooting so much as worried that he'd lost his job. "No, it's standard procedure when a suspect is shot and killed by an officer during a crime. It's a paid leave; they hold an investigation and make a report. As long as everything was on the level, the officer reports back in three or four weeks."

"Oh. I didn't know that." She took a bite of her sandwich.

"My captain told me not to worry about it. There was nothing else I could do." He thought about telling her how close he'd come to getting killed himself, but it didn't seem like the right time. "When I get back they're promoting me to detective." He grinned. "That's the long answer to your question. I'm here because I need the training, and Joe picked New York City."

"Oh." Understanding filled her eyes. She put her hands around her cup of tea and held it to her lips. "Because of Wanda."

"Right."

The conversation moved to what the training would include and how long he'd been an officer, then went back to the men on the ferry.

"Did you really see a gun?" She tilted her head, her eyes doubtful. "You were all the way across the deck."

He grinned. She was very perceptive. "I saw the guy move in on you, and I could tell by your face that you didn't know him. I told Joe, and we both kept an eye on you. When the second guy came over and pressed in against you, the look on your face was clear even from where we were sitting."

"I was scared to death."

"Yes." His hand itched to hold hers, but the idea was ludicrous. He clenched his fingers. "That's what I saw. Then the second guy jerked something near your ribs, and you jumped. I asked Joe if he saw a gun, and he said, 'Why, yes, I did.' So I said, 'Well then, I better go get it from him.' And Joe said, 'Me too.'"

Jamie giggled and took a long sip of her tea. "But you never actually saw one?"

"Well, see, the thing was, it *felt* like we did."

"And as it turned out—" Jamie was smiling, playing along with him—"your feeling was right."

He waited a beat, breathing her in. "It's been right a lot lately."

Her eyes told him she understood what he was saying. Her cheeks grew a shade darker. "Clay?"

"Yes, Jamie." *God . . . let me see her again. Don't let this be the last time we're together.*

"Can I see you again? While you're here?" Her fingers were shaking, though she tried to still them on her teacup.

Clay wasn't sure whether to laugh or look for angels again. The answers were pouring down as fast as the rain. He wouldn't tell her about his prayer. That could come later. Besides, he didn't want her to think he took her question lightly. In light of what she'd just told him about her husband, it couldn't have been easy to ask it. He nodded. "I'd like that."

"You're staying on Staten Island, right?"

"Yes. Cheap hotels, or so I'm told."

"Much cheaper." The nervousness—or whatever it was—lifted. She smiled the comfortable way she'd smiled at him on the ferry and at St. Paul's. "Could I make dinner for you and Joe?"

Clay felt his heart soar. He never took his eyes from hers as he nodded. "That would be perfect."

Jamie had to catch the ferry back to Staten Island to pick up her daughter, so they finished their lunches and took cabs in different directions—him to the NYPD station staging the training orientation, her to Battery Park. He resisted the urge to hug her. She was no longer a victim needing to be held. She was a woman who, in an instant's time, had captured his thoughts and imagination.

Maybe even his heart.

Was it her vulnerability or the way she looked straight to his soul? *Cool it, Michaels. Slow down.* He turned his thoughts to Joe. How had his friend done with Wanda? Had Joe been able to apologize the way he planned, or was Wanda still upset with him?

He tried to imagine their encounter, but instead saw Jamie's face, the way she'd looked on the ferry when she walked past, her terrified eyes when the thugs accosted her, the way she'd let him hold her in the captain's office . . .

All of it played again and again in his mind. As the cab let him off at the police department, two very strong thoughts stayed with him. First, this new friendship would have to develop slowly.

And second, how many hours he had until he saw her again.

FOURTEEN

By the time Jamie put the casserole into the oven, she was so nervous her throat was dry.

She stared at the dial above the glass door. Was she supposed to set it at three-hundred-fifty degrees? Or was it four-fifty? She gritted her teeth. *Focus, Jamie . . . come on.* She turned back to the counter and the recipe still lying there. Her enchilada casserole was something she could make in her sleep. So why couldn't she remember how high to heat the oven? She scanned through the list of ingredients and finally found it on the back side. Three-fifty. Of course.

Four times that day she'd picked up the phone to cancel the dinner.

There were a hundred reasons why she shouldn't have Clay and Joe over. It was too soon. Her entire house was a shrine to Jake. The buffet table in the dining room still had the same six photos— pictures of him and Sierra, him and Jamie, the three of them at the beach, him in his uniform the day he was hired by the FDNY.

And then there was the bigger framed photo taken on their wedding day.

She would keep those pictures forever, but she didn't want Clay and Joe looking at them. Didn't want their pity. Poor firefighter's widow, still stuck in the past. The fact was, until the past two weeks the thought of other men hadn't crossed her mind. Sure, several FDNY widows had remarried, and she knew others who had started dating.

But her? Jamie Bryan?

The idea was laughable. No one could fill the place in her heart but Jake. No one. She felt scared and sick and guilty just thinking about starting over with someone new. But then, Aaron brought up the question, opened the door to possibilities she hadn't wanted to consider before.

And now . . .

There was no denying the way she felt with Clay. She'd relived the moment on the ferryboat at least once an hour in the past twenty-four. How he'd taken charge of the scene and kept her safe, his body shielding hers. Things she hadn't been conscious of at the time were now vivid in her memory. The pungent fragrance of his leather jacket, his fresh-showered soap smell mixed with a subtle cologne. How she had inched closer to him, wanting his protection, his closeness.

It was crazy.

She hadn't asked for these feelings or looked for them or ever even imagined them. She'd only felt them for one other man in all her life. And now, in just a day's time, she was willing to serve Clay dinner in the house where she and Jake had built their life together?

It was all wrong.

Still . . . every time she picked up the phone to make the call, she stopped herself. She couldn't go back on her offer. It wasn't polite, for one thing, and the men *did* save her life, after all. Clay picked up the lunch tab. The least she could do was make dinner for them—a home-cooked meal, something they wouldn't be getting much of in the next three weeks. She would make good on her invitation because it was a nice thing to do, a Christian thing.

Unfortunately, as soon as she told herself that, the truth screamed at her so loud she couldn't think: her dinner offer had nothing to do with Christian goodwill.

She wanted to see Clay again.

It was that simple. He was all she'd thought of since their first meeting, no matter how wrong that might've been. That truth ran wild through her heart for a few hours until she walked across the house and picked up the phone, determined to cancel.

Then the whole goodwill thing came back around again.

The cycle was driving her crazy. Finally she stopped fighting herself. Yes, she was attracted to him. So what? Jake was dead; it wasn't a crime to have a nice-looking man over for dinner. He would be gone in three weeks, back to California. What harm could come from a single dinner together?

She looked at the clock on the kitchen wall.

They'd be there in half an hour.

"Sierra?" She wiped her hands on her jeans and ran lightly to the base of the stairs. "Did you finish your homework?"

"Yes, Mommy. I was just playing with Wrinkles." Jamie heard her daughter's small feet padding toward the top of the stairs. "Can you play too? We're playing house and we need a mommy."

Jamie smiled. Sierra always put everything into perspective. "Okay, baby. I'll be up there in a few minutes."

"Good! I'll go tell Wrinkles."

"Okay." Jamie turned and gave the house a critical glance. What needed last minute touch-ups? She took quick steps into the dining room. The table was set, Sierra had put the vase of silk roses in the middle, and—

Jamie looked at the buffet table. She hadn't done anything with the pictures of Jake. They would stay, of course. But tonight? Both men would pity her for sure, pity her and think her delusional, trapped in a life lived more back in yesterday than today. She moved to the buffet.

The pictures were dusty, and that shot another arrow of guilt through her. How long had it been since she dusted them, since she'd come this close and actually looked at them? She picked up the one of Jake in his uniform and went to dust it with her shirt, but stopped herself.

She had on a new sweater—a ribbed pale blue pullover. Dust would show on it for sure.

The buffet had extra linens, didn't it? She opened the top drawer and pulled out an old cloth napkin, wrinkled from lack of use. Jake's pictures shouldn't get dusty. She ran the napkin over the glass until she could see his smile, the pride in his eyes, as easily as if she was taking the picture all over again.

The dust fell to the floor. She started to shove the napkin back in the drawer when an idea hit her. It wasn't that she wanted to hide his pictures. Rather she wanted to protect them from the curious looks and silent questions that were bound to come if she left them up. The drawer was deep enough for all of them. She swallowed back a tidal wave of guilt and one at a time she dusted the pictures and layered them in the drawer with more cloth napkins.

There. She shut the drawer and dusted off her hands. As she did a picture came to mind. Pontius Pilot, rubbing his hands together, convincing himself he wasn't guilty when he clearly was.

Just like her.

Here she was, hiding Jake's pictures, burying her past in a buffet drawer and then dusting off her hands, as if that could make her innocent.

She stared hard at the closed buffet drawer, willing herself to see through the wood at the pictures laying there, put away like so many outdated knickknacks.

"Jamie," she whispered out loud, "you're losin' it."

If only Jake had stayed home that day, gone with her and Sierra to the zoo. If he hadn't gone in that Tuesday morning they would have other, newer pictures on the buffet, and dinner would be for Jake and Sierra. Not two strangers she'd met just the day before.

Jake ... it's so hard. I don't want to live without you, but ... I keep waking up. Life keeps coming whether I like it or not. She gripped the edge of the buffet and closed her eyes. *God ... am I bad? Should I keep the photos up? Help me ...*

No holy words came to her, no Scripture verse. But after a few seconds, a calm settled over her. She could put the photos away for a night if she wanted to. If it helped her take one step toward tomorrow then it was the most right thing she could do. She opened her eyes.

She wouldn't be able to think straight if she had to get through the night with Jake's eyes on her the whole time. With hers on him.

"Mommy?" Her daughter's voice came from the upstairs bedroom. She sounded frustrated.

Jamie gave one last look and then turned her back on the buffet. "Coming."

What was the big deal, anyway? It was one dinner, one simple dinner for two police officers far from home. She could do this one thing, show them some East Coast hospitality and be done with it. She darted up the stairs and stopped at the top.

She'd forgotten perfume.

"One sec, Sierra." More quick steps, through her bedroom, to the bureau near the end of her bed. She grabbed the amber bottle and gave first her neck, then both wrists a quick spray.

When she walked into Sierra's bedroom, her daughter sat up straight and studied her. "How come you're dressed up?"

"I'm not." Jamie dropped cross-legged on the floor across from Sierra and Wrinkles. The cat had a pink scarf tied around his head and white lace socks on his front paws. His look was one of attempted dignity and mild disgust. "Wrinkles is the one who's dressed up."

Sierra grinned at the cat. "She's my big sister."

"I see." Jamie loved her daughter's imagination. That she could dress up a tomcat and convince herself he was her sister was testimony to the delightful reaches of her creativity. For the occasion, Sierra wore a blue velvet hat and long white gloves.

"You be the mommy, okay?" Sierra bounced up and grabbed an old straw hat with loud purple plastic flowers glued to the sides. It was her favorite dress-up hat for Jamie. "Here, this is for you."

The hat was big and obnoxious; it flopped over Jamie's ears, but she didn't mind. The game was a welcome distraction. "Well?" She held her arms straight out. "How do I look?"

"Fabulous." Sierra giggled. "Isn't she fabulous, Wrinkles?"

Jamie petted the cat. "Wrinkles is speechless, I think."

The cat started to get up, but Sierra stopped him. She cooed near the cat's face. "It's okay, Wrinkles, he isn't the only pretty girl in the family, actually." She looked at Jamie. "Wrinkles is jealous because he doesn't have a pretty dress."

"Tell Wrinkles it's okay. I don't have a pretty dress either."

Sierra blinked and her eyes grew serious. "Wait, Mommy. Who's coming for dinner again?"

"Two police officers. I met them on the ferry yesterday, going to my volunteer work."

"Oh." She kept one hand on the cat's back. "Were they hungry?"

"The police officers?"

"Yes. You invited them for dinner so they musta been hungry."

"No." She hid her smile behind her fingers. "I mean, not at the time, they weren't hungry. I hope they're hungry tonight, though."

Jamie studied her daughter. "Actually, they saved me from some bad men."

Sierra opened her eyes wide. "Bad men? Like with guns?"

"Yes." Jamie adjusted her hat. "Three bad men tried to scare me." She wanted to keep the story simple. "And before they could make me too scared, the officers came and took them away."

"Wow." Sierra adjusted Wrinkles's scarf so that it came down closer to his eyes. "He looks more like a girl now."

Jamie studied the cat. "Yes, you're right."

"So they took the bad guys away and then you asked them to dinner?" Sierra kept one hand on the cat's head. In case he had any ideas about ending the game prematurely, Jamie guessed.

"Well, no. I talked to them for a while. They're both very nice."

"What's their names?"

"One man is Clay . . ." Jamie felt her heart skip a beat. What if Sierra could see through her? What if she could tell the minute the men arrived that Jamie had feelings for Clay? "The other man is Joe. They're from California."

"Oh." One of the socks was slipping off Wrinkles's paw. She pulled it back on. "So they didn't know Daddy?"

It took Jamie a moment to catch her breath. "No, sweetie. Why would they know Daddy?"

"You said they're policemen. Sometimes policemen and fire-fighters know each other." She patted Wrinkles's head. "Didn't you know that, Mommy?"

"Yes, I guess I did." She never stopped being amazed by the things Sierra said. "But these two men don't know Daddy, okay?" Jamie pointed at Wrinkles. "Now listen, daughter. Where have you been, out so late and dressed like that?"

Sierra giggled. "Mommy, don't be mad at us. We had dancing lessons with our boyfriends."

"Boyfriends?" Jamie used her best mock mean mother tone. "No boyfriends for you! Besides, where are the boyfriends?"

The wheels in Sierra's head must've been turning. She looked around the room and in a rush she pointed at the closet. "There. We keep our boyfriends in the closet."

Again Jamie had to stifle a laugh. She sat a bit straighter, more authoritative. "There will be no more boyfriends in closets anymore."

The cat tried to pull away, but Sierra stopped him again. He settled back down and meowed.

Jamie pointed a finger at him. "No talking back, sister. And don't try to run away, either."

The doorbell rang. They were here! Certain moments since yesterday Jamie was sure she'd dreamed the whole thing up. Men couldn't have tried to accost her on the ferry in broad daylight, and certainly two police officers didn't happen to be watching. She hadn't spent the morning with a man who had mesmerized her from the first few seconds, and she didn't have lunch with him, talking with him like they were old friends. And she certainly didn't invite them for dinner.

But she really did. The whole day really happened, and now Joe and Clay were downstairs waiting to be let in.

She jumped into action. "Come on, Sierra, let's go meet them."

Sierra swept the cat into her arms and the two of them bounded down the stairs to the front door. Jamie shot Sierra a look. "Best manners, okay?"

"Okay." Sierra held the cat to her chest. "Best manners."

Jamie opened the door and found Clay on her porch. He held something behind his back. "Hi." Warmth stirred inside her at the sight of him, and she felt her cheeks get hot. Sierra came up beside her, still holding the cat, and suddenly Jamie remembered what she was doing. She put her arm around her daughter. "Come in."

"I don't know." Laughter danced in Clay's eyes. He looked himself up and down. "Looks like I'm underdressed."

Jamie gasped and grabbed the hat from her head. "We were playing—"

The laughter came all at once, and after a day of worrying and overthinking, it felt too good to stop it. Dress-up games were normal fare for Jamie and Sierra. But how must they have looked? Sierra with her old-lady blue velvet hat and white gloves; her with the cheap plastic flowers? And what about Wrinkles?

She was laughing too hard to say anything. Instead she backed into the house, gesturing for him to join them.

Sierra apparently didn't see anything funny. She gave Jamie a strange look and then turned to Clay. "Mommy's silly sometimes."

Jamie let out another burst of laughter.

"Yes." Clay stooped down to Sierra's level. "I see that." He petted the cat's chin. "I'm Clay."

"I'm Sierra." She smiled at him, not quite smitten, but close.

Clay winked at her. "You have nice taste in outfits, Sierra."

"Thank you." She was still in character, assuming it perfectly normal for a cat to have a scarf and lace socks. But she did a little giggle and spoke in a loud whisper, as if she were sharing secret information. "We're playing pretend."

Jamie had tears in her eyes. Still laughing, she leaned against the foyer wall so she could catch her breath.

Clay's eyes widened. "Oh, I see." He gave Jamie a quick smile. "She must be the crazy neighbor lady?"

Sierra giggled. "No, she's the mom."

"Are you the princess?"

"No, I'm the little sister." She held Wrinkles up and one of the socks slid off his paw onto the floor. "Wrinkles is the big sister."

"I see."

Jamie sucked in two quick breaths and dabbed the corners of her eyes. Sierra held Clay's attention, so she took the moment to study him. He wore a tan sweater, khaki dress pants, and the leather jacket. His hair was short, cut conservatively in a way that complimented his face.

He looked at her. "I don't know, Jamie. I kind of liked the hat."

Another giggle worked its way up, but she held back. She was on the verge of being rude as it was. She exhaled hard. "Whew! I'm sorry." She lifted her shoulders and gave him a grin. "What a bad hostess I am." Jamie drew another breath and fanned her face. "Welcome to our home. We're a little loony, but we have fun."

"I like it." His eyes were full of teasing. "But under the circumstances, I think I need a hat."

Sierra's eyes lit up. "I'll get you one!" She started to run off, and the motion frightened the cat. He jumped from her arms, losing the other sock and causing the scarf to slide down around his neck.

"Wrinkles!"

The cat was off and around the corner before Sierra could stop him. She watched him for a minute and then she shrugged. "I'll be right back."

"Wait, Sierra." Clay straightened. He was still hiding something.

Sierra pulled her gloves up a little higher and turned around. "I can get you one, really. I have a whole box."

"Okay." He gave her a kind smile. "First I have something for you."

Jamie watched from her place against the wall. Her heart swelled as she took in the scene. In all the time they'd known Aaron, he'd never brought Sierra a present.

Sierra came and stood in front of Clay. "Really?"

"Yep." He pulled a pink bag out from behind his back. "Here. This is for letting me come over for dinner."

"Wow!" She took the tissue paper from the top and gasped. "It's Nala!"

Nala? Jamie blinked, stunned. Nala was the girlfriend of Simba in *The Lion King*. Jamie met Clay's eyes and caught his knowing look. The gift wasn't an accident. He had remembered their conversation at lunch, remembered that Sierra's favorite movie was *The Lion King*.

With great care Sierra pulled a honey-colored stuffed lion from the bag. She turned to Jamie and held it up. "Look, Mom! She's perfect! Next time, *she* can be the big sister!"

"I'm sure Wrinkles will be glad to share the scarf."

"Yeah, I'm sure too." She stared at Clay, awed. "Thanks very much." She gave him a quick hug and then ran to Jamie. "She's super soft, Mommy, look!"

Sierra gushed about Nala for another few minutes before running off to find a beat-up hat for Clay. The conversation shifted to their orientation and Clay's expectations for the three weeks of training.

"I'll go home a better detective." They moved into the kitchen. "Joe'll see to that."

"Isn't he coming?" The silliness at the front door made her forget about his partner. She grabbed an old pair of pot holders, opened the oven door, and pulled the casserole out. The cheese on top was barely golden brown.

Clay looked over her shoulder at the dinner. "Whatever that is, I'll take two." He helped clear a spot on the counter. "Smells delicious."

"It's a family favorite." A memory flashed in Jamie's mind—the first time she'd made the casserole for Jake in the days after they were married. She'd burned the cheese and mixed the sauce wrong. They couldn't eat it, but it gave them something to laugh about for days afterwards. She blinked and the images were gone. "So what about Joe?"

"Wanda invited him to her place." He leaned against the counter and crossed his arms, watching her.

Jamie took the milk from the refrigerator and poured Sierra a glass. "Things must've gone well."

"I guess." Clay made a slight frown. "Joe felt awkward; he couldn't find the right time to tell her he was sorry." He unfolded his arms and rested the palms of his hands on the counter behind him. "I guess she sent her kids to the neighbor's house for the night yesterday. Joe thought it was sort of strange."

"They both have a lot to work through." Jamie took the casserole to the table.

Clay followed behind with the salad and milk. "Definitely."

They heard Sierra before they saw her. She raced around the corner, a jester hat in one hand, the oversized hat with the purple plastic flowers in the other. On her head, the older velvet hat had been replaced with a sailor's cap. Sierra collected hats for her dress-up box, and these were three of her favorites. "Hi, guys!" Her cheerful voice struck Jamie. Sierra was a happy child. More subdued, maybe, than before the terrorist attacks. But happy all the same. But now—for whatever reason—she was practically bubbling over with enthusiasm, her eyes dancing with a joy that Jamie hadn't seen in years.

"Here, Clay." She handed him the jester hat. "I think you're right. Let's wear hats for dinner."

Jamie was about to tell her no, but Clay took the hat and adjusted it on his head. "Whaddaya think, Jamie. Would I scare off the bad guys with this?"

She had to bite her lip to stop another wave of laughter. She looked at Sierra and angled her head. "Honey, I'm not sure our guest wants to spend dinner wearing a jester hat."

"Actually—" Clay lifted his chin with mock dignity—"I'm quite fond of jester hats."

Sierra clapped her hands. "Yeah, Mommy. This'll be the funnest dinner in forever." She put the sailor's hat on her own head and handed the one with the plastic flowers to Jamie. "Please, Mommy. Wear it, please."

"She'll wear it." Clay stooped down some, so he was more on Sierra's level. "Hats are required at this dinner."

"Fine." Jamie rolled her eyes. "Give me the hat."

Clay took it from Sierra, stood up, and placed it on Jamie's head. "You look pretty in purple."

"Thank you." Jamie's knees felt shaky, her stomach warm from the effects of her melting heart. Not since Jake had anyone told her she looked pretty. She gathered herself and looked at Sierra. "All washed up?"

"Yep." Sierra sat down at the table and folded her hands.

Jamie sat beside her and Clay across from them. His jester hat flopped to one side as he held his hands out. "Can I pray?"

"Yes." The warmth moved up to her cheeks, and she smiled. He looked silly, but his voice, his eyes, were as deep, as vulnerable as they'd been the day before. She took Clay's hand and watched Sierra take the other.

They bowed their heads and Clay began. "God, thank You for this food—" he gave Jamie's fingers a gentle squeeze—"and the hands that prepared it. And thank You for new friends. In Jesus' name, amen."

Throughout the meal, Jamie expected to be nervous, unsure of how to carry on a conversation with a man she'd only just met. She was sure she'd be distracted, guilty at having moved Jake's picture. Instead, the meal flew by, and all she could think about was how wonderful she felt. Having Clay there, his hand in hers during the prayer, his presence at their table. All of it felt impossibly good, right in a way she couldn't begin to understand.

During the meal, Jamie caught him looking at her, glancing away from Sierra and finding her eyes, almost as if he wanted to see for himself that the attraction or chemistry or whatever they shared was still there.

It was. Jamie used her eyes to tell him so. He'd been dropped into her life and nothing had been the same. She hadn't had time to analyze how or why God had brought them together, just that He had. Only one thought threatened to mar the night. It wasn't of Jake or his picture or how she would get on with life without him.

Rather it was what would happen to her in three weeks—when Clay went home.

Sierra felt it in her heart the minute she pulled Nala from the gift bag. Clay liked her. Because how else did he know about Nala? Nala was the coolest present ever, and it wasn't even her birthday. All her friends had Lion King, but not Nala. Plus Nala was a girl, which meant she could wear hats and scarves and fancy socks and bows in her hair and play the big sister.

Without getting mad, the way Wrinkles sometimes did.

Clay wasn't a regular kind of grown-up like Captain Hisel. Captain Hisel would smile at her and pat her head, and sometimes he'd talk to her for as long as a TV commercial. But he didn't really like her because he never asked her questions.

Sierra was counting. While they ate dinner Clay asked her eight questions, like who was her teacher and how many kids were in her class and who were her bestest friends and what did she want for Christmas?

By the end of dinner, Sierra was having a secret thought. Secret thought was when she had an idea in her head but she didn't share it with anyone else. Not even Mommy. Her secret thought was this: Since the other second daddy had to go back to his real family, maybe Clay would make a good second daddy.

She spied on him when he wasn't watching, and her heart had a sense about him. A sense that he acted sort of like a daddy, actually. He smiled big and wore his jester hat all night. Also, after dinner he played Uno with her and her mommy. The three of them laughed a lot, and Sierra didn't even care who won.

When Clay left, he stooped down and told her to have fun with Nala. Then he gave Mommy a short hug, sort of like when Captain Hisel came over.

Before he left, Clay looked at her one last time and winked. And Sierra did a little gasp because that's something she'd seen before. Maybe it was her daddy who used to do that, or her second daddy— the one who lived with her after the Twin Towers fell down. But instead of feeling confused, her heart felt happy. Because maybe the wink was a sign that God knew how lonely she was without her daddy.

And maybe God would take away the lonely forever.

FIFTEEN

Jamie reported to St. Paul's the next day, but for the first time she didn't stop and look at the gaping hole where the towers had stood. Her head was still spinning from the night before, from the new feelings stirring up her heart and soul. How could she care so much about a man she'd only known a few days? Was she using the situation to avoid Aaron Hisel? Or was Clay Miles really as wonderful as he seemed?

Allen, a young man in college, was the first person she talked with that morning. His father, an investment broker, was trapped near the top of the North Tower when it collapsed. Allen had a small photo of his father, one that he wanted to leave as part of the memorial. Jamie helped him find a spot for the picture, and then asked him if he wanted to talk.

"Not really." He shrugged. "I don't talk about it much. It happened, Dad's gone, end of story."

Jamie leaned against one of the thick white pillars that separated the memorial along the perimeter from the sanctuary area of the chapel. Memories of Clay and her dinner the night before came to mind and she willed them away. "Allen, would it be okay if I prayed for you?"

The surprise in the young man's eyes changed to anger, then vulnerability. "The last time I prayed was the morning of September 11." He clenched his jaw and gave a shake of his head. "Apparently God didn't hear me, so I stopped talking."

"But you're here." Her eyes found the pew where she'd sat with Clay the other day. Was he in training now? Would he call her again the way he'd promised? Was she crazy? She blinked hard and focused on the young man.

Allen looked over his shoulder at the tables of memorabilia. His eyes were damp when he found Jamie's eyes again. His chin quivered. "I don't know how to move on."

So many visitors to St. Paul's faced the same thing.

Their loss was so great, they practically limped through the doors. Anger, hurt, and grief kept the calendar at a standstill. Regardless of time's incessant marching, every day was September 12—and without God's divine intervention it always would be. She led the young man to the closest pew and sat down with him.

Her mind drifted back to the night before, to something funny Clay had said about his jester hat. She tightened her hands into fists. *Focus, Jamie . . . focus.*

"I understand." She looked at the stained-glass window across from them. "My husband was a firefighter; he died in the South Tower."

The young man looked at his knees. "I'm sorry."

"It's okay. He's in heaven; I'm sure about that." She told him about Jake, about finding the faith her husband had always held to, how she wouldn't have survived without that faith.

Sometimes even while she was counseling at St. Paul's her mind wandered. But always she would rein in her thoughts and focus on the matter at hand. Usually the distractions came because of Jake. His picture across the room, or the thought of him kissing her goodbye that brilliant sunny Tuesday morning, hearing his voice telling her he loved her that last time.

But not today.

Today she had to remind herself to stop thinking about Clay Miles and the way her spine tingled when she was with him. Distractions about Jake were a normal thing, especially working at St. Paul's. They were constant reminders that she was in the right place, working alongside people most touched by the tragedy of the terrorist attacks.

But thoughts of Clay?

Every time she had a spare moment that morning she saw Clay's face, the way his eyes met hers over dinner the night before, felt her body protected against his as he handled the men on the ferry.

She dismissed the thoughts. The young man across from her deserved her complete attention. He was going on about his relationship with his father, and Jamie had to listen to him as if there'd be a test later.

She struggled through two meetings that way before she sensed someone behind her.

"Hey." Aaron's tone held a layer of hurt. "You haven't fallen off the planet after all."

The sound of his voice shot darts at her conscience. She turned around and smiled at him. "Hi." She was suddenly short on words, not sure what to say. "Did you just get here?"

"A few minutes ago." He searched her eyes. "I called you twice last night."

"I know." She forced a light laugh. "Sorry I didn't call back. Sierra and I were crazy busy." It wasn't a lie, not really. But with her feelings so jumbled it was the most she was willing to say.

"Whatever." Aaron tried to look nonchalant, but he didn't pull it off. He lifted his shoulders. "I was just worried. You always call back."

"I'm sorry." Jamie didn't know what else to say. Another visitor walked through the doors and turned to look at the memorial set up on the first table. "It's been busy."

"That reminds me—" Aaron pointed at the displays along the back wall—"let's talk to the others about redoing that area. We have stacks of kids' drawings in the back, letters from children sending wishes to the New York survivors, that sort of thing. It's okay the way it is, but if we built it up some, maybe added an additional shelf along the wall, we could bulk up the display."

Odd. The idea left Jamie flat. A week ago she would've made plans for someone else to pick up Sierra so she could go through boxes of letters, looking for a way to make the makeshift memorial more emotional, more meaningful for the people who passed through.

But today . . .

"Jamie?" Aaron crossed his arms, his feet spread just enough to give him the look of a New York City fire captain. "Did you hear me?"

"Yes." Her answer was quick this time. She cleared her throat. "Yes, that'd be great." The words sounded forced, even to her.

He took a step back and studied her. "Are you okay?"

More darts. She let her gaze fall to her shoes. His friendship meant a lot to her; she had to tell him at least something of what she was going through if she was going to stay close to him. She looked up. "Can we have lunch today?"

"Sure." Hope replaced some of the uneasiness in his eyes. "Casey's Corner?"

"Perfect." She wanted to tell him it wouldn't be the type of lunch he was looking forward to, that she had some difficult things to discuss with him. But a visitor was approaching them, a woman in her thirties with red, swollen eyes.

Aaron nudged her. "You get this one; I'll be in the back if you need me."

Jamie struggled through the next two hours.

Not only with thoughts of Clay, but with the work at hand. Instead of the usual meaning and emotion that came with her job, she felt trapped. At one point she breathed in through her nose and looked around, alarmed. Was there a gas leak or a ventilation problem? There had to be, because the oxygen was gone. As hard as she tried she couldn't draw a relaxing breath. Finally, she had to go outside to grab a few mouthfuls of fresh air. Back inside it was more of the same. Just the old, musty smell of the building, and too little air.

She glanced about. Unless she was imagining things, the walls looked closer together, as if the whole place was shrinking, trying to swallow her up whole.

Of course all of it was a delusion. It was her confusion with Aaron and Clay and her memories of Jake, that's what was sucking the air from her. The building wasn't running out of oxygen any more than the walls were closing in, but that didn't change the tightness in her lungs or the way she longed for her shift to be over. It was the first time she'd ever felt this way. Trapped, anxious to leave.

She pondered the idea until finally it made sense. Of course. September 11 was everywhere around her—in the voices and conversations and pictures and artwork. In the streaming video that ran on the TV against the back wall and the displays set up along the exit wall, the ones honoring the massage therapists and cooks and counselors who volunteered their time during the cleanup.

It was all so suddenly overwhelming. Jamie couldn't quite catch her breath until she and Aaron were in a cab headed for Casey's Corner—a bright and cheerful café where they'd shared dozens of lunches. She was glad they were going there. The day was gray and cold, threatening snow. Combined with the strange mix of thoughts in her head and the things she wanted to tell Aaron, she would need an upbeat atmosphere to get through the lunch.

They were almost at the café when he leaned against the cab door and watched her. "You're quiet."

"Yes." She looked over her left shoulder at the city, the buildings and people, all of it passing before her eyes like a familiar river. Thoughts from earlier came rushing back. "Today was hard."

He didn't push her until they were seated at a booth in a quiet part of Casey's Corner, sipping coffee and waiting for their sandwiches. Aaron leaned back against the padded seat. "Why was today hard?"

"I don't know." Her hands were cold. She cupped them around her coffee mug and watched the traffic outside. "I didn't want to talk about September 11 with anyone."

Aaron leaned forward. "Maybe you need a break."

"Maybe." The idea sounded good, but she wasn't sure. "I know I'm supposed to be there; it's the least I can do for Jake."

He didn't add anything. Casey Cummins, the owner of the café, brought their sandwiches over. It was part of the charm of the place—that the owner took a personal interest in his customers. "Coldest day of the season." He smiled at them as he set the food down. "Let me know if you want a cup of minestrone." He brought his thumb and forefinger together in the shape of an *o*. "It's perfect today."

They both thanked him but turned down the soup. When he was gone, Aaron took the toothpick from his sandwich and poked it at his water glass. "You want to talk about something?" The look of hope was gone from his eyes. Clearly he could sense some of what she felt.

"I do." She gripped the bench she was sitting on and sucked in a quick breath through her teeth. Whatever happened, she didn't want to lose his friendship, didn't want to hurt him after all he'd done for her. She wasn't entirely sure she wanted to shut the door on the future. Still, something needed to be said.

"Well?" He uttered a small laugh. "You gonna tell me or make me sit here guessing?"

"Aaron." Jamie closed her eyes. When she opened them, she was looking straight at him. "I need space."

His brow lowered into a subtle *v*. "Am I crowding you?"

They hadn't even seen each other in the past few days. Jamie folded her hands and rested them on the table. *Please, God . . . give me a way to make him understand.* She ran her tongue over her lower lip and tried again. "I told you I could see things getting more serious, that maybe all I needed was time."

"Right."

"Well—" she held her breath—"things have changed." She couldn't tell him about Clay. The entire story sounded ridiculous. She raked her fingers through her hair and cupped her coffee mug again. "I need time away from you, Aaron. So I can sort through my feelings."

He rested his forearms on the table and looked out the window. He shifted his jaw from side to side, the way he did when he had a lot on his mind. Finally he looked at her again and let out a quiet breath. "We barely see each other."

"I know. But I need time from that too."

"Everywhere? Even St. Paul's?"

"Yes. Even there." She wanted to disappear under the table. He **was** her friend, after all, the person she'd leaned on and turned to **more** times than she could count. But as much as she appreciated his **friendship**, she couldn't let him believe there'd be more between **them**. Not now. Not when she was almost certain there wouldn't be.

Aaron sat a little straighter. "Is it something I did?"

"No." She reached out and touched his hand, but only for the **briefest** moment. "None of this is your fault. I think it's something I'm going through. I need to close the last chapter in my life before I can start a new one. Does that make sense?"

His expression told him it didn't, but after a few seconds he swallowed hard and looked at her. "Whatever you need, Jamie. I care that much." He was clearly shocked at the change in her, especially after the nice time they had at Chelsea Piers. "I'll talk to the coordinator and tell them I'm only available in the afternoon." Since he worked nights, afternoons were bound to be more difficult. More hours awake without a break.

"I'm sorry, Aaron. When I have things figured out I'll tell you. It just . . ." A lump filled her throat; she waited until it was gone. "It isn't fair to keep you guessing. And unless I take some time, maybe I'll never know what I want. What God wants for me."

At that last part, his eyes hardened. "I understand." He pointed to their sandwiches and the regret in his small laugh tore at her. "We better eat."

Jamie tried, but she barely forced down three bites. She wasn't hungry, not as long as her heart was in a tailspin. The rest of the lunch was awkward, and Jamie wondered if she was losing her mind. Why cut Aaron out now just because she'd met Clay? Just because she had a bad day at St. Paul's?

Not until she was on the ferry, two minutes from Staten Island, did she have an answer for herself. She didn't need time away from Aaron because of her feelings for Clay, but because of her feelings for Aaron—feelings that seemed more and more like friendship with every passing hour. She needed her distance to be sure this thing with Clay wasn't some sort of desperate ploy to avoid getting serious with Aaron. With the captain out of the picture for a while, she could think clearly.

And maybe, when a few weeks had passed, she would know without a doubt that she belonged with Aaron Hisel.

The thought simmered in her mind until she reached her car where she found an envelope in a plastic bag tucked beneath her windshield wipers. She wrinkled her nose. Funny. The ferryboat people didn't usually allow canvassers through their parking lots. She pulled the envelope from the bag and saw her name written across the front.

It was from him; it had to be. She knew it before she opened it, and her fingers trembled as she slipped them beneath the envelope flap and pulled out the note.

> *Jamie, Thanks again for the great dinner and dress-up party, even though I was disappointed I didn't get to keep the jester hat. I thought it would be a nice touch for the ferry ride.*

He'd jotted down his room number at the hotel. She laughed out loud and turned so she could lean against her car. Her eyes moved further down the page.

> *Anyway, Joe's going to see Wanda again tonight. I'll be at the Holiday Inn if you want to talk. Thinking about you, Clay.*

She read that last part three times in a row. *Thinking about you, Clay . . .*

He was going to be at a lonely hotel room. She folded the note, put it back in the envelope, and slid into her car. The least she could do was invite him over. They could order pizzas and maybe watch a movie after Sierra went to bed.

Her heart rate picked up at the thought. Yes, that would be a great idea.

She glanced around the lot. What type of car was Clay driving? Some sort of rental, but she wasn't sure what. Then she remembered the note. He was staying at the Holiday Inn. She checked the clock on her dashboard. Forty minutes until Sierra was home. With a heart half a ton lighter than it had been at lunchtime, she headed for the Holiday Inn, parked, and grabbed a piece of paper from a notebook she kept in her van.

> *Clay, I can't let you stay here alone all night. Especially without your jester hat. After you catch your breath, come over. We'll get pizza and watch a movie if you want. Hats are optional.*

She stared at the rest of the page, the blank part. If she told him she was thinking about him, it would be the truth. But was that more than she should say? After all, she hadn't known him for a week. Still . . .

Her pen was poised over the page, ready to tell him he wasn't the only one, that she hadn't been able to stop thinking about him all day. But at the last second she just signed her name, folded the paper, and ran in to the front desk. She wrote his room number on the front, handed the note to the clerk, and asked her to see that Clay Miles got it.

When she picked Sierra up at school, her daughter looked at her longer than usual. "Something's different about you, Mommy."

Jamie waited until Sierra was buckled into the backseat. She gave a small, nervous laugh. "You're silly, Sierra. I'm same as always."

"Nuh-uh." Sierra set her backpack on the seat beside her. "Didn't you have your volunteer work today?"

"Yes." Jamie focused on the road, but in her mind all she could see was Clay, coming off the ferryboat, tired, not sure if she'd gotten his note or what her response would be, then getting back to the hotel and reading her letter.

Sierra was saying something. "Most times when you do your volunteer work you look sad, Mommy. But not today, a'cause you know why?"

"Why?" Jamie turned right, onto their street.

"Because today you look happy, so it's a nice change. Don't you think so?"

Suddenly her distracted thoughts settled down long enough to understand the thing her daughter was saying. Most of the time when she worked at St. Paul's she came home looking sad? Was that really how Sierra saw her? If so, what sort of life was that for her daughter? No father, and a mother who was sad more days than not?

Sierra chattered on, something about school and music class and the girl next to her singing too loud. Jamie tightened her grip on the steering wheel and turned into the driveway. She looked different today.

What a profound observation. One more bit of proof that God was bringing about some sort of change in her life—if only she understood exactly what it was. As they walked into the house, Jamie wondered which was more telling: how working at St. Paul's left her downcast, or how today—for a change—she looked happy. Because after working the hardest shift since becoming a volunteer, and then telling the captain she didn't want to see him for a while, there could be only one reason why she'd look happy.

His name was Clay Miles.

SIXTEEN

Clay was in his room changing when he noticed the light blinking on his motel phone. Probably the front desk asking if he wanted fresh towels. He ignored it and searched through his closet.

The day had been a long one, full of drills and workshops on technique. The group of officers in training would spend the first part of the three weeks learning the most up-to-date detective skills—crime scene forensics, blood-spatter evidence, ballistics testing. The last eight days would send them into the streets of New York, working alongside some of the city's top detectives.

One of the captains briefed them that morning about the realities of the job.

"Some of our crime scenes are, well—" sarcasm filled his tone and his smile—"let's just say they're not in the penthouse district. And some of our investigations take place at night." The grin faded. "You'll wear flak jackets and carry weapons. The streets of New York City aren't for the faint of heart."

Clay received approval to carry a weapon during training from his captain in Los Angeles. Some of the paperwork had to be fast-tracked, but during his first week off the department was able to clear him of any guilt in the shooting of the carjacking suspect.

Good thing. Clay couldn't have made the trip without clearance to carry a weapon. It was why he'd been armed on the ferryboat, and why he'd met Jamie Bryan. Jamie, who'd made it difficult to concentrate these past few days. He was drawn to her in a way that consumed him, left him breathless. Even now he wondered if she'd gotten his note, if she'd considered leaving one on his car, as well. He slipped on a pullover and glanced at the phone again.

What if the message was from Jamie?

He took light running steps to the phone, dialed 0, and sat down on the bed.

"Front desk."

"Yes, hi." Clay kicked his feet up and leaned back against the headboard. "My message light was flashing."

"Okay, sir, let me check that for you. Just a moment." She was gone for a few seconds. "Yes, a woman came in and gave us a note. It has your first name and room number on it."

The smile took hold of his face and didn't let go. It had to be Jamie. "Could you send it up?"

"Certainly, Mr. Michaels."

A minute later there was a knock at his door. "Bellman."

Clay opened it, took the note, and tipped the man. He unfolded the note and read it.

She'd gotten the note, after all. He felt giddy as a schoolboy with a first-time crush, and no wonder. After three years of bad setups and superficial dates, he'd finally met a woman like he'd always hoped. One with goals and values and a faith that colored everything about her.

But this relationship wouldn't be easy.

He folded the note, tossed it on the nightstand, and grabbed his keys. On the way across the island he thought about how there had been no pictures of her dead husband anywhere. Not that he was looking, but it seemed strange. She was still single, after all. It would make sense to have pictures up.

Of course, maybe it was part of her healing process. Keeping his image out of sight so she could move on with life. Clay wasn't sure. Just that the look in her eyes when she'd talked about him said very clearly she'd never loved anyone the way she'd loved him.

Sadness settled over him, weighing his heart down like a sodden wool cloak.

How smart was it to fall for a woman with that sort of devotion to someone else? Even dead, the man might always hold the first place in her heart, and what sort of life would that be? Second place?

He dismissed the thought.

All of it was insane, anyway. He'd only met her two days before. They'd be friends for the three weeks he was in New York, and maybe write once in a while. What more could ever come of it with him living so far away?

Not until she opened the door did he admit he was fooling himself. Big time.

Through their pizza dinner, he could hardly take his eyes off her. During the ice cream sandwich dessert and a story, compliments of Sierra who was learning to read, he could hardly tear his gaze from her.

Jamie Bryan had captured his imagination from the moment he saw her. There was no logical reason, no explanation, but he was falling. Hard.

And nothing in his power could make him stop.

The story was finished and Jamie moved to the edge of Sierra's bed. She looked back at Clay. "Wanna pray with us?"

"Sure." His heart thudded against the wall of his chest. This was the picture, wasn't it? The family scene he'd been longing for all his adult years? He took his place between them and bowed his head, not sure of their routine.

Sierra reached out and took one hand while Jamie took the other, giving his fingers a light squeeze. She spoke the prayer in hushed tones.

"Dear Jesus, please be with Sierra as she sleeps and please watch over her. Help her to have peaceful dreams and wake up happy about a new day. We know You have great plans for Sierra, God. Please help her to look for those every day of her life. We love You, Lord. Amen."

Clay held onto Jamie's hand a few seconds after the prayer ended, then let go. When they left her room, he stopped outside Sierra's door. "I love that."

Jamie smiled. "What?"

"The way you are with her, projecting God's blessings onto her."

"Oh." Jamie started down the stairs. She looked over her shoulder as she walked. "You mean the part about God's plans for her?"

"Right." He stayed close behind her. "Jeremiah 29:11. Kids need to hear that so badly."

"They do." She turned around at the foot of the stairs and her smile eased some. "It'd be easy for her to grow up mad at God, because of what happened to Jake." Her eyes shone with a strength that Clay knew only came from walking in faith. "But God has plans for us no matter what bad thing has happened. Even losing Jake."

They went into the family room, and Jamie pointed to a shelf of videos. "Feel like a movie?"

"Hmmm." He sat down at one end of the sofa, glanced around the room, and spotted a backgammon board. "Hey, you play?"

She followed his gaze. "Backgammon? Sure." She grabbed it and brought it back to the sofa. "Just a minute." She slipped a CD in the player and before she was sitting down, Kenny Chesney started playing in the background.

"Country, huh?"

"There's something about a good country song." She took the spot at the opposite end of the sofa so there was enough room to open the game between them. She held his eyes for a few beats. "Country songs tell a story; I like that."

"Me too." Clay set up the backgammon pieces and tried to sort through his feelings. They had everything in common, and a chemistry that couldn't be denied. But in less than three weeks he'd be back in LA. He didn't want to think about it.

They played five games and several times his fingers brushed against hers. Each time he could feel the sensation throughout his body. Once in a while he would look at her, almost certain she was feeling the same thing.

"I believe I'm the winner." Jamie lifted her chin and closed the board. It was almost ten o'clock, and they both had to go into the city in the morning. She set the game on the floor and leaned against the sofa arm. Her eyes were soft again, shining with the vulnerability that had caught his attention the first time they'd spoken. "I had fun tonight."

"Me too."

They were silent for a moment, studying each other. Clay had so many questions. What was happening between them? How was she feeling, and why were they playing with each other's hearts when he had to go home in a few weeks? Did she and her husband play backgammon together?

Instead of voicing his thoughts, he put his arm up on the sofa back and tried not to dwell on the fact that he had no answers.

"How's Joe doing?"

"He was glad Wanda invited him back; after last night he wasn't sure he'd get to see her again."

"Maybe tonight's the night."

"The apology?" Clay leaned sideways and rested his head in his hand. "I hope so." He shook his head. "Crazy guy. If someone's got something to say to a person they care about, they should come out and say it."

Not until the words were out did he realize what he'd said. She raised her brow and gave a subtle sideways nod. "Good idea." Her eyes found a deeper place in his heart. "But it's not always easy . . . or wise."

"No, it isn't." Clay watched her. Was she talking about herself or him? He wanted to ask, but she was right. It wasn't easy or wise to talk about what was happening between them. It was simply too soon. Besides, what if he was imagining the chemistry between them? Maybe Jamie was merely a lonely widow hungry for company. Since Clay was a police officer, and he'd rescued her on the boat, and he was only in town for a few weeks, he was a pretty safe bet.

He checked his watch, stood, and stretched. "I guess I better go." His neck still hurt from the shooting, but it was getting better. "Thanks again for dinner."

"It was fun." Jamie stood and led the way toward the foyer. "Let's do it again."

"Sure."

They reached the door and Jamie turned to face him. The entry-way was dark and shadowy, the only light coming from two rooms away. Somehow the mood of the moment became more intimate. She leaned against the door. "Can I tell you something?"

"Okay." He rested his shoulder against the wall, careful to keep several feet between them.

"I haven't . . ." She bit her lip, her eyes locked on his. "I haven't done this since . . . since Jake died."

Though her eyes were vulnerable, transparent, she hadn't said anything that dipped below the surface all night. Until now.

"Jamie." His heart melted. It must have been so difficult to have him over, give him dinner, and share a night of backgammon with him in the place where she and her husband had loved and laughed and started their family.

She hung her head and in the shimmer of distant light a single tear fell to the floor. "I thought you should know."

The hug was inevitable. Everything about the moment cried out for him to take her in his arms and soothe away the pain.

He reached out to her. "C'mere."

"I'm sorry." She sniffed and took two slow steps toward him. "I'm really not sad." Her eyes lifted to his. Though they were wet, they shone with something more than sorrow. "I like you being here, Clay."

Their faces were inches apart, but Clay wouldn't kiss her. Not even when everything in him wanted to. Instead he folded his arms around her and held her close. He stroked her hair and let her rest her head against his chest. "Guess what?" He leaned down some and whispered near the side of her face.

"What?" She uttered a sound that was more laugh than cry. "You think I'm crazy?"

"Nope." He pulled back and spoke into her eyes. "I like being here too." He let go of her and smiled. "Maybe you and Sierra can join me in the city tomorrow night . . . find something fun to do."

Her smile in the shadows warmed him in a way nothing else had. "I think we'd like that."

He stepped closer to the door and opened it. "Good night, Jamie."

"Good night." A cool breeze shot its way into the house and she crossed her arms tight. "Thanks for understanding."

He nodded, and then he was outside and the door was closing. The air was freezing cold, but the sky was crystal clear. It was amazing, this close to Manhattan, that he could see any stars. But that night the sky was full of them. He stopped and stared up. *God . . . it's too soon, but it feels like something's happening.* He pulled the edges of his coat tighter around him. This time he spoke out loud. "Lead me, God . . . don't let me get ahead of You."

Halfway to the car he was going over the evening in his mind— especially the last few minutes, the way Jamie leaned on him, the way she held him—when something occurred to him. One of the main questions he had about Jamie and whatever it was they'd found together had just been answered.

The chemistry between them definitely was *not* a figment of his imagination.

SEVENTEEN

Jamie stood with her face against the door until she heard Clay drive away. What had she done? Opening up to him in the dark foyer, practically begging him for a hug? How could she be so shameless? Here in her own house, the place she'd shared with Jake? And what did Clay think, now that she'd practically thrown herself at him?

She rubbed her hands along her arms. Dirty, that's what she felt. Dirty and cheap and completely disloyal to Jake. It was one thing to invite Clay over, to give him dinner and play backgammon with him. But the hug at the end was over the top.

Even if she didn't have Jake's memory to protect, she'd acted too quickly. Still . . . that was the strange thing about Clay. He seemed so familiar, already so much a part of her life.

She drew a long breath, then made her way through the house turning off lights and locking doors—what used to be Jake's nighttime ritual. Finally she pushed herself up the stairs to the bedroom. No matter if Clay felt familiar or not, she'd acted inappropriately. Guilt and embarrassment mixed in her gut and shot through her heart, leaving her cheeks hot.

While she brushed her teeth, she could only stare at her reflection. What was *wrong* with her? How could she have changed so quickly, let go of the past in a forty-eight-hour window? And what about Aaron? No one would ever understand her loss the way Aaron did. Because it was his loss too, they forever shared a connection. But Clay? He was sympathetic, of course, but he'd never known Jake, could never understand the relationship she'd shared with him.

It was all so confusing.

She rinsed her toothbrush and set it back on the charger. The best idea was to forget about both of them, Aaron *and* Clay. All she needed was God and Sierra and memories of Jake. That was more than enough to get her through life until she could be with her husband again. She would work at St. Paul's, and when the new Twin Towers were built, she would apply for a position at the official memorial.

If she spent her life helping the victims of September 11, she would be honoring Jake's memory and never—not ever again— would she suffer the horrible pangs of regret that jabbed her now. She gripped the bathroom counter and hung her head. *God . . . I'm sorry. I acted on my feelings, but it was wrong. I know it was wrong. Help me to live a life that would please You and Jake and Sierra. And help me keep my distance from Clay Miles.*

She looked up and her eyes fell on a small wooden plaque, one that had hung in her bathroom since her first birthday after Jake died. It had been a gift from her friend, Sue Henning.

"I bought us each one," she told Jamie at the time, "because there'll be days when we can't leave home without remembering the message written there."

Jamie looked at it now, studied it, and a chill ran down her neck and arms. The words were from the Bible. They read, *Trust in the Lord with all your heart and lean not on your own understanding; in all your ways acknowledge him, and he will make your paths straight.* Beneath that it said, *Proverbs 3:5–6.*

Her path felt crooked, for sure, after the evening with Clay, after their hug. If she was honest with herself, she wanted to kiss him. But how *could* she, when in her heart she was still married to Jake?

The Bible words gave her a different perspective, a peace. Never mind about Clay or Aaron or any of the emotions churning up her soul. Don't try to figure it out. Rather trust God. He'd take care of making her paths straight; that was His promise. That's what He was telling her, wasn't it?

She straightened and headed into the bedroom.

Tonight she needed more than a single Bible verse. She wanted to get lost in Scripture, to swim through the verses and chapters until she found the safe harbor she desperately needed.

Jake's Bible was on the dresser—where it always was. She picked it up, dropped into the nearest chair, and flipped it open. Some nights she used a study guide and read specific parts of Scripture. Other times, like tonight, she flipped through until something caught her eye. Jake had read this Bible thoroughly, and nearly every book was replete with highlighted sections, underlined verses, and notes written in the margins.

Jamie started at the beginning and thumbed through the books of Genesis, Exodus, Leviticus, and Numbers, passing various high lighted areas. But as she passed over Deuteronomy, something caught her attention.

It was her name; she was sure of it. Her name in a part of the Bible she'd never read before. She flipped back, turning the pages until she saw it again, scrawled in Jake's printing above Deuteronomy, chapter 30. Jake had drawn a line from her name to a section of Scripture that read, "I have set before you life and death, blessings and curses. Now choose life, so that you and your children may live."

Next to the text Jake had written this:

> *Jamie, this is for you. If I could get anything into your head, your heart, it would be that one point. Choose life, Jamie. Whenever you have the chance, choose life.*

Choose life?

She read his words again and again and one more time before her tears blurred the letters. Sweet Jake, still lending her his wisdom and understanding. But what did it mean? She sniffed and wiped at her eyes. Then she started at the beginning of the thirtieth chapter of Deuteronomy and began to read.

Clearly the story was about God's people on their journey to the Promised Land. Jamie remembered hearing a sermon series on the topic at church the year after Jake's death. Chapter 30 told the people that God was giving them a choice. Choose His ways, His truth, His leading, and they would be choosing blessings and prosperity. Choose their own ignorant, prideful ways, the ways of idols or false gods, and they would be choosing destruction and curses.

Jamie stored the words in her heart as she finished the chapter. Yes, that's what it meant. Life or death—the choice belonged to God's people back then much as it belonged to every person born on earth. Choose God, choose life. Choose an alternate way, choose death.

Jamie, this is for you. If I could get anything into your head, your heart, it would be that one point. Choose life, Jamie. Whenever you have the chance, choose life.

Jake's words had been aimed straight at her lack of faith.

An ache started in her chest and consumed her heart and soul. She hugged the Bible's open pages close.

Jake had loved her with a love so great it could only have come from God. A love that left her to make her own decision. But not until she had a chance to read his Bible did she understand the angst she'd caused him. He prayed daily for her eyes to be opened, for his faith to become real to her.

That's why it hurt so much now.

Jake died longing for one thing—the chance to share his faith with her. Yes, God answered his prayers. Through his journal, his Bible, through the confusion of trying to teach a stranger to be her husband, God answered Jake's prayers. She found God and she would hold on to Him until her dying day.

But she never got to share Him with Jake.

The enormity of all she had cost the two of them had never been more clear. She'd missed the intimacy of praying with her husband, missed holding his hands and coming before their God with a single heart, single purpose. She'd missed looking into Jake's eyes and seeing the love of Christ reflected there. Sure, she'd seen love in his eyes. Every time he looked at her, she saw love. But not God's love, because she wasn't aware of that sort of love. A deeper love, a bond that could only come through shared faith.

She'd missed all of it because of her stubborn pride.

Faith in Christ was the most important thing to Jake Bryan, and she'd missed the chance to understand that, to connect with him on that eternal level. She'd missed it and there wasn't a thing she could do about it.

A canyon of sorrow cut through her heart. If only she could have one day to hold him again, look into his eyes, his soul, and tell him that she had done what he'd asked of her. She had chosen God's life. One time to share the intimate bond of faith, an intimacy that would've made them even closer, more connected.

But it was a closeness she'd never know with Jake, and the truth of that pushed the canyon deeper until she could feel her heart breaking. For a long time she let the tears come, sadness that hadn't taken the form of weeping for months.

Eventually her sobs subsided, and she blinked so she could see clearly. Then she lowered the Bible and read the underlined part once more.

I set before you life or death . . . choose life.

Choose life . . .

Bit by bit, realization formed. She'd made the choice for life when it came to Jesus. But what about the way she *lived* her life?

Images flashed at her, the days and months she'd spent at St. Paul's, the conversations with Aaron about keeping the memory of September 11 fresh in the minds of people, helping the country to never forget. Then she heard Sierra's innocent voice telling her she looked happy today, but not usually. Usually after her volunteer work she looked sad.

How could she have been so blind? She'd surrounded herself with death and destruction ever since Jake died. Talking about the dead, remembering the dead, commemorating the dead, honoring the dead. Reliving the destruction, imagining the destruction, putting herself next to Jake amid the destruction, staring at the place where the destruction happened.

It consumed her.

Not that working at St. Paul's was a bad thing. They needed volunteers, and her time there had been a necessary part of her healing.

She closed her eyes. What was the prayer she'd said in the bathroom a few minutes ago? *Help me live a life that would please You and Jake and Sierra?* Wasn't that it? Then she walks in, flips open Jake's Bible, and reads a verse about choosing life?

Another chill worked its way down her spine.

Was it an answer from God? Was He telling her she'd spent enough time living in a cemetery, existing in a memorial? Was God giving her permission to move on, to choose life?

She read her husband's words again and for a moment she could see him standing before her, smiling at her, running his thumb beneath her eyes to dry her tears. "Jake . . ."

His name hung in the air and the image of him faded.

All this time she'd volunteered at St. Paul's so she could feel closer to him, closer to his memory. She'd done it to honor him and make him proud, because it was the sort of thing he would've done.

But not for two years straight.

The truth was suddenly clearer than air. Jake embraced life, lived it to the full without fear or doubt. He woke up each morning praising God and loving his family, and headed to work with a full heart. Always he had known he might die on the job, but the fact had never stopped him. The windy possibility of death had never so much as dimmed the brilliant candle that was Jake Bryan's life.

Maybe she'd acted too quickly that night by hugging Clay; maybe it would be years before she was ready to fall in love with someone new. But if Jake were standing here now he would tell her it was time to step out of the darkness, time to turn away from death and destruction.

Time to choose life.

Now Jamie had only one question for God. How? She dug her elbows into her knees. Should she leave St. Paul's? Invest her time somewhere other than memorializing the victims of September 11?

Find someone new to share her life?

The options were overwhelming.

She stood and set the Bible back on the dresser. Maybe she should call Sue, ask her what she thought of the verse. It was late, but Sue was a night owl. She'd still be up. Jamie was about to pick up the phone when it rang. The unexpected sound of it made her jump back.

Caller ID told her it was from a cell phone. Clay Miles. It couldn't be anyone else.

She picked up the receiver. "Hello?"

"Hi." The smile in his voice sounded over the phone lines. "I know it's late, but I had two things."

"Okay." She felt herself smile, felt her eyes lighten and the burden lift from her shoulders. "Tell me."

"First, I got a call from one of the guys on the department. He had a bunch of Broadway tickets donated to the police force; they had three left for *The Lion King*, and I snagged 'em. It's Friday night. I thought you and Sierra might want to join me."

"*Lion King?* At the Amsterdam Theater?" Four different times Jamie had looked into tickets for Sierra, but the show was sold out months in advance. "Are you kidding?"

"Serious. They're orchestra level, ten rows from the stage."

"Clay!" She did a light scream. "Sierra will flip!"

He laughed. "I had a feeling. How about we head into the city about five o'clock. That way we can get some pizza before the show. Sound like a plan?"

Jake's words came flying at her. *Choose life, Jamie . . . whenever you have the chance, choose life.* "Yes, Clay." Happy tears stung at her eyes and she swallowed against the thickness in her throat. "A wonderful plan."

They made a decision to have lunch the next day, then hung up. Jamie stared out the bedroom window at the shadowy bare trees, swaying in the early winter night. The timing of Clay's call was unbelievable. There she'd been, overwhelmed with the idea of choosing life, of moving on. What did it look like and where should she start? She smiled, the tide of sorrow waning. Most of her questions were still unanswered, but at least she knew what she was going to do first.

She would take in *The Lion King* on Broadway with Clay and Sierra.

God would show her what to do after that.

Eighteen

Sierra had barely enough time to talk to God when she got home from school.

Clay was taking them to *Lion King!* The real live *Lion King!* She bounced into her bedroom and found Wrinkles on her bed.

"Wrinkles, guess what?"

The cat yawned and stretched out his skinny arms. He didn't look that interested. Sierra dropped down on the edge and rubbed the soft fur between his ears. "Clay's taking us to *Lion King,* can you believe it?"

Wrinkles looked at her and blinked. Sierra did a big breath because maybe that cat was jealous. Or maybe he didn't understand. But God would, so she closed her eyes super-duper tight and tried to be serious. Only instead a squeally sort of laugh came from her mouth, so she jumped up and danced around the room until she bumped into the wall.

Then she settled down. *Settle down* is what Mommy said when she had a little too much energy. "God . . . Clay's taking us to *Lion King!* Isn't that the bestest news in the whole wide world?"

Of course God didn't talk to her like her friend, Katy, or like her mommy would. But she could feel Him listening all the same. She licked her dry lips and did a smaller, shorter dance. "I think I like that Clay, God. Thanks for letting him meet Mommy on the boat when he saved her life from the bad guys."

She opened her eyes and gasped. She didn't have a nice dress picked out yet, and Mommy said to hurry. The closet had six nice dresses in it, so she picked out the frilliest and prettiest one, the one with blue and white and ruffles and a big bow in the back. Then her white socks with the lacy tops, the ones Wrinkles wore the other day.

Speedy fast she was ready and running down the stairs. That's when she stopped, because Clay was already there and he and Mommy were smiling at each other. Real quick she added a P.S. for God, because she had something else to say. But this time she said it in her head so Mommy and Clay wouldn't hear her. *God . . . I know Clay lives in California, but maybe he could change his mind and live here. Because he would make a nice second daddy, don't You think? A second daddy like James has? Please think about it, God. Thanks.*

Clay looked up at her. "Don't you look pretty."

"Thank you." She did a curtsy, the kind she and her mommy did when they played princess. "And you look like Prince Charming." He really did. He was tall and he had blond hair and his eyes looked like Prince Charming in the movie.

Clay did a prince-type bow and smiled at her. "That's very nice of you, Sierra."

Her mommy covered her mouth and laughed. Then she made smiling eyes at Sierra and said it was time to go. The trip into the city was the longest in the world. It felt like the week before Christmas because it lasted forever. But finally they ate their pizza and took a cab to the theater and went inside. The theater was the prettiest place in the world, with fancy decorations on the walls and ceilings and even the floor and seats.

They walked down toward the front until Mommy said, "This is it."

Sierra went down the row first, then Mommy, then Clay. She wanted to stand up and dance around a little because this was the real *Lion King!* Instead her stomach did the dance by itself, twisting and jumping and proving how much excitement she had inside her. Plus also her head and shoulders did some moving and turning and looking at the other people and then her knees got involved.

Mommy leaned close to her. "Sit still, Sierra. Young ladies sit still at the theater."

Sierra already knew that because Mommy took her here to see *Annie* once. But because of *Lion King* getting ready to start, she forgot. "Okay, Mommy. Sorry."

"It's okay." Her mommy smiled. "You're excited."

"I'm *so* excited, Mommy. My tummy and head and shoulders and even my knees are excited."

Clay leaned over Mommy's legs. "That's exactly how I feel." He gave a nice nod, then he looked at Mommy. "I might need a reminder about sitting still too."

Sierra giggled, and just then the lights went out. A squeal started to come from her mouth, but she smacked her hand over her lips and looked at her mother with a quick look that said she wouldn't squeal again. Promise.

But she definitely did a lot of gasps.

The giraffes came up the aisles around them, and the lions covered the stage, and painted people were singing in the trees, and more of them from someplace near the ceiling, and it was all so amazing she could hardly stand it. A dancing person started singing "Circle of Life," and that's when the most amazing thing of all happened.

In the corner of her eyeball she saw Clay holding Mommy's hand. And that's when she was sure she would remember this night all the way until forever.

The moment Clay arrived at her house, Jamie knew the truth. No matter what she'd told herself the night before about jumping in too quickly or being ashamed of herself for her attraction to him, seeing him in person told the real story.

There was no turning back.

If she was going to choose life, if she was going to embrace it, then she couldn't berate herself for hugging a man whose company she enjoyed. Never mind whether they ever saw each other again after these three weeks, for now all she wanted was to be with him. When he walked through the door, their eyes met. They stood there, looking at each other. Then—almost in slow motion—they came together in another hug. Not the sorrowful hug of the night before, but a hug of friendship and promise and something that defied time and reason.

A hug she neither regretted nor wanted to end.

Conversation had been light and upbeat since then, with Sierra providing the main source of dialogue. From her perspective, everything about the city was super bright and super busy and super big. She talked about all of it right until they took their seats.

It was when the music started, when the fullness of it surrounded them and swept them away on the story, that Clay reached out and took her hand. At first she expected him to squeeze her fingers or pat them, his way of telling her he was glad they were getting a chance to see the show, glad they were together.

But then he eased his fingers between hers, and the sensation sent a tingling feeling all the way to her knees. She was afraid to look at him, afraid the emotions tossing her soul around would be too transparent. Instead she focused on the way her fingers felt against his, the warmth of his large hand covering her smaller one.

The play was amazing.

She'd heard people say that *The Lion King* was in its own category theatrically, that nothing compared to it, and they were right. The costumes, the singing, the sets, it was more than Jamie could've imagined. Once in a while she looked at Sierra, and always her daughter's eyes were wide and dancing, her mouth slightly open. She neither talked nor fidgeted, mesmerized by the experience.

And through it all, Clay held her hand.

At the part where Simba, the young lion king, meets up with his old childhood girlfriend, Nala, and the two sing about feeling the love in the air that night, Clay ran his thumb over hers. Tears stung at Jamie's eyes, though she wasn't sure why. Whether it was because she and Jake had been childhood friends ... or because that very night love, or something like it, was indeed in the air. And it had nothing to do with Jake.

Then when Mufasa's memory spoke to Simba, Jamie felt tears again. The message was the same as what she'd read in Deuteronomy. What Jake had written to her in the margins of his Bible. Loss was part of the package of living, but the fighter remains. He fights the good fight, he gets back in the ring, he never gives up.

He chooses life.

Jamie's heart almost broke when the play ended. Not because the story was so moving, so brilliantly performed. But because when the lights went up, Clay released her hand. Probably for Sierra's benefit. The two of them hadn't had time to talk about what was happening between them, let alone involve Sierra.

On the way home she was more aware of him, the way he walked beside her, his arm brushing against hers, how he sat next to her in the cab, their legs touching. Once in a while she'd catch him watching her. Their eyes would meet and hold, and she'd feel the tingling again, a floating sensation that made her look down to see if her feet were still on the ground.

Back at the house, they went through the nighttime ritual with Sierra, and this time Clay took her hand and Sierra's and offered to pray.

"God, thank You for a wonderful night. Thanks for singing and music and drama." He paused. "And stories that touch our hearts."

Jamie was supposed to have her eyes closed, but she couldn't. She kept them open just enough so she could watch Clay, the way he bowed his head and prayed so easily, with a heart for God alone. She'd missed this with Jake, the praying. The thought shot a quick burst of pain into her heart, but it faded as Clay continued.

"You have a plan for each of us. A good plan. Help us keep our eyes open so we won't miss it. Thank You, Lord. Amen."

Her heart skipped a beat. *Help us keep our eyes open so we won't miss it?* Was he talking about her, the two of them? She didn't ask, and a few minutes later they were downstairs fixing snacks.

The atmosphere remained easy, uncomplicated throughout the evening. They watched country music videos and played backgammon—with Clay winning five out of seven. Jamie told him that Wanda had called her the night before. Joe finally had a chance to meet her children, and when he saw her little boy he broke down.

"I guess he looks exactly like the boy they lost." Jamie bit her lip. "The kids went upstairs, and Joe wept. The thing was, Wanda didn't know what to do with him. She hadn't drawn comfort from him when their son was killed, and now she didn't know how to give him comfort."

Clay frowned. "Tough for both of them."

"But get this." Jamie dropped the dice she'd been fiddling with, her eyes locked on his. "Joe apologized. He sat her down and even through his tears he told her he was sorry for walking out, for not being there for her when she needed him most."

"Wow." Clay crossed his arms. "God's doing something between those two."

"Definitely." She looked at the game board. "But I guess he left with things still awkward. Wanda asked me to pray for something to happen, something that will help them break the bonds of the past so they can find a new way to relate to each other."

The conversation switched to the carjacker Clay had to shoot, and a handful of other calls—gang fights and domestic violence and drug busts—runs that had taken all of his training to pull off.

It was the first time Jamie considered the danger of his job. Just as dangerous as Jake's had been—more so, in some ways.

Her reaction was proof she was different now; she wasn't afraid for him. Whether he remained her friend or something more, she would never again live in fear for the safety of someone she cared about. Besides, like Jake, Clay loved God. And that was enough. Every day when he hit the streets he put on two kinds of armor. His bulletproof vest, and the armor of God.

Fear couldn't add anything to that.

He closed the game board and dug his shoulder into the back of the sofa. "So tell me about you, Jamie. Other than St. Paul's and playing dress-up, what do you do? Hobbies? Sports? Jester training?"

She giggled. "Definitely jester training." Her smile eased. The question was harder than it seemed. What did she do with her time, after all? "I like to jet ski." An image of Jake and her flying across the water filled her mind. She willed it to disappear. "And I used to take a ceramics class. You know, pottery, painting little statues, that kind of thing."

"Not anymore?" Clay angled his head, his expression mildly curious.

"No." She made a slight lift of her shoulders. "I haven't gotten back into it, I guess."

"What about the jet skiing?"

She looked at her hands. He wasn't probing, really. Just learning more about her, maybe learning more about how far she'd come since losing Jake. Her eyes met his again. "Not as much as before."

A knowing filled his eyes. "It was something you did with Jake?"

"Yes."

He winced a bit. "Sorry ... I wasn't ... I didn't mean to bring up something that ..."

"Something about Jake?" Her heart hit another level of respect for the man across from her. On top of everything else, he was compassionate.

"I guess." He exhaled through pursed lips. "Sorry."

"Don't be." She hesitated. "For the rest of my life Jake's name will come up. It has to; I shared twenty years with him." Her voice softened. She was letting Clay see a part of her that few people saw. "At first, after September 11, I couldn't talk about him without breaking down." She tucked her feet beneath her. "What happened to Jake will always be sad, but I can talk about him now." She lifted the corners of her mouth. "Time does that to you."

"You loved him very much, didn't you?" He set the game board on the floor and slid closer.

"Yes." She shifted her gaze to the chair across the room, the one that had been Jake's. "His memory is always with me." A Shania Twain song came on the television, a love song that lent an intimacy to the moment. She looked at him again. "And you, Clay? What hearts have you broken?"

"Not many." He chuckled and shifted so his back was against the sofa. Only a few inches separated them. "The LA girls I've met don't have hearts; just brains and beauty."

"New Yorkers can be that way too."

"I'm sure." His laugh was slow and easy. "Actually, there was one girl, someone I met in high school."

She studied him, the way his eyes didn't change when he talked about the girl. Whoever she was, Jamie guessed she no longer had a hold on Clay Miles. "Did you date her?"

"No. We were friends. In fact—" his light chuckle made her smile—"she married my brother."

Jamie raised her eyebrows. "Really?"

"Yep." He sounded comfortable, as if whatever pain had been involved no longer hurt him.

"Did it make things hard between you and your brother?"

"No." Clay looked straight ahead at the wall. "My brother's a nice guy. They're happy together; she belongs with him. Besides . . ."

She waited, but when he didn't finish his thought she had to know. "Besides what?"

He turned to her and searched her eyes. "She never made me feel like this."

And there it was.

The admission they knew was coming. The special something that had been between them from the moment they met was now out in the open. Her pulse picked up speed. What was she supposed to do? How could she respond when she was blind as a bat in the ways of new love?

She looked down; her hands were trembling. "I . . . I've felt it since the ferryboat." Her eyes met his again. "I thought it was just me."

"It's not." He took her hand, and worked his fingers between hers. "It's crazy; I haven't known you a week." She understood the bafflement in his tone, felt it herself. "But I feel something with you I've never felt before."

They were quiet for a while. Tim McGraw was singing something slow and pretty, and Jamie felt no need to talk. What would they say? Regardless of their feelings, he would go back to California in two weeks.

He spoke first. "I lay awake at night in the Holiday Inn wondering what I'm doing, what could come of this after only three weeks." He gave her a crooked grin. "I guess that's why I brought it up."

"Mmmm." She gave the back of his hand a gentle squeeze. Her heart still tore along, but no longer at breakneck speed. She was nervous, not sure where the conversation was going or whether she could bare her heart enough to tell him her true thoughts—that she struggled with feeling guilty because of Jake, that he would've wanted her to move on. "I've done my share of wondering."

Clay released her hand and put his arm around her, positioning her so she could rest her head on his shoulder. "When I pray about it, I feel God's hand on this—" he gestured to her and then back at himself—"whatever this is between us." He held his breath for a moment. "I guess we need to let Him answer the other questions."

"Exactly." His statement was the perfect wrap-up for the night, a way to stop herself from overthinking the situation and let the night come to an end. She smiled at him, savoring the feel of her head on his shoulder. "Thanks for a great night."

"Well . . ." He raised his brow in mock sarcasm. "We didn't get to wear the hats, but still . . ." His eyes danced. "It was a pretty good night."

He stood, helped her to her feet, and walked with her to the front door. His hug didn't linger, didn't suggest anything more than the closeness he'd already admitted to. When he was gone, she stared out the window and watched his car pull away. She explored her feelings. No guilt. No shame.

Something was changing inside her.

Talking about their feelings had been a good thing. Neither of them was willing to rush ahead, to assume they should start a relationship simply because they shared a chemistry. In the meantime, they would enjoy the next two weeks and believe God had a plan for them. Whether that plan found them together.

Or apart.

NINETEEN

The next week passed in a blur, in which Jamie Bryan was Clay's single focus.

They met at St. Paul's every day Jamie worked and walked through Battery Park, stopping for a few silent moments at the giant globe that was once the courtyard between the Twin Towers. It had been damaged in the terrorist attacks but not destroyed, and now it was on display to commemorate the city's fighting spirit, its will to survive. They took a tour boat to Liberty Island and held hands as they walked along the base of the Statue of Liberty.

There were lunch dates, and dinners with Sierra, and once Clay wore the jester hat when they went bowling.

Now it was Sunday night, and Clay wanted to stop time.

He and Jamie had spent the day in Central Park with Sierra. The temperatures were in the thirties, so they bundled up in coats and hats and scarves, and Sierra convinced them to consider coming back later in the week for an hour of ice skating.

The city was taking on the look of Christmas. Lights were strung across much of the park's perimeter and preparations were being made for the Macy's Thanksgiving Day Parade, coming up a week from Thursday. Clay's flight was set for Saturday; five days later he'd be sitting around the Thanksgiving table with Laura and Eric and Josh, wondering if his time in New York was all some sort of marvelous dream.

Wondering how soon he could find his way back.

Time had flown by. In six days his training would be over, and he and Joe would be on a plane back to Los Angeles, ready to start his department training for his new position as detective. He should be excited, focused on the future, the fascinating cases he'd be working on and getting involved in his local church—as he'd planned before he left for New York.

Funny, the last thing he'd told himself was that he'd meet a girl at church. Who knew it would be a church in the heart of New York City?

He stretched out on his hotel bed and stared at a blank spot on the wall. It was just after nine o'clock; Sierra and Jamie had homework to focus on, so he'd made an early night of it. But the day had been amazing, full of the sweet glances and joined hands that had come to mark their time together.

He wanted to get back in his car and drive to Jamie's house so they wouldn't miss a minute of the time they had left. But this was good, this time apart. Even for a single evening. He needed time to think of a plan, a way to connect her world with his. The holidays were coming up, so maybe that was the answer.

Pictures played in his mind: Jamie and Sierra sitting around the table with Eric and Laura and Josh. Jamie would love all of them, but then what? Would she consider relocating if things between them continued? She had nothing concrete holding her in Staten Island—nothing except a lifetime of memories and her work at St. Paul's.

There was the possibility he could find a job in Manhattan with the NYPD, but that wasn't what he wanted. The weather was already near freezing, when back home it was still in the midseventies. Then there was the obvious—it would be close to impossible to start a life with Jamie in the place where she and her husband had shared a million memories, the place where he worked and died.

He exhaled and glanced at the nightstand. His cell phone was finished charging. Maybe he could call Eric and ask for advice, suggest the Thanksgiving idea and see what he thought. He picked up the phone, dialed the number, and waited.

Eric answered on the second ring, his voice upbeat. "Hey, it's my little brother! We thought you fell off the face of the earth."

"Sort of." Clay laughed. "I haven't had a free minute."

"They have you working twenty-fours, huh? I thought for sure they'd give you a few hours off here and there to call home." Eric was enjoying the moment. "Laura and I were trying to guess what had happened to you, so I told her you probably met someone, fell in love, and decided to get a police job in New York."

"Well ..." Clay formed a stack of pillows behind his back and leaned into them. "I'm not getting a job in New York."

Eric was silent for a moment. Then he uttered a single chuckle. "You telling me the other part's true?"

"I don't know." He tried to picture his brother, face expectant, certain Clay was messing with him. "I think so."

"*Really?*" This time Eric sounded excited. "You met someone? Hey, that's great! Where'd you meet her?"

"It was the strangest thing." Clay laughed again and told Eric the story. "They had a gun in her ribs by the time we pulled our weapons on them."

"Serious? That's amazing!" Eric paused. "So basically, you saved her life?"

"Pretty much." He smiled. The room was cold, but he didn't mind. Any time he thought about Jamie he felt warm inside. "I've seen her every day since."

"Every day?" Concern tinged Eric's tone. "What happens when you come back home?"

"We haven't talked about it really. Jamie's told me she has feelings for me, and I've told her the same thing. But that's as far as we've gone." He let his head fall back against the headboard. "I'm thinking about inviting her for Thanksgiving dinner. She and her daughter could fly out and join us at your house." He paused. "What do you think?"

The line was silent.

"Eric?" Clay checked his cell phone; he hadn't lost the call. "Hey, Eric, you there?"

"I'm here." His voice held none of his previous excitement. "Her name's Jamie?"

"Yeah." Clay forced a chuckle. What did his brother care about her name? "Anyway, I've spent a lot of time with her and her daughter. Even their cat. I'd love to invite them for Thanksgiving."

"Definitely." Eric's answer was quicker than before but his tone was still distracted. "Invite her; if she's got your attention we'd love to meet her."

The conversation stalled after that. Clay promised to call again toward the end of the week—to let them know if Jamie and her daughter would be coming. Then he hung up and stared at the phone. What was Eric's deal? Was he hesitant about Jamie because Clay had only known her for a few weeks? Or because something at home had his attention?

It didn't matter.

What did matter was how he was going to convince Jamie to fly to LA for Thanksgiving. The plan was crazy because who did that? Who invited a woman across the country for dinner when they'd only known each other a few weeks? But it wasn't impossible. People found love at first sight all the time, didn't they? Besides, they weren't fresh out of college. They were adults; they knew enough about love to recognize it when it hit them square in the face.

Not that what they shared was love. Not yet. They still hadn't kissed, hadn't allowed their conversations to get deeper than that one night over backgammon. But they held hands, and he could read her eyes well enough to know she cared.

Would she come for Thanksgiving? Clay didn't know, but he was sure of one thing. If she and Sierra came for Thanksgiving, they would hit it off great with Eric and Laura and Josh. His brother was bound to make Jamie feel comfortable, a part of the family.

Clay would have to be patient. He would simply tell Jamie she was invited and let her make the decision about whether to come. He set the phone back down on the nightstand. She would come; he was sure of it.

He could hardly wait to tell Jamie about the idea.

Eric set the receiver on the base and stared at the phone. Jamie and her daughter? From Staten Island? Adrenaline had shot through his veins at the mention of the name, and now—now he wasn't sure what to do next.

"Who was on the phone?" Laura padded into the bedroom. She wore jeans and thick fuzzy slippers. She had a small pink gift bag in her hands.

"Clay." He couldn't change his distant tone. Eric caught his wife's attention. "He met someone."

"Is that so?" Laura's eyebrows lifted and she gave him a sly smile. "Good for him." She watched him for a moment and her mouth relaxed. "What's wrong?"

"What's wrong?" He blinked and tried to focus on what she was saying.

"Yes, you look like someone died." She took a few steps toward him. "Didn't you say Clay met someone?"

Eric stared at her, wondering if he should put his fears into words. Finally he did a quiet gulp. "Her name's Jamie." He slowed his words down, so each one would have an impact. "She has a daughter and she lives on Staten Island."

"So, she—" Laura stopped and the color drained from her cheeks. "What's her last name?"

"I didn't ask."

"What about her daughter?"

"Didn't ask that either."

She groaned and her shoulders slumped some. "Why not?"

"Because." He shook his head. "I didn't want to know."

"Eric . . ." Laura dropped to the edge of the bed. "Staten Island is a big place. Ten million people live in the New York City area. You don't think it's the same woman."

He turned so he was facing her. "What if it is?"

"It isn't."

"No, seriously, Laura. What if it's her?"

"I'm telling you, it's not." She brought her voice back to an even level. "There must be a thousand women named Jamie living on Staten Island. Half of them probably have daughters." Her eyes told him that she was flustered, but she smiled. "Forget about it. Clay would've told you if it was the same Jamie."

Eric gripped his kneecaps and studied the wall for a moment. Then he found her eyes again. "Clay doesn't know her name; I only talked about her with you." He shrugged. "It was too weird, the whole thing was something most people wouldn't believe in the first place." His voice fell a notch. "God used my time with Jamie to save my life, Laura. I'm the man I am because of her husband. But that sort of thing doesn't exactly come up over lunch. Even with my brother."

Laura stood and came around in front of him. This time she kept the pink gift bag in front of her. "You're worrying about nothing." She stopped near his knees and smiled. "She lives on Staten Island, right?"

"Right." Eric pictured her, working in the kitchen, making blueberry pancakes for Sierra, sitting across from him sharing coffee each morning.

"Did she work?"

"No." Eric tried to focus on his wife, but the memories were strong. Jamie had plenty of money—an accident settlement she'd inherited when her parents died in a car accident when she was barely twenty years old. She'd shared that with him when he was recovering, one of many facts meant to trigger his memory. He shook his head. "She had money in the bank; she didn't need to work."

Laura's smile faded. "She didn't?"

"No. Her husband didn't need to work either. Fighting fires in New York City was a family thing, something in his blood."

"You never told me that." She shifted her weight to one foot. Her voice was higher than before, threatened. "So Jamie had a lot of money."

"Yes." He hadn't talked much about his actual time with Jamie as much as he'd shared the ways of life and faith he'd learned from her husband's journal, from the pages of his Bible. What was he supposed to do if she'd made a connection with Clay? He smiled and tried to hide the pounding of his heart. "Where's this going?"

Laura hesitated. The doubts lifted and cleared from her expression. "What I'm saying is, if she didn't work, then why on earth would she head into the city on a weekday morning?"

Eric hadn't thought about that. He looked at the ground for a minute and stroked his chin. "You're right." He found his wife's eyes again. "She would never have had to work, not with the money she had put away and the insurance settlement she would've gotten from her husband's death." His heart rate slowed. This was good. Thinking things through helped. His shoulders relaxed and he drew a calming breath. "If she decided to get a job—you know—just for fun, she never would've worked in the city; she hated that her husband worked there."

"Okay." Laura's tone was pleasant again. She was still standing in front of him, and she moved closer. "See? There's nothing to worry about."

Eric looped his arms around her waist and smiled. "I guess I overreacted a little. Like you said, there are millions of people in and around the city."

"Exactly." She bent down and kissed the tip of his nose. "Enough talk about that, all right?" Her eyes danced as she straightened. She held the pink bag out to him. "I've got my own news."

News? Wrapped up in a small pink gift bag? Eric felt his heart flip-flop as he took the package. "News?" His voice was a hoarse whisper.

"Go ahead." Her eyes were suddenly damp. She sat down beside him and motioned to the bag. "Open it, Eric."

He gulped. Was it what he thought it was? They'd tried to have another child ever since he came back home, after the terrorist attacks. Laura's doctor wasn't sure why she hadn't gotten pregnant, but in the next few months they were planning to look into some options that might help speed the process along. He met her eyes, looked deep into her heart, and he knew. Before he lifted the tissue and found the tiny pink pair of booties, he knew. "Are you . . . ?"

She nodded. "Six weeks already." Her eyes welled up and she massaged her throat, looking for the words. "I bought pink because I just know, Eric. I know she's a girl."

Eric memorized her face, her expression, the look in her eyes. It was all worth it—the horrible injuries he'd received on September 11, the time with Jamie, his three months of recovery and learning to be a man of God. All of it led to this. "Laura . . ." In a slow rush they came together, holding each other, and Eric couldn't describe the feeling inside him. Warm and full and grateful beyond words. He whispered against her hair. "You think it's a girl?"

"I do." She let out a happy cry. "God is so good. He had a plan all along."

Indeed.

Eric held his wife and thought about the little girl they'd lost, the one Laura miscarried before Josh's birth. He'd known he had a daughter, even in the throes of amnesia. It was why he felt right fathering Jamie's daughter, Sierra, for three months. And it was one of the hardest things about realizing his real identity. He had a loving wife, a wonderful son.

But no daughter.

He nuzzled Laura's cheek, her ear. "I'll be happy with a baby—boy or girl."

"I know." She pressed her face against his and sighed. "It's just that God has already worked so many miracles in our lives."

And in that moment, the way everything was going—even things for Clay—Eric could do nothing but take Laura's face between his hands and kiss her, long and slow, with the kind of love he'd never felt for anyone but her. Because she was right. God *had* already worked so many miracles in their lives. Why wouldn't He be pulling together one more? A baby girl? A daughter? The thought was more than he could imagine.

Eric couldn't think of a better miracle.

TWENTY

Jamie had a new favorite spot on the ferry from Staten Island. If it was sunny—and that Monday morning the sky was brilliant—she stood against the ferry's back railing. It wasn't a place she would've considered before—not on the trip to Manhattan. Because she couldn't see the empty place in the skyline from there.

But now . . . Every hour the message from Jake's Bible, the words he'd written in the margins, became more clear. *Choose life.* That meant she didn't have to stare at the empty skyline every day. She could stand at the back of the ferry, protected from the wind by the indoor seating area. She could stare back at Staten Island, the place where she was trying to learn how to live again, and she could think about things relevant to her new life.

The one without Jake.

She lifted her chin and let the sun hit her face square on. Something in her heart told her to savor the ferry ride, because she might not be making the trip much longer. Not to St. Paul's anyway.

Father. . . She breathed in the feel of God around her, the sensation of His Spirit inside her. The brisk air, the brilliant spray of shine from the early morning sun on the water. Being out here always made her feel closer to God. *I'm trying, Lord, trying to choose life. But what about Clay? Where does he fit into my—*

There was a tap on her shoulder. She turned around and gasped. "Clay!"

"Hi." He looked deep into her eyes, straight to her heart. "Fancy meeting you here."

Her breath caught in her throat. She'd wondered if he might be on her ferry since he had training that morning, but she hadn't seen him during the boarding process. She turned back toward the water and he took the spot beside her. Without the headwinds, it was easy to hear each other. "I was just praying about you."

"Hmmm." He edged closer, his arm full against hers. "Sounds interesting."

"It was." She stared at the rough water behind the boat. Her tone was light, teasing even—not giving away the electricity coursing through her veins, the way her mouth was dry because of his nearness.

He leaned his head back, taking the sun on his face the way she had earlier. "Let me guess. Praying that I'd find a new hat? Or that just once I might make dinner for you?"

She giggled and angled sideways to see him. Something about the winter air and the crisp blue sky made it feel as if they were the only two people on the boat. Her silliness faded and she looked at him, searching his eyes. "Wanna know what I was praying?"

"Wanna tell me?" His tone was measured, asking her questions his words did not. Questions like whether she was ready to share the heart behind her faith, whether she was ready to give even a glimpse of what she'd been feeling those past two weeks.

"Yeah." Her eyes stayed locked on his. For days Jamie had wanted this moment, a reason to go beyond the obvious—that she enjoyed his company. And now—even as she was praying for wisdom—God had provided it. "I do want to tell you, Clay." She hesitated. "I was asking God where you fit into my life."

He had no clever volley, no thoughtful comeback. Instead his eyes grew more narrow, his gaze deeper than before. "Tell me, Jamie."

She lifted one shoulder. "I don't know, except . . ." She glanced at the water, then back at him. "Except I don't want you to leave in a week."

"Me neither." He turned so they were both leaning against the boat's railing, facing each other. "I worry about you, Jamie. That maybe you're not ready for this." He angled his head. "Any of this. Have you thought about it?"

She did a small laugh, but it was lost on the sound of the ferry engines. "That's like asking me if I'm breathing." Her smile faded. "Yes, I think about it." She reached out and took hold of both his hands. The sensation took her breath away, his fingers intertwined with hers. "I read something in Jake's Bible the other day; it's helped."

"What did it say?" He rubbed his thumbs along the sides of her hands.

The sudden thickness in her throat made it hard to talk. The conversation was more intimate than anything they'd shared. "It was in Deuteronomy, chapter thirty."

"Ahhh." Clay's face was only inches from hers, their voices such that only the two of them could hear. "'I set before you life and prosperity, death and destruction.'"

She hesitated, allowing their eyes to carry on a conversation of their own. "'Choose life.'" Tears built up in her eyes. "Jake wrote me a note in the margins. 'Jamie, if you ever get the chance, choose life.'"

He felt her pain. It was written in his eyes and across the canvas of his heart, a place she could see clearly in this moment. "You miss him."

"I do." She used her shoulder to wipe a single tear. This wasn't a time for crying; she was happy, really. Happy because this—standing here with Clay this way, talking about Scripture—was what God wanted from her. For her. This was life; attention on the living. "I miss him, but he's never coming back." She sniffed. "If he were here, he'd tell me not to live my life in a memorial. He'd want me to start living again."

"I'm sorry, Jamie." His eyes shone, though she didn't think it was from the cold. "I'm sorry."

She wasn't sure which of them moved first, but slowly, as if drawn by a force neither of them could control, they came together. Their lips met in a gentle, soft kiss, one that was still building even as she drew back.

His breath was warm against her cheeks, and as though it was destined from the first time they were together on this very boat, his hand left hers and took gentle hold of her jaw, his fingers spreading along the side of her face. "Jamie . . . is it okay?"

"What?" She breathed the word against his face, so close his skin was touching hers. Her heart was doing somersaults; it was all she could do to remember to inhale.

"Is it okay if I kiss you? Really kiss you?"

The moment he breathed his question against her lips, she was his. She moved closer, giving him permission to do what she'd been imagining and fearing, desiring and dreading, every day since they met. They kissed, and it was something from a dream. Her tears came again because she was kissing someone other than Jake— something she'd never done in all her life. And because it didn't feel wrong and shameful, but sad and wonderful, impossible and right. God had answered her prayers not with quiet holy whispers but with Clay Miles. With this man standing there kissing her, putting his arms around her and holding her close, the way she wanted him to hold her forever.

He pulled back, catching his breath. "Jamie . . ." He looked at her, his eyes full of questions. Was she okay? Was it all right? Was it what she wanted?

"I'm fine, Clay. I am." She closed the distance between them and kissed him this time, full on his mouth, silencing his doubts the only way she knew. This time when they drew apart, she laughed. Not loud or hard, but with an abandon that expressed the joy welling within her. She found his eyes and searched his soul. "God brought you into my life for a reason." Her heart grew suddenly heavy; she felt the corners of her mouth fall. "I just wish we had more time."

He took her hands again. His eyes sparkled with something, maybe anticipation. "Funny you should ask."

"Funny why?" She loved how she felt, warm and safe and appreciated. The captain made his announcement. They were a few minutes from shore.

"Because I've been praying about us too."

"You have?"

He leaned in and kissed her, his lips tender against hers. "Yes, I have. I even talked to my brother back in Los Angeles. Everyone's in agreement."

She giggled. "About what?"

"About you joining us for Thanksgiving."

"In LA?" In a split instant, the idea bridged the gap between despair that he was leaving so soon and hope that maybe—just maybe—they'd find a way to see each other again. "You want me to come to LA for Thanksgiving."

"No." Clay's face got serious, but his eyes still danced. A huge grin spread over his face. "Not just you, crazy. You and Sierra." His words came faster. "Thanksgiving's always at my brother's house. He said he and his wife would love to have the two of you. You could fly in a few days before, and I could take you to the beach. I don't know, maybe take Sierra to Disneyland, that kind of thing. Make a week out of it."

He sounded like a kid talking about spring break, but she was as caught in the wave of enthusiasm as he. She thought for a moment. It was possible, wasn't it? She had Jake's father, but he'd understand if they didn't head upstate for the holiday this once. Besides, she and Sierra hadn't been on a vacation since Jake died. "You're serious? You really want us to come?"

"Of course." His eyebrows were raised halfway up his forehead. "It'll be great, Jamie. Say you'll come."

She laughed again. She'd laughed more those past two weeks than in the past three years combined. "I have to make my orange salad; it's Sierra's favorite."

"That's the nice thing about California in November." He frowned at the sky and shivered. "Oranges are in season."

Everything was happening so fast, but Jamie didn't mind. That was the strangest part of all. They walked off the ferry together and Clay admitted he didn't have to be at work until noon. The captain had changed the schedule at the last minute because of a big drug bust going on that morning in Chinatown.

They held hands as they headed across Battery Park, toward the line of waiting cabs. Jamie kept her steps slow; she didn't want the morning with Clay to end any sooner than it had to. "Why are you coming in so early?"

He stopped, faced her, and took both her hands in his. "I came to find you." He kissed her, just long enough to make her breathless again. "I had to tell you about Thanksgiving."

"Clay . . ." Her heart sang inside her. How had God done this? Brought a man into her life who was everything she needed, everything she hadn't even known she was looking for. "You came in early just for that?"

"Yep." They started walking again, their hands linked. "And now you're stuck with me. I might as well do my waiting at St. Paul's." His voice was upbeat. "Besides, I never finished looking at the memorial tables. Remember? I started on the last wall."

"True." They reached the curb and she hailed a cab. "Maybe it'll be slow and we can find somewhere to talk." Anywhere in the chapel would be comfortable. Aaron Hisel was working a later shift so there wouldn't be any need to explain Clay's presence or why they were together.

Traffic was busier than usual, and by the time they walked through the doors, one of the other volunteers waved Jamie down. A small crowd of people stood around her. "Help!" she mouthed.

Jamie nodded, and gave Clay a helpless smile. "I'll be back."

"Okay. No big deal." He squeezed her hand before letting it go. "I'll look around."

For the flash of an instant Jamie realized that for the first time Clay would see a picture of Jake—because it was still set up next to Sierra's letter at the first table near the door. Not that he'd know he was looking at Jake. And whereas the idea had bothered her the first time Clay came with her to the chapel, now it was something she'd come to accept, that one day Clay would see Jake. A part of her wanted him to see the man she'd loved since she was a girl. It would be one way of blending her worlds, life before Jake and life after him.

She joined the other volunteer and answered questions for ten minutes before Clay caught her attention. He was staring at the picture of Jake, staring at him with an odd intensity. Did he know? How could he? There was no way he could know that the man in the picture was her husband.

Then again . . . The letter next to the photo was signed *Sierra*. How many little girls named Sierra would've lost a firefighter father? She started to excuse herself, head back toward him, when he looked straight at her. Forty feet separated them, but even from that far away she could see his face.

It was ashen.

She slowed, suddenly afraid. Why did Clay look that way? Had he changed his mind about her, maybe decided she must not be ready for something new? His eyes were wide, his mouth open, looking like a person in shock.

"Jamie . . ."

Though she couldn't hear him, she could read her name on his lips.

Her heart skittered about, warning her that something—something she couldn't understand—had in a moment's time gone very wrong. She closed the distance between them, her eyes moving from Clay to the photo of Jake, and back again. "Clay?" She remembered to breathe. "What is it?"

"Is that . . . that's your husband, right?"

She let her eyes find Jake's. The clear blue eyes and short dark hair, the chiseled features of the man who loved her and promised her a lifetime. "You saw Sierra's note."

He nodded, his face still pale. For a long time he said nothing, just looked at Jake, realization coming into his expression.

Jamie relaxed. His reaction was understandable. Here was the picture of a man Jamie never would've left, of Sierra's father. And his likeness—in some cruel twist of senseless hatred—was not gracing the home where Jamie and Sierra lived, but a table in St. Paul's Chapel.

Of course Clay looked shocked. This was probably the first time he'd felt the terrorist attacks personally. She just needed to talk to Clay the way she'd talked to so many other visitors at St. Paul's. She would grieve with him, and they would come away richer for the experience. She was about to take his hand, when he turned to her.

"Jamie." The fear in his eyes was worse than before. "He looks exactly like my brother."

"Like your—" His words hit her in slow motion, each one ramming into her heart and kicking her in small circles until she had to brace herself against the table to keep from falling to the floor. She could feel the blood leaving her face, feel her knees trembling. Her eyes were locked on his, searching for some sort of explanation. He was kidding, or maybe his brother had dark hair or blue eyes. Not an exact replica, certainly. Because God never would've brought this marvelous man into her life only to have it all end in some cruel joke.

Words gathered in her throat but she couldn't say them. She searched Clay's eyes, his face. Bits of conversations came rushing back and she sifted through them for a sign. He couldn't be Eric's brother; it wasn't possible. Sure, he was from California, but that didn't mean anything. His name was Clay Miles, not—

The impossible breathed its hot breath against the nape of her neck. She moved back a few steps, leaning against one of the white pillars. "What's . . ." Her words were scratchy. It took everything to complete the question. "What's your last name?"

He looked as devastated as she felt. He moved closer, leaving only a foot between them. "Clay Michaels."

No! No, it wasn't true. His name was Clay Miles, not Michaels. The spinning in her head got worse and nausea swept over her. "No." She looked away. Navigating with her hands, she made it around the pillar and dropped into the first pew. Then she leaned her forearms on the back of the seat in front of her and hung her head.

She felt him move into the pew and ease into the space beside her. "Jamie, look at me. Talk to me." Anguish was raw in his voice, mixed with shock.

It took everything to lift her head. This wasn't happening; it couldn't be. "You . . . you told me your name was Clay Miles."

"No, Jamie." Alarm joined the emotions burning in his eyes. He lowered his brow, concentrating. "I told you my name on the ferry. We were outside in the stairwell; it was loud."

He was right. She could picture the moment, standing before him, the horn sounding when he told her his name. No wonder there'd been something familiar about him. He had his brother's eyes.

Clay was still watching her, staring at her, caught in the middle of a nightmare that couldn't possibly be true. "So you're the one." His words were slow, full of disbelief. "Of all the people in this city, how could you be the one?"

"I'm sorry, Clay. I can't . . ." She didn't finish her sentence; she didn't need to. The look on Clay's face told her he understood. That because of his relationship to Eric, she and Clay could never move forward.

She closed her eyes and lifted her face. *God . . . why? Of all people, why him?* If only she'd heard him right the first time, heard him say Clay Michaels. She would've known instantly why he looked familiar. They would've figured out their strange connection, talked about it for the rest of the ferry ride, and gone their separate ways.

"Jamie, nothing has to change." Clay leaned closer, his eyes wide, imploring her. "You don't have to come back for Thanksgiving if you don't want to; your time with Eric has nothing to do with this."

She shook her head. "I can't." She met his eyes and willed him to understand. Looking at Eric again would be like looking at Jake. She couldn't carry on even a friendship with Clay if it meant spending time with Eric. It'd be like trying to ignore Jake's ghost in the room.

Clay looked at his watch and pursed his lips. "I have to go." He put his hand on hers. "Jamie, please. We'll talk about this. Nothing's changed."

Jamie wanted to cry. She leaned toward him and slipped her arms around his neck. "Go, Clay." She couldn't tell him good-bye, couldn't bear it. A part of her was dying, the part that was connected to the man in her arms.

He stroked her back. She could feel his heart pounding against her shoulder. "I'll call you as soon as I'm done today."

The walls were up. His words no longer penetrated her heart the way they had before. She drew back and nodded. There was wetness on her cheeks, and for the first time she noticed. She was crying. He used his knuckle to wipe the tears from her cheeks. Then he stood and backed out of the pew, his eyes on her the entire time. "I'll call."

She didn't argue. She wanted to be alone, to gather her feelings and stop the dizziness in her head. To look in the mirror and convince herself that the impossible had happened. Eric Michaels's brother really had come to town, saved her life, and made her feel things she hadn't felt since Jake.

"Don't, Jamie, please." He stopped. "This doesn't have to mean anything. Nothing's changed." His eyes told her he was desperate for her to see things his way, that even though this was a twist, a strange coincidence, it didn't need to mean the end of what they'd started.

"Go." She held up her hand, her eyes locked on his until he walked through the doors.

When he was gone, she knew it was too late. What they'd found was gone. If they'd figured it out that first morning, they could've spared themselves all of this. Because while she might be ready to start living again, ready to face a future without Jake, she couldn't start a relationship with Eric's brother.

Not if it meant seeing Eric again.

After all they'd been through, Jamie knew the only way she'd ever move on was to let him go. Bid him good-bye and never look back, not for anything.

Not even his brother, Clay.

TWENTY-ONE

Sue Henning would know what to do.

Jamie picked up Sierra at school and headed straight for her friend's house. She had barely survived the day, convinced it all had to be some sort of bad joke. As long as she'd lived she'd never believed in love at first sight. Until she met Clay.

Their first meeting was like some sort of cosmic metaphor. She, alone and vulnerable, unaware of the dangers that surrounded her. Him, looking out for her, rushing to her rescue, protecting her the way she still needed protecting. He loved God and his country and *The Lion King*. What more could she ask?

Crazy girl, she'd told herself a hundred times that day. She didn't even know him, didn't know his faults other than one: he was impulsive.

The thing was, she'd never been quick with her decision-making. But she'd been drawn to him in a way that kicked common sense out the door. So much so that this morning when he'd asked her about Thanksgiving in California, the idea had seemed practical. Logical, even.

But that was before she knew about Eric.

She gritted her teeth as she rounded the corner to Sue's house. Why would God allow it? Why let them meet, why light the fire in her long-cold heart only to snuff it out this way? *God . . . You promised You'd see me through this.*

The thought hung in the stale air of her car. A few feet away, Sierra turned and looked at her. "Did you cry today, Mommy?"

Jamie sniffed and shot her daughter a quick glance. "Of course not," she lied.

"Then how come your eyes are puffy?" Sierra's knobby knees stuck out from her woolen jumper, the uniform she wore to school.

Poor Sierra. She was still a little girl, her feet not quite touching the floor. She deserved a man like Clay in her life.

"Mommy, how come? How come your eyes are puffy?"

"Mrs. Henning says Katy's looking forward to seeing you."

Sierra stared out the car window. "What about Clay? Will we see him today?"

Her words hit her like so many rocks. "I don't think so."

The conversation stalled. Jamie turned into Sue's driveway. Anger welled up in her, anger at God for letting this insane thing happen. She cared about Clay, could easily love him. But being around Eric Michaels would be like being around Jake. Maybe she hadn't heard God about choosing life. Maybe He wanted her to choose her old life, with Jake's memory, her obsession with helping the victims of September 11, her work at St. Paul's.

Maybe she was never supposed to do anything more than thank Clay Michaels.

Sue was waiting out front, arms crossed, leaning against the door frame. Even from fifteen feet away Jamie could read her; she was worried.

Sierra jumped out, waved hello to Sue, and ran inside calling Katy's name. Jamie felt tired and old, battered by the turn of events. She dragged herself up the walkway and met Sue's gaze. Jamie hadn't told her anything except the basics. She'd met someone on the ferryboat, a police officer from California. He was the reason she hadn't called in a few weeks.

But now things had gone terribly wrong.

"I still can't believe you didn't call sooner." Sue's words were quiet, muffled by the icy breeze outside. They entered the house and went into the living room. Sue had two cups of tea already poured, waiting.

Jamie sat down across from Sue and clasped her hands. "I wanted to tell you." She barely lifted her shoulders. "I guess I didn't know how. I still can't believe it myself."

"Do you . . . do you have feelings for him?"

"I did." Jamie felt tears in her eyes. She swallowed hard and found her voice again. "I've seen him every day since I met him. Whenever he isn't training or sleeping, he's been with Sierra and me." Jamie told Sue how he'd taken them to *The Lion King* and shared a number of dinners with them. "It was all happening so fast, but it felt real. For the first time since Jake, it felt real."

Sue frowned. "So where's the problem? Jamie, it's been three years. You're allowed to care about someone else."

"You haven't."

"But I would." Sue's voice grew soft. "If God brought someone into my life, I would. I've thought about it lately."

Jamie still hadn't gotten to the most important part, but now she had this to consider. Sue would care about someone else? Date someone else? She'd been thinking about it lately? Maybe they'd both been thinking about it, too afraid to tell the other that they couldn't imagine being alone for the rest of their lives. Even if the idea was unthinkable in light of the men they'd lost.

Sue took a sip of her tea. "What's so bad, Jamie? If it's guilt that's stopping you, let it go. Jake would want you to let it go."

Jake's words filled her heart: *Choose life, Jamie. Whenever you can, choose life.* She closed her eyes. "You don't know the whole story." She blinked and searched her friend's face. "It's the worst thing, Sue. You won't believe it."

Worry colored the fine lines on Sue's forehead. "If he hurt you, he's not the guy you made him out to be."

Jamie shook her head. "No, nothing like that." She slid to the edge of the sofa, her heart beat fast and hard against the wall of her chest. "You remember Eric Michaels?"

Sue squinted. "Eric Michaels?"

"Yes." Jamie exhaled hard. What did she expect? She'd seldom talked about Eric, just telling everyone—even Sue—the straight facts. The man she'd thought was Jake was really a businessman from Los Angeles, a man suffering from amnesia, one who looked enough like Jake to pass for him. She kept her answers short, and Sue had always known better than to ask. Now she had to revisit that time again—something she'd never wanted to do.

Sue shook her head. "The name's familiar, but I can't figure out why."

"He's the man who lived with me, the one I thought was Jake."

A knowing look filled her face. "Oh, right. Okay." The frown was back. "Why bring him up?"

Jamie felt the blood leaving her face, felt herself reacting to the news as if she were hearing it for the first time again. Her tone was pinched, scratchy. "Clay's his brother."

Seconds passed while Sue processed the news. "Clay, the police officer you met on the ferry, is Eric Michaels's brother?" Her eyebrows lifted and she lowered her chin. "That's impossible."

"That's what I thought." She stood and walked to the window, her back to her friend. The girls were upstairs, playing in Katy's room. Outside the trees were bare, a light snow had fallen the night before, and everything was the color of winter. "It's true, Sue. Clay's his brother. We found out this morning." She looked over her shoulder at Sue. "He saw Jake's picture. A few minutes before he had to leave for his shift."

"Oh, Jamie." Sue's expression relaxed, but her face was taut, pale. "I can't believe it."

"I told him I couldn't see him tonight." She faced the window again. "I can't see him ever again."

Sue was quiet. After a while, Jamie returned to the sofa and drank down half her tea. "I already miss him. I can't believe this is happening." She set her cup down. "There's nothing you can do to help, but I had to tell you."

A minute passed, and then Sue stood and crossed the room to the fireplace. Next to it was a bookshelf, and from a place in the back she pulled out a small urn. Jamie had one like it—given to them by the city. The urn held a few cups of debris and ash from the collapsed Twin Towers.

With slower steps, Sue carried it back to the coffee table and set it down on a spot between them both. She leveled her gaze at Jamie. "You know why they gave us those urns?"

Where on earth was her friend going with this? She didn't want to look at the urn or think about what might've been inside. The ashy remains of any of the two thousand victims. Jamie had kept hers out of respect for the lives lost that day. But it was hardly a reminder of Larry or Jake. "No." She shook her head. "Mine's tucked away somewhere; I don't look at it."

"I keep mine out." She angled her head and looked at the detail on the small container. "It's a reminder of something that might be easy to forget otherwise."

"What?" Jamie still didn't know what the urn had to do with her situation, the one she was battling that day.

"That Larry's not coming home." Sue's voice cracked. "It reminds me that every terrible thing about September 11 really happened. That my husband and your husband were two of the heroes, two of the men who ran up the stairs when everyone else was running down." She sniffed and pressed her finger to her lip. Sue rarely broke down, and this would be no exception. "Larry's gone. When his name is on my lips, when I jump up to ask his advice about something or wonder what he might want for dinner, I remember the urn and it's all real again. He's gone and he's not coming home."

Jamie leaned closer. "I already know that about Jake." She pressed her fingers against her chest. "I'm the one who's been dating these past two weeks. I don't need an urn to remember the truth about Jake. He's gone; I get that."

"Yes." Sue's voice was even, her eyes unwavering. "But there is something you have trouble remembering."

"What?" She didn't come here for a lecture from Sue. "What do I have trouble remembering?"

Sue's voice slipped to a whisper. "That Eric Michaels wasn't Jake. That you didn't lose Jake the day Eric left on an airplane back to California. You lost him in the terrorist attacks, same as the rest of us."

Jamie felt her breath catch. She couldn't breathe, couldn't inhale for the emotions strangling her. She wanted to tell Sue she already knew that about the timing, that she'd lost Jake when the Twin Towers collapsed, same as the other firefighter widows. But she couldn't. Because what Sue had just said made her feel raw and hurt and aching inside.

"Jamie . . ." Sue's voice was a little louder now, filled with compassion. "Do you understand what I'm saying?"

Her head was spinning, her heart bleeding from wounds that still weren't healed. "Not really."

"So *what* if Eric and Clay are brothers? What does it matter?"

Jamie's heart rate doubled. Panic seized her by the neck and threatened to strangle her. "What does it matter? If Clay and I got close, I'd have to see Eric again." Tears blurred her vision, spilling from a well so deep Jamie barely acknowledged its presence. "I can't do that, Sue, I can't."

Sue wouldn't let up. "Why?"

"Because every time I saw him, I'd feel like I was with Jake."

This time Sue waited, and when she spoke her words were slow, measured. "Eric isn't Jake; he never was." She drew her feet up beside her on the sofa. "I wonder, Jamie. Have you ever worked through the memories you made with that man and told yourself that every single one of them was with a stranger? Have you allowed yourself to take Jake's name off each of those days you and Eric had together?"

Jamie felt the nausea rise inside her, felt her head swimming. She'd done that, hadn't she? Her head knew Jake hadn't come home, that he'd died right beside his best friend when the South Tower collapsed.

But did her heart know? Or had she, by suppressing details of that time, by never taking it out and spreading the memories on a table and examining them, allowed her heart to believe that Jake *had* come home. That she'd been given some sort of reprieve, a mulligan, a time with Jake, that none of the other survivors got to have with their loved ones.

Was that why she never talked about Eric? Maybe a part of her wanted to believe the man in her house hadn't been Eric at all, but Jake. At least until he'd taken the blood test and they'd known he was someone else.

Jamie stood and realized she was shaking. She needed to be alone, needed to think through this, to shine a light on the darkest corners of her heart. "Can you watch Sierra for a while? I need to go to the beach."

"It's winter, Jamie. It'll be freezing."

"That's okay. I have a coat in the car." The place where she and Jake liked to go was just a few miles from Sue's house. Cold weather wouldn't matter, not when she had so much to work through. "Can you watch her?"

"Yes." Sue stood and came to her. "Can I say something before you go?"

"Go ahead." Jamie's teeth were clattering, not because she was feeling the effects of winter, but because she was about to go places she hadn't gone in three years.

Their eyes locked, and Sue looked as serious as Jamie could remember seeing her. "Maybe God brought Eric into your life so he could become the man *he* needed to be. He was different when he went home, right? Isn't that what you told me?"

Jamie looked at the floor near her feet. "Yes."

"He wasn't supposed to replace Jake." Sue put her hand on Jamie's shoulder. "He was supposed to learn from him. Learn the value of faith and family and friendship."

"Then what about Clay?" Jamie lifted her eyes. "Why would God let me have feelings for Eric's brother?"

"Because." Sue gave her shoulder a gentle squeeze. "Maybe Eric's brother was the man you needed. Not because of Jake or Eric or anyone else. Just because of Clay." She hesitated. "Maybe that was part of God's plan too."

TWENTY-TWO

It was almost dusk when Jamie walked across the sand to the spot where she and Jake had set out their chairs and towels so many times before. This time she brought nothing with her, just pulled her long coat tight around her and eased down to the sand. Her eyes found a pale blue section of sky. "God . . . what is this feeling in my heart?"

When she remembered the three months after the terrorist attacks, one day stood out as changing everything. The day they went to the hospital and discovered the man living with her didn't have Jake's blood type. From that point on, Jamie had grieved. No longer could she spend every moment teaching the man in the downstairs bedroom how to be Jake, how to think like him and pray like him and father like him. How to love like him.

From that point on she knew a stranger was living with her, and it was up to her to care enough to help him find his way home. She had understood, hadn't she? When she said good-bye at LaGuardia she was saying good-bye to a nice man, a stranger named Eric Michaels. Jake was already dead.

But what about those twelve weeks when he'd *been* Jake to her in every way but one? When she longed for him and took him to church and held his hand?

A breeze rolled off the water and brushed against her cheeks. Could it be that she still savored memories of that time as if he wasn't a stranger at all but Jake?

She pulled her knees up to her chin and stared at the harbor. Had she done the thing Sue asked? Had she consciously told herself the truth about those weeks? That Jake hadn't been with them, hadn't sat beside her at the breakfast table, or cooked up blueberry pancakes for Sierra?

A deep ache began within her, and with it came a realization: if she could admit the truth about Eric, her fears about seeing him again were unfounded. If she could admit he'd never been Jake. Not for the first few days after the terrorist attacks. Not for the first few weeks or months.

Not at all.

"God," her voice took wind. "I was mad at You . . . but it wasn't Your fault, was it?"

She looked up. If only God would give her a sign, something to tell her He was still on her side. A single seagull soared into view and dipped toward the ocean. For a moment, Jamie felt sorry for the bird, making his way through a late winter afternoon alone, without a friend or a mate.

But almost at the same time, she saw another seagull swoop down and join the first. Jamie blinked against the cold air and felt the burn of moisture in the corner of her eyes. The bird wasn't alone, after all.

But she was, and all because she had believed in some dark hallway of her heart that Eric really was Jake; that she hadn't lost her husband in the collapse of the Twin Towers, but three months later. And yet, Eric wasn't Jake. No matter how much he looked like him or learned to act like him, he never could be.

Her heart splintered, and she bowed her head. "I'm sorry, God. I'm so sorry."

Remorse filled her. Remorse and guilt and understanding.

Remorse, because she'd never had Jake a minute past the time when he told her good-bye and headed off for work September 11; guilt, because how dare she believe another man to be Jake—even under the strangest circumstances; and understanding, because Sue was right. Jamie realized that now.

She'd never gone through the memories of those twelve weeks one at a time and painted in Eric's name, his face and likeness. She'd been okay with keeping that time locked up in her heart, protected from scrutiny so she didn't have to admit to herself that Jake had never been a part of any of it.

The sky was getting darker, colder. If she was going to unlock that time in her life and give it a proper burial, she needed to move quickly.

She started with the afternoon of September 11, the moment she got the call from Sergeant Riker. Jake was alive, he told her. Alive and hurt and at Mount Sinai Medical Center. After a day of desperate fear and worry, the news gave Jamie permission to breathe again.

The memory filled in, and she pictured herself responding to the amazing news. The telephone receiver fell slowly to her lap as she screamed her husband's name. He was alive! Relief, like a gust of air, filled a room where she'd been suffocating. Jake hadn't been in the South Tower after all. He was alive! Just like he'd promised!

Jamie held her breath and looked out to sea.

She exhaled, shaking. Sergeant Riker went on to tell her that Captain Hisel was searching the rubble at Ground Zero when he found Jake beneath a fire truck.

Awe filled Jamie's mind now as she realized the truth. She'd never quite convinced herself that Aaron hadn't found Jake there that day. But now she didn't want to miss a moment, had to remove Jake from every one of the places where he didn't belong.

Eric Michaels had been coming down the stairs, escaping the building when the tower collapsed. The force had sent him—not Jake—underneath the fire truck. Which meant that the man Aaron Hisel saw and helped and sent to the hospital wasn't Jake, either.

The hurt was so bad. Jamie remembered, years ago, when Jake broke his arm playing football in high school. He hadn't wanted to wear a cast because it might limit his playing time. So he continued on with the pain, not telling his parents or anyone else how bad it was.

But then he began to notice a bend in his forearm, a bend and a bump that finally his family doctor spotted. By then only one thing could be done to fix the arm. Rebreak it and let it heal correctly.

That's exactly how she felt now.

She'd let her heart heal in the wrong position, believing at least on some level that those memories of late September, October, and November still involved Jake. Now—with a pain that knew no bounds, she was letting God break her heart again so that it might heal correctly.

Jamie wasn't sure she could continue. But she had no choice. She dug to another level, the moment she rushed into the hospital room, certain Jake had survived, the hours she'd held vigil at his bedside, the days of stroking his hand, whispering to him, and begging him to wake up.

Jake hadn't been there for any of it.

Not when Sierra saw him for the first time, and he remembered her name. Eric had merely run into Jake in the stairwell and by some bizarre series of events, he'd seen the inside of Jake's helmet. The place where he'd kept a photo of Sierra and her name written below it.

Eric saw it and remembered it that day in the hospital.

Jamie no longer felt the cold air around her. Her battered heart took up all her energy, her determination to remove Jake from those moments after September 11 wore on her, leaving gaping wounds at her very core.

She kept on, working through the homecoming from the hospital. The man who rode the ferry with her and sang with Sierra, the man who stared at their wedding portrait and gasped, convinced he was in the picture. All of it took place with Eric Michaels.

One at a time Jamie continued, dissecting memories, painstakingly removing Jake and placing Eric there instead. Halfway through the process, she felt drops of water on her arms. She was crying and she hadn't even known it. She'd been too absorbed in the matter at hand to acknowledge how much it all hurt.

When she finished—when she staggered to her feet, dusted off the sand, and peered through the dusky evening toward the water one last time—the hole in her heart was so big she felt hollow, as if people could see straight through her. She walked closer to the shore, close enough so she could bend down and get her fingers wet.

"Jake . . ." Her voice was hoarse, raspy. This was where she liked to come to connect with him, to touch the water where the two of them had played so often together.

But everything was different, maybe because she had a firm grasp on the truth. The water wasn't warm and inviting, it was freezing cold, the same way her empty heart felt. She stood and slipped her wet fingers deep into the pocket of her coat.

Now came the hardest part.

She took herself back further than before, back to the week and days and hours before September 11. Back to her life with her husband. The jet skiing with Sue and Larry and the little girls, the small ceramic figurine of an angel she'd painted for him the Sunday before the attacks, the hugging and laughing and lovemaking.

Though her head knew the truth since Eric's blood test, her heart needed to understand once and for all. *Those* were her final days with Jake. That Tuesday morning, waking up beside him, wanting him to stay and go to the zoo with her and Sierra, wishing he'd play hooky and skip work for the day.

And then watching him consider the idea and decide instead to go to work. Tomorrow, he'd told her. They could play together tomorrow. Then her promising to get Chinese food for dinner and one last kiss, a final quick good-bye. Hearing him head down the hall to Sierra's room, enjoying his laughter as Sierra asked him for butterfly kisses and Jake promised to play horsie with her when he got home.

That was the end, his final moments with them.

She straightened and let her coat ease open, let the wind off the water blow over her, taking with it the remaining shards of her denial. This should have been the hardest part, the time when she would turn away and head for the car, so hollow and empty she could barely support herself.

And she was empty, no doubt. But through her tears, she could feel God doing something inside her, knitting her broken heart back together again. Correctly this time. She turned and trudged through the sand, a grieving widow leaving the scene of a burial. But amid the pain and loss and acceptance working its way through her was something else, something she hadn't expected.

Hope.

Because the emptiness meant Eric was no longer living in her heart, masquerading as Jake. And if Eric wasn't living in her heart, then maybe someday she could handle seeing him again. Not as Jake's substitute, a man she had wanted to keep as her own even after she knew the truth about his identity. Next time—if there was a next time—she wouldn't see him as Jake Bryan's double.

But as Clay Michaels's brother.

TWENTY-THREE

Clay and his partner were five minutes from the scene of the crime.

A drug lord had been shot in the head in a busy alley on the lower East Side, and the trail was getting colder by the hour. The NYPD detective force had a good idea that the key suspect was an ex-con who headed up a rival drug ring, but so far they had no proof.

Four of the detectives-in-training—including Clay and his buddy—had been selected to conduct street interviews with the New York detectives. Fan out, talk to regulars at a few of the taverns, chat with the locals and street vendors. That type of investigation almost always netted witnesses or leads that would help in the investigation.

Clay had no idea how he'd stay focused.

"You're quiet." Joe was in the backseat with him; two NYPD officers were in the front seat holding their own conversation.

"Yeah." Clay stared out his window.

"Jamie again?"

Clay turned and met his friend's eyes. "Is it that obvious?" He hadn't told Joe all the details, just that something had gone wrong, and he and Jamie weren't speaking. Not that Clay hadn't tried.

"Yep, it is." Joe pursed his lips and stared straight ahead. "As obvious as it is for me."

"I think Wanda will come around." Clay swallowed thoughts of his own heartache and thought of his partner. Joe hadn't seen Wanda in a few days, either. Ever since his breakdown after seeing Wanda's little boy—the one who looked exactly like the child they lost.

"She doesn't know what to say; I don't either. I told her I was sorry, but it's not enough. It's like she doesn't believe it."

Clay waited. They were almost at the alley, the one where the murder had taken place. "I still say she'll come around." He looked at his friend. "You belong together."

"Same as you and Jamie." Joe was the office cutup, dry and never missing a chance to get a laugh. Until now. Now his voice was quiet, even tender. "I've watched you after you've been with her, man. She's got you good. You can take a few days off from talking to her, but that won't change a thing. Your kind of gotcha doesn't go away ever."

Clay narrowed his eyes. Every inch of his heart ached for Jamie, but he couldn't do a thing about it. He'd called her twice a day each day since that terrible morning. Now he was leaving in a few days, and they hadn't even had a chance to say good-bye. Could that have been God's plan? Let them meet and feel something for each other that they'd never felt with anyone else, only to find out it was all for nothing?

The hardest part was Eric.

Clay had called him that Monday night, the day he'd found out the truth. Eric had answered the phone, upbeat. Maybe a little too upbeat. "So, little brother, how're you doing?"

"Been better." An awkward silence played over the phone line. That's when Clay knew; with a sixth sort of brotherly sense, he knew. Eric had been worrying about this since their last phone call, worrying that maybe by some horrible twist of fate, Clay's Jamie was actually Jamie Bryan.

"Yeah, well, training's almost done." Eric cleared his throat. "Hey, uh, tell me, Clay. What's the name of that girl you're seeing? The one you met on the ferry. You know, from Staten Island?"

"Why didn't you ask me the first time I called?" Clay tried to keep the bitterness from his voice. It wasn't Eric's fault. A sad chuckle eased through his lips. "You guessed it, right?"

Shock crept into Eric's tone. "What's her name, Clay?"

"Jamie Bryan." Clay stared at the ceiling of his hotel room. "That's her, right? The woman you lived with."

It was, of course.

Eric could no more believe the strange coincidence than Clay or Jamie could. What were the odds that Clay would go to New York

City and fall in love with the woman who for three months had played the role of Eric's wife?

Before the phone call ended, Eric tried to tell Clay it didn't matter, that they could all get past the strangeness of having Jamie Bryan around for Thanksgiving. But Clay could hear the doubt in his brother's voice. Eric didn't want a reunion with Jamie anymore than she wanted one with him.

And so Clay had lost again; lost to his brother twice.

This time so much worse than with Laura. Back in high school, he'd had a shot at dating Laura long before Eric entered the picture. But he hadn't been sure, hadn't been bowled over the way he wanted to be. Really, it was only after Eric started dating Laura that Clay became more interested.

Then, after September 11, when it looked like Eric was dead, Clay was convinced God had a plan for Laura and him to finally wind up together. But even then his feelings for her were more along the lines of brotherly love and deep concern.

Yes, he was attracted to Laura.

But he was blown away by Jamie Bryan.

The police car pulled over just outside the alley, and the detective at the wheel turned off the engine. "It's four o'clock." He looked at the other men in the car. "We have an hour before dusk, and that's about all we want. You know the routine." He grinned, his eyes hard and focused. "Get in, get the information, and get out. People know what happened." He patted his holster. "Be aware of your weapon, especially as the sun starts to set. The killer's loose. If it's the man we think it is, then his cronies are probably still around. It's no secret that they're packing more than dime bags of weed." He gave them a final look and nodded at his partner in the passenger seat. "We'll take the west side. Stay in pairs."

They climbed out of the car, and the detective and his partner crossed the alley. All four men were uniformed, armed, and carrying pens and notebooks. Joe turned to Clay and raised his eyebrow. "Man, you know what time it is?"

Clay fell in step beside him. "Late and getting later."

This time Joe shook his head. "Nope. Time to forget the women for a while."

The first establishment was a shoddy strip bar with no windows—typical for a back alley entrance. Though the shooting took place at the opposite end of the alleyway, they would try everyone they could find in a hundred-yard radius.

Clay pushed the door open and took a few seconds for his eyes to adjust to the darkness. He was immediately hit by a thick wall of cigarette smoke.

Joe nudged him. "Cockroach trap." He kept his voice low. "Buncha dirty old bugs who can't stand the light."

"That's for sure." Clay could see better now, but not much. The blue smoke was thick inside, and a heavy beat, loud and pulsing, filled the air. Neon lights spun and roved around a dimly lit stage where someone was dancing. Clay didn't look; he never did. Instead, when his job took him to places like this, he remembered Scriptures that spoke of evil being done in the darkness, and how the darkness can't stand the light.

Once, when he was a kid, Clay stumbled onto his father's *Playboy* magazine collection. Even back then something in his spirit had reeled at the idea. Made him sick to his stomach. His father looked at naked women? Women other than his mother?

As he got older, his faith solidified the feelings he'd had as a boy. Women dancing in a place like this didn't interest him. They made him sad, sorry for whatever experience had led the dancer through the doors in the first place.

The bartender was staring at them. He was bald with a single thick hoop earring and a tight T-shirt. He grunted at them. "Can I help you?"

Joe took the lead. "Guess you heard about the murder." He strolled toward the bar. "The one at the other end of the street?"

The bartender picked up a wet glass and buffed it with a dish towel. He never took his eyes from Joe's. "Well, Officer." His voice was measured. "Can't say that I did."

Clay shifted his weight, studying the man. He knew something, no doubt. But as they'd expected, he wasn't talking. People didn't simply open up and start spilling details to detectives. They had to be coaxed.

Joe had a reputation for brilliant coaxing.

"Right." He sat down and patted the stool next to him.

Clay took that seat and glanced at the few patrons sitting alone at dark tables. Joe would ask the questions; he would cover. "We'll take a couple of waters."

The bartender scowled. He grabbed two glasses, filled them with water and slid them across the bar. "I don't know nothing, okay? Now get outta here before you hurt business."

Joe leaned on the bar and glanced around the room. "Business isn't exactly booming."

"We've been down a bit, so?" He snapped his towel at the glass and glared at Joe. "Crime goes up, business goes down, okay?"

Joe's smile faded. "Cut the line." He leaned in, a snarl in his tone. "You heard about the murder. You probably know who did it. We didn't come here for ice water, okay?"

"I told ya, I don't know nothin'." The bartender's accent was so thick he was hard to understand.

"Fine." Joe settled back onto his stool. "We'll stay all day."

Clay leaned his forearms on the bar. "We could always get the inspector. He'd love a look around here, don't you think?"

"Great idea." Joe started to stand.

"Wait!" The man blinked three times and ran his tongue along his lower lip. He dried a few more glasses, but his hands shook so hard he finally stopped. An exaggerated huff came from him, loud enough that a few patrons turned and looked. "Listen." He braced himself against the bar, his voice a whisper. "The dead guy was a crack dealer. His boys hang out down the street. At the Top Hat." He lowered his head a little. "Their rivals come from ten, eleven blocks south. They wanted to expand and the guys down the street wouldn't give." He straightened and Clay noticed his lip. It was covered with a fine layer of sweat beads. "I swear that's all I know. I ain't never seen any of 'em in here."

"Okay." Joe didn't miss a beat. "But you know who did it, who was the shooter, right?"

"Not his name, no." He gave a quick shake of his head. "Just where his boys come from."

Clay didn't believe him; he doubted Joe did either. But it was a start. If they were going to interview people down at the Top Hat, they needed to get going. Joe must've thought the same thing. He jotted something down in his notebook. Took the man's name and the bar's phone number.

Outside, they headed down the street. "Amazing," Joe turned to him and grinned, "how much a person can remember when they want a cop to leave 'em alone."

"You did good."

Joe shrugged. "I figured the Top Hat was the place. That's what the guys at briefing said this morning."

Already dusk was falling; shady types lurked near doorways and talked in a cluster as they leaned against the occasional dumpster. Clay squinted at the opposite side of the street. The other pair of detectives were nowhere around.

"Get the feeling all eyes are on us?" Joe raised his eyebrows. He spoke from the side of his mouth, just loud enough for Clay to hear.

"No question." Clay kept his pace brisk. He wasn't worried, just aware. The situation could easily become dangerous.

They reached the Top Hat and spoke to three people. After going round and round with each of them, they came away with a possible shooter name—the one that matched the name of the man the NYPD detectives already suspected. They also had a tip from a homeless man who refused to give his name. He said the shooter was working with two other guys, and that they were all still in the area.

They left the Top Hat at dusk, though the shadows along the alley made it seem darker. Again the other detectives were not in sight. "Better head back to the squad car." Joe motioned toward the opposite end of the street.

Clay's caution grew. Though the establishments where they'd conducted interviews had front entrances on a busier street, the murder occurred in the alley. Any information they might get would have to come from there, but like most big-city alleys, it was intersected by even smaller alleyways. And in the shadowy darkness, as they passed the smaller alleys, Clay kept one hand on his revolver.

"We got some good stuff," Joe whispered. Voices carried, and neither of them wanted to be heard talking about the interviews they'd done that afternoon.

"Yeah." Clay looked across the alley again, his eyes darting up and down the length of it. "I was hoping for something—"

A form jumped out from a dark doorway, and Clay felt a hand clamp on to his arm and jerk him off his feet before he had time to pull out his gun. Joe had been grabbed as well.

"Shut up!" A voice hissed at them. The smell of alcohol and old tobacco filled the tight space. "I've got a gun! Don't move."

Next to him, Joe stopped scuffling and grew still. "We're police. Don't do something stupid."

A different voice laughed at them, and the sound was anything but humorous. Clay blinked and tried to make out their faces. Two Asian-American men, both young and high as kites.

"That's right, Superman; you're finished."

His partner kicked Clay's leg. "You didn't think you could come snoopin' around without an official welcome, did you?" His snort was half laugh, half nervous energy. "We'll lose business because of you jerks."

Business? The pieces came rushing together. They were drug dealers; maybe part of a ring. And now they were wanted in a murder.

In a rush of movement, Joe pulled his gun and pushed the guy who claimed to be armed. "Up against the wall!" His voice was loud, stern. He pulled away enough to get his hand on his revolver, but as he did, both men lunged at him.

Clay pulled his own gun free when a gunshot exploded through the small, cramped space. Joe slumped against the door frame and inched down. His eyes found Clay's and his mouth formed the word, "Help!"

"Joe!" Clay grabbed hold of his friend, stopping him from sliding all the way to the ground.

Both men stepped back and stared at Joe. "Now you did it!" one of them snarled. He pushed his buddy aside and ran down the alley, toward the Top Hat.

"I . . . I didn't mean it. I didn't shoot him; I swear it." Before the last word was out, the second man turned and followed after his friend.

"Backup!" Clay shouted over his shoulder. Where were the other detectives? *God, let them hear me. Please* . . . "I need backup. Officer down!"

His hands were shaking so hard he could barely use them. But he kept one set of fingers firmly around Joe's arm, and with the other he yanked his cell phone from his shirt pocket and dialed 911.

"911. What's your emergency?"

Clay gritted his teeth. The other detectives had to be close. *Come on, God ... please let Joe be okay.* "Officer down!" He gave his location. "I need emergency backup."

Clay heard screeching tires in the distance and then footsteps, lots of them, running hard and growing closer. NYPD detectives ran up, breathless. "We called for help. Four cars have a bead on the suspects." Clay grabbed a quick breath. "An ambulance will be here any minute."

"Clay ..." Joe's voice was fading. His eyes were open, but they looked frozen, in shock. He gasped for breath and stared hard at Clay. "Tell ... tell Wanda I ... I love her."

"Keep him upright." One of the detectives moved in along the other side of Joe and held that arm. "He's losing a lot of blood."

Something caught Clay's eyes and he saw it was a red stain on the door frame, a smeary blood trail caused by Joe's body sliding down it. Joe'd been shot clear through the abdomen just beneath his flak jacket. He had blood at the corners of his mouth and near his nose, and his eyes were closing. His breathing was labored and slow.

"Joe!" Clay gave him a shake. It was okay; he was going to be okay. He had to be okay. "Hang in there. Wanda wants you to tell her yourself, man. Come on!"

Sirens drew closer, but would the ambulance even matter? Joe was bleeding to death; he had maybe a few minutes by the looks of it. Clay hung his head. "God ... please stop the bleeding. Make it stop, God ..." His prayer was loud enough for the other detectives to hear, but even as Clay prayed, Joe closed his eyes and his head fell forward.

"No!" Clay tightened his grip on Joe's shoulder. His heart raced and he wanted to shake something. No, Joe couldn't die. "God, don't let him die, please!"

The ambulance sped up and slammed to a stop a few feet away. Clay stayed beside Joe as he was placed on the stretcher, as the men loaded him into the back. He would go with him, of course. Travel in the back to the hospital and stay with him until they found a way to save his life. "Joe, hang on!" Clay shouted the words, in case Joe could hear him.

One of the other detectives grabbed Clay's shirt and pulled him back from the scene. "You can't go with him."

"Why? He needs me there." He jerked away and took a step toward the ambulance.

"Stop!" It was the other officer, the lead detective.

"I'm going with him!" Clay spun, breathless. The paramedics were closing the door; if he waited another few seconds it would be too late.

"You can't, Michaels." The detective's expression changed. "The medic told me they're doing CPR; they need all the space they can get."

"CPR?" Clay felt the ground beneath him turn to liquid.

The detective motioned toward the NYPD squad car, fifty yards away. "Come with us; we'll get you there just as fast."

He was in the squad car, the other detectives driving him to the emergency room, when he figured out what to do next. He grabbed his phone and dialed Jamie's number.

She picked up on the second ring. "Clay ... I'm glad you called."

"Jamie." He hesitated, not sure how to tell her. "Joe's been shot. I'm ... I'm not sure he's going to make it."

Her gasp was sharp, and he could picture her face. Beautiful, terrified. "What happened?"

"We were doing street interviews." He didn't want to tell her the other details—not yet. He closed his eyes and pinched the bridge of his nose. The detective at the wheel had the siren on, making the best time possible to the hospital. "Pray, Jamie. Please." He told her what hospital they were headed for. "And call Wanda, okay?"

"Clay ... are you all right?"

Her voice was balm for his soul, but he couldn't think about her that way; not now. He opened his eyes and stared at the city street ahead of them. The hospital wasn't far away. "Just pray."

As he hung up he realized something that ripped him apart inside, something that made him turn and lean his head against the car window. If they were doing CPR on Joe Reynolds, then he wasn't breathing. Which meant there was another reason they hadn't wanted Clay in the ambulance. Not so much because they had to start CPR.

But because they might have to stop it.

TWENTY-FOUR

It took Jamie twenty minutes to board the ferry for Manhattan.
Her first call had been to Wanda, and as she'd expected, her
friend was terrified, too scared to speak. She was able to say only that
she was on her way to the hospital and that she wanted Jamie to meet
her there.

Next she called a neighbor, who was more than willing to take
Sierra for the evening. Before she did that, she told Sierra that Clay's
friend had been hurt and she needed to be with him. Sierra didn't say
much, but her eyes shone. A strange mixture of fear and hope.

Jamie thought she knew why.

She hadn't seen or spoken about Clay in days, and Sierra wasn't
happy about the fact. Now, though, if Jamie was going to the hospital to meet him—even for a sad reason—then maybe she would
get to see Clay again.

Even so, they didn't talk about Clay. Every second counted, and
she wanted to be at the hospital when Wanda arrived. She took time
to do just one thing before she left. She went to her bedroom dresser,
where she kept Jake's Bible, and she lifted her left hand.

She'd always believed she would know. That when it was time
for her wedding ring to come off, she wouldn't have any doubts. She
studied the ring. Jake, her marriage to him, their days of loving and
laughing and making a life together, would always be a part of her.
But the ring . . .

It was time.

She worked it off her finger, held it in her hand a moment, then
opened the lid on a small blown-glass box. With careful fingers, she
set her wedding ring inside the box, and shut the lid.

Her hand seemed empty. She ran her thumb over the bare spot,
the pale indented circle at the base of her finger. It would bear for a

very long time the proof that Jake's ring had been there. Much as her heart would forever bear proof of Jake himself.

She took a quick step back, then left the room. She ran Sierra over to the neighbor's, then headed toward the ferry. The news was still working its way through her, convincing her that this latest, terrible thing really had happened. That Joe had been shot and critically wounded on the streets of Manhattan.

Jamie parked and made her way to the line for the ferry. Once aboard, she crossed to the opposite side, so she'd be first off when the boat docked. It was dark, the sky providing a cloud cover that kept temperatures from dropping too much. She found a place outside, near the railing, and stared at the skyline.

God . . . let him live. Guide the doctors and be with Wanda. Please, Father.

Peace wrapped its arms around her and she leaned into it.

Tragedy used to scare her to death. The news of it almost as much as the event itself. That was something else the terrorist attacks had taught her—how to handle bad news. Nothing could be as terrible as coming into the health club lobby that awful Tuesday morning and seeing the World Trade Center in flames on television.

She was anxious, lifting her voice to God every few minutes on Joe's behalf. But she was calm at the core, convinced that survival was possible—even in the face of great loss. And so it wasn't only thoughts of Joe that filled her mind as the boat sliced through the harbor. It was thoughts of Clay and Jake and Sierra and life.

And of her epiphany on the beach.

It wasn't that she'd avoided life all this time. She hadn't chosen death over life, not at first. Working at St. Paul's had been her way of choosing to live. It was that or crawl into bed and never get up again.

But after two years of volunteering, after hearing the stories of loss and praying with grieving relatives and letting strangers cry on her shoulder, Jamie had grown. She no longer needed a reason to get out of bed in the morning. God gave her that just by sending the morning, by giving her another day with Him.

Whether she spent that day with Sierra or the people at St. Paul's, she no longer felt like one of the walking dead, the empty-eyed grievers who still colored the Manhattan landscape. Rather she was excited about life, about what God wanted to do with her and through her as long as she drew breath. It only made sense that she'd outgrown her time at Ground Zero. She could find purpose at St. Paul's, but she couldn't move on there.

She looked at the sky and saw Jake's image, his face smiling at her, giving her that knowing look. The one that told her he knew what she needed to do, and she knew it too. Now all she had to do was make the decision.

"Choose life, right, Jake?" Tears blurred her eyes. "Even with someone new. That's what you want me to do, isn't it?"

His eyes were as clear as if he were standing in front of her, clear and blue and filled with a love that she hadn't understood when he was alive. "Jake . . ."

The image held for a moment longer. Then it faded and blurred and became night sky. Yes, that's exactly what he would want her to do. Him and God Almighty.

See, I set before you now life and prosperity, death and destruction . . . Choose life!

That was why God brought Clay into her life in the first place. That she might be moved forward in the healing process, past the point of St. Paul's and toward the possibility of new life.

New love.

Just the thought of Clay made her breath catch in her throat. As desperate as the situation was, she felt a little bit like Sierra. Frightened and filled with concern, but with eyes that shone with hope. Because in a very little while she would see Clay again. And at some point, she'd tell him about her day, how she'd figured things out on a cold lonely beach, and how wrong she'd been before.

How much she needed him.

But what about Joe? What if he didn't make it? Clay had sounded desperately worried. She wanted to be with Clay, to pray with him and help him believe everything would work out. She pressed into the railing, urging the boat to move faster.

They needed to sit by Joe and coax him to hold on, because with God Almighty calling the shots, life—with all its painful turns and

gut-wrenching losses—still had tremendous hope even in the sim-
plicity of a sunrise.

Jamie had made the choice to choose life. Now, where Joe was
concerned, she would pray for it.

The boat pulled up to the dock, and Jamie had a cab in record
time. She was still praying for Joe when they arrived at the hospital
and she paid the driver. Now that she'd come this far, she couldn't
wait to find Clay, and she ran into the lobby and down the hall
toward the emergency room.

Clay was the first person she saw.

He had his back to her, his arms crossed, head hung. He wore his
uniform, and next to him sat two detectives, talking to a third uniformed officer with a notepad. Their conversation was hushed, rel-
egated to the far corner of the waiting room.

Jamie made her way closer, and when she was halfway there,
Clay turned. His eyes found hers, and her heart skipped. How could
she have considered leaving this man, losing him, just because his
brother was Eric Michaels? The entire situation seemed ludicrous
now. After all, if Eric made her uncomfortable, she could keep her
distance from him.

But she couldn't keep her distance from Clay. Not a minute longer.

In as much time as it took him to look at her she understood
that, understood it to the core of her being. He came to her, and
they met in the middle, falling into an embrace that was seeped in
sorrow and relief. Sorrow over Joe; relief that despite the strange
circumstances, they'd found their way back together.

Clay held her for a long time, his arms around her waist, hers
around his neck. Being with him like this was better than she
could've dreamed. She closed her eyes and savored it. Life. Bubbling
through her and filling her with a sort of joy that left her speechless.
God . . . I don't want him to ever let go. Please, God.

She opened her eyes. The officers had looked away. The waiting room offered little privacy, but at least the others weren't watching. She pressed her face against Clay's, still relishing the feel of his
arms around her waist. "How is he?"

"Alive." Clay drew back. He searched her eyes. "They're operating, but it doesn't look good. The bullet messed up his insides pretty

good." His cheeks were red and blotchy, his expression pained. "They told us to expect the worst."

Jamie felt her heart sink to her ankles. "No . . ." She shook her head and tightened her grip on Clay's arms. "We can't give up."

"I know." Determination filled his eyes. "I've been praying."

"Me too." She paused. This wasn't the time, really. But she had to tell him, had to share what had happened to her that day. "Clay, there's something I want you to know."

Concern filled his face. Clearly he expected her to say that though she had come, it was only as a show of support because of Joe. Not because she'd changed her mind about Clay or the situation with Eric.

"Relax. It's a good thing."

He studied her, his brow knit together. "Good?"

"Yes." She felt the corners of her mouth lift some. She eased her thumb along the fine lines in his forehead. "Sierra and I would like to spend Thanksgiving with you and your family." Even with the sadness and pain in her heart because of Joe, she felt her eyes dance a little. "If we're still welcome, that is."

"What about Eric?" He moved his hands up to her shoulders and studied her. As if she might vanish if he didn't hold on to her. "You're okay with him? Dinner's at his house."

"God showed me something today." She looped her hands around the back of his neck. "I lost Jake on September 11; he was never alive after that." A wave of sorrow came over her, but she rode it out. "Every memory I have from that point on wasn't with Jake; it was with Eric. A stranger who came to our house to learn how to be the kind of father and family man God wanted him to be."

Clay nodded, studying her, making sure she believed the words she was saying. "You mean it?"

"Yes." She hugged him for a long while before pulling back and finding his eyes. "Eric was never Jake, and if he wasn't Jake, then what's the problem? He's just a nice guy who looks a lot like my husband."

For a moment, Clay's mouth hung open. Then he shook his head. "I prayed for this, Jamie. That you'd understand about Eric. But when you didn't take my calls, I—"

"Shhh." She held her finger up to his lips. "I understand." They released their hold on each other, and she led him to a pair of seats a few yards away from the other officers. When they sat down, she wove her fingers between his. "We need another miracle tonight. Let's pray for Joe."

Clay held her eyes a moment, then bowed his head and began to pray. He begged God for the same things Jamie had been asking for. That Joe would live; that he would have no lasting effects from the terrible gunshot wound.

When the prayer was over, they spotted Wanda. She was just entering the emergency room, frantic fear scrawled across her face. Right away she saw them and she started to cry. "Jamie!"

She stood and met her friend, holding her even when her legs buckled. Clay was on his feet, helping ease Wanda into a chair, but she was unstable. Dizzy from the shock. When she was seated between them, she leaned forward, clearly trying to fight what must've been a consuming panic. "How is he? Can I see him?"

Clay gave her the update, and when he got to the part about his chances, Wanda broke down, weeping, clinging to both of them.

"I . . . I waited too long!" She could barely breathe for the sobs. "I can't . . . lose him now." She looked at Jamie, her expression frozen in regret. "I love him, Jamie. I love him."

They stayed that way most of the night, long after the other detectives reported that the suspects had been arrested, along with four other men—all part of the drug ring responsible for the murder in the alley, as well as a host of other unsolved crimes. Once they'd delivered that news, the other detectives said their good-byes and their condolences.

And still the three of them stayed, Jamie and Clay on either side of Wanda, taking turns holding her while she cried, comforting her and listening to her talk about Joe and how much she'd missed him and how come she couldn't have told him so sooner.

"Pride, that's what it was." She came up with this conclusion sometime around four in the morning. "I would've called him back the day he left if it weren't for my cursed pride."

Jamie shot a look at Clay as relief made its way through her. *Thank You, God . . . that it's not ten years from now and me saying those words about Clay.*

The night wore on, and twice doctors reported no change. Joe was still in critical condition, still on life support, his body trying to adjust to the massive blood loss and internal injuries. Jamie was exhausted, but they had to hold on. News could come at any minute.

The group grew quiet, lost in their own prayers and thoughts. Sometime around seven that morning, Clay was pacing along the window area, and Wanda had her face in her hands when a doctor entered the waiting room.

He was grinning.

All three of them were on their feet, meeting the doctor. Only Clay could find the words to speak. "How is he?"

"I'm amazed, really. A half hour ago his vital signs had a sudden improvement. We took him off life support, and he's doing well." The doctor gave a shake of his head. "*Very* well. Almost as if someone breathed life into him."

"Oh my . . ." Wanda lifted her fingers slowly to her mouth. Her eyes found Clay's and then Jamie's. "For the past hour I changed my prayer. I told God if he'd let Joe live, I'd spend the rest of my days by that man's side, following the Lord together, the way we should have from the beginning."

Chills ran down Jamie's arms.

The doctor gave Wanda a knowing nod. "I've seen this kind of thing too often to doubt it. God still works miracles today; I'm convinced." He paused. "You've been here all night. You can come in and see him if you'd like. He's trying to come around."

"Oh, thank God!" Wanda hugged the doctor. "He's giving me one more chance!"

Jamie rubbed her arms to ward off another series of chills. How was it possible? Two hours ago Joe barely clung to life, and now he was breathing on his own, waking up? The power of God at work in their presence was enough to drop her to her knees.

Instead she took Clay's hand and the three of them followed the doctor to Joe's room. He was hooked to half a dozen machines, and he had tubes running into his nose and arms. But otherwise he looked well. His midsection was bandaged and a light sheet covered him to his waist.

Wanda looked at the doctor. "Can I . . . can I touch him?"

Joe moved his lips and made a weak attempt at clearing his throat. "Doc . . ." His voice was scratchy. "That's my Wanda." He struggled, wincing from the pain. "You better . . . tell her yes."

"Joe!" She framed his face with her hands and kissed him square on the mouth. "I'm sorry! It wasn't all your fault, it was mine." She was crying again, crying and smiling and holding on to Joe the same way Jamie had hung on to Clay hours earlier. Her words spilled out almost too fast to understand. "I should've gone after you when Jimmy died, and instead I made a stupid mistake and lost you. I lost you, but it was my pride." She took a quick breath. "My pride, I tell you. It kept me from calling when I should've, and now it almost kept me from telling you the most important thing, because Joe Reynolds, I have pride something fierce! But guess what?"

He blinked and his eyes opened just enough to see her. "You won . . . the speed-talking award?"

She stopped and sat a bit straighter. Then her eyes lit up, and she looked at Jamie and Clay. "He's gonna be fine! If he's got his humor, he's gonna be just fine."

The slits in Joe's eyes grew wider. He looked around the room, wincing again as he shifted himself higher on his pillow. "Michaels?"

"I'm here." Clay took a step forward.

"Tell me they got those punks." His words were slow, but he was coming back a little more every few minutes.

Clay smiled and Jamie moved in beside him. "Got 'em good, buddy. Real good."

"Attempted murder?" He managed a weak smile.

Jamie understood. *Attempted* murder, because Joe had every intention of surviving the shooting. She felt something warm work its way through her, and she knew what it was. Blessed assurance. The certainty that God had indeed worked not just one miracle in their midst by bringing her to the understanding that she could see Clay again. But He'd worked the miracle of Joe's life as well.

Clay took another step closer and put his hand on Joe's knee. "More than that." He looked at Jamie. "The guys were wanted for a bunch of drug deals and one other murder. They were part of a ring."

"Scary." Jamie felt the blood leave her face.

"Yeah." Clay gave her a look that told her he'd known this information all night, but hadn't wanted to share it until now.

Jamie looked at the floor near her feet, too shocked to speak. Fear tap-danced around Jamie but didn't touch her. It could have been Clay just as easily. She met his eyes and looped her arm through his. "I'm so glad they caught them."

Joe gave a slow nod and looked at Jamie. He shifted his gaze to Clay. "What else they get 'em for?"

"Besides attempted murder?" Clay grinned at his friend. "Homicide in the alley killing and a number of drug charges."

Joe lifted his head a few inches off the pillow. "They were the killers?"

"Not sure which one was the shooter, but the police think one of 'em is their guy."

"Okay, then ask the doc . . . when I can leave." His voice was still scratchy, his words still slow. He smiled at Wanda. "That news calls for a party."

"No parties." Wanda kissed him on the cheek. The mood changed as she grew quiet, searching his eyes. "You have to get better, Joe. And when you go back to L.A. you have to take me and the kids with you." Her voice was softer, not the hysterical weeping or giddy excitement from earlier, but a deep warmth that filled the room. "I love you, Joe Reynolds. God gave me the chance to tell you. This time I'm not going to miss it."

Clay shifted and pulled Jamie into another embrace. Not as desperate as the one they'd shared when she first arrived at the hospital, but one of joy and contentment.

He whispered close to her ear. "I think we should leave them alone."

"Me too." Jamie stifled a giggle and let herself get lost in Clay's eyes. "Besides, you have a call to make."

"I do?" He nuzzled his nose against hers.

"Yes." Now that Joe was doing better, she allowed herself to be lost in the feelings he stirred in her. She wanted to kiss him, wanted it as much as she wanted her next breath. But they had other details to take care of first.

"Okay, Miss Jamie." He held her closer, a lazy smile hanging on his lips, his eyes filled with desire. "Who do I have to call?"

"Your brother, so you can tell him the news. Sierra and I are coming for Thanksgiving."

TWENTY-FIVE

Jamie was nervous.

Whatever she told herself or Clay or Sue or anyone else, her stomach was tight and her heart raced even when she was sitting still. For three years she had accepted she would never see Eric Michaels again, and now, in a few days, she was about to do just that. The level of anxiety over the matter hit her again the Wednesday morning before Thanksgiving. She was about to have dinner with Eric and his wife; the idea still seemed like something from a dream.

Or a nightmare.

The flight took forever, and Jamie tried not to think about Eric. There were more pressing matters. How fast the plane could fly, for instance. Only two days had passed since she'd been with Clay, but she couldn't wait to see him. It seemed forever before the plane finally circled over Burbank and came in for a smooth landing.

"I'm excited, Mommy. I've never seen California." Sierra squeezed Jamie's hand as they stepped off the plane and onto the jetway.

"I think you'll like it." Jamie grinned at her. They held hands as they headed down the concourse toward security. She spotted Clay just as his eyes found her through the crowd.

"Look!" Sierra let go of her hand and did a few jumps. "It's Clay! Can I go see him?"

Jamie laughed, her eyes still locked on his. "Just don't knock anyone down."

She took off toward Clay, her red backpack bouncing, and when she reached him, she threw her arms around his waist. He stooped down and handed her a long-stemmed white rose. Then he gave her a red one and nodded toward Jamie.

"Mommy!" Sierra ran the few feet that separated them and handed the flower over. "Here! It's from Clay."

Jamie stopped and took the rose. She looked at Clay and thanked him with her eyes. A few seconds later she and Sierra were at his side. He leaned close and kissed Jamie. "I missed you." He spoke the words low, near her ear. "Two days felt like forever."

"I know." Her cheeks burned, but she didn't chide herself. So what if she felt like a schoolgirl in Clay's presence? She refused to feel guilty or ashamed. God had brought him into her life, everything about him was a blessing from God. The feelings he stirred in her heart were something everyone should be so blessed to feel.

The three of them went to the baggage area, where they found Jamie's suitcase and Sierra's duffel bag, then they headed for Clay's Jeep. As they walked, Sierra rattled on about Wrinkles staying with the neighbor and how she'd explained the trip to the cat so the cat wouldn't worry about her.

"But did you take the dress-up clothes to the neighbor's house?" Clay tried to look serious. "What will Wrinkles do without his fancy socks for a whole week?"

Sierra giggled and skipped along between them. "You're silly, Clay."

"Only with my jester hat."

By the time Jamie and Sierra checked in to their hotel, and the three of them found lunch, the day was almost over. They spent the afternoon touring Hollywood and Malibu Beach.

Every hour or so Jamie remembered that the meeting with Eric was coming. But for the most part her anxiety didn't interfere with the day.

They had dinner at Gladstone's on the beach and were back at the hotel by nine o'clock. Clay walked them to their door and made sure they got inside safely. Sierra was digging through her duffel bag looking for her nightgown when Clay bid them good-bye.

Before he left, Jamie stepped just into the hallway, pulled the door partially shut behind her, and smiled at him. "I can't believe we had dinner on the beach in November."

"I told you." He raised an eyebrow at her. "California's not too bad." His arms circled her waist and drew her close.

"Mmmm." She looked deep into his eyes. "I'm beginning to see that."

He searched her face, and it was clear what he was thinking before he said it. "Are you okay? About tomorrow?"

"Yes." Her smile eased. It was the truth. She was nervous, yes. But not enough to stop her from going ahead with the meeting. "I'm fine."

"Good." He took one hand from her waist and slid his fingers along the side of her face. "I'm so glad you came, Jamie."

"Me too." He was going to kiss her, and she could hardly wait. But just as he moved closer, a split second before his lips touched hers, Sierra opened the door.

"Hey, guys!" She had her nightgown in her hands. At the sight of the two of them, she giggled.

Jamie exhaled her frustration, then shook her head with a laugh. "Did you need something, dear?"

She giggled again. "My toothbrush."

"On that note . . ." Clay took a step back and chuckled. "Guess I better get going." He winked at Sierra and gave Jamie a look that would make it hard to fall asleep later. "I had a wonderful day."

"Me too." Sierra grinned at him, clearly happy that the two of them had been hugging.

"I think we all did." Jamie hoped he could read her eyes, that given the chance she would've spent as long as he liked kissing him in the hallway. But once again the moment would have to wait.

Clay left, and Sierra was asleep in fifteen minutes. But not Jamie. She lay there, staring at the ceiling, half the time wondering what she was doing, the other half wishing morning would come.

She wasn't sure when she drifted to sleep, but when she woke the next morning, she sat straight up, overcome by a burst of anxiety that made her head spin and left her sick to her stomach. Once as a young girl she visited Six Flags with her parents on a day when there were no lines. Ten rides on the giant wooden roller coaster and she wasn't sure she'd ever feel normal again.

That's how she felt now.

She looked at Sierra, sleeping in the other bed. Maybe they shouldn't have come; she hadn't told Sierra the truth about Eric, that he was Clay's brother. Now it might feel rushed, forced. She wasn't sure why she'd waited so long. Maybe because the news would be difficult for Sierra; maybe because it would be too difficult for herself.

She glanced at her suitcase. She could still do it. Grab her clothes, stuff them inside, wake Sierra, and catch a cab to the airport. It wasn't too late.

The air in the hotel room was stuffy. Jamie stood, went to the window, and opened the drapes. She pressed her forehead against the cool glass and realized she was holding her breath. No wonder the air felt stuffy; she wasn't getting any of it.

She exhaled.

As she did so, she found a point of balance again. She was here because she wanted to be, because the strength of her feelings for Clay Michaels wouldn't be denied. Maybe they would wind up friends, Internet pen pals who kept in touch from opposite sides of the country. Or maybe one day they'd be something much more.

But Eric?

She took in a slow breath and stared at the already busy Ventura Boulevard, just beyond the parking lot. Eric was a nice man with an uncanny resemblance to Jake. But Eric wasn't Jake, nor was he some ex-lover she needed to avoid. He'd never belonged to her, not even when she thought she was married to him.

So what was the problem? Why the nervous stomach and—

"Mommy?"

Jamie spun around and found a quick smile. "Good morning, honey." She crossed the room and sat on the edge of Sierra's bed. "Happy Thanksgiving."

She rubbed her eyes and gave Jamie a sleepy grin. "What time is Clay coming?"

"In a few hours."

It was time to tell Sierra the truth. Jamie brushed her daughter's bangs with her fingertips and felt a lump in her throat. Sierra had been just four when the terrorist attacks hit. Chances were she wouldn't recognize Eric if they passed on the street.

"I like when you play with my hair, Mommy." Sierra leaned back into the pillow, a dreamy look on her face.

"I like it too."

Jamie studied her daughter. No, Sierra might not recognize Eric, but what if something serious did come of Jamie's relationship with Clay? One day she would have to know the truth. The same way she'd needed the truth about Eric not being Jake. Sierra deserved to know who Eric was.

Jamie cleared her throat. "Honey, I have something to tell you." She brushed her knuckles against Sierra's cheek. "Something about Clay's brother."

Sierra made a face. "Clay's brother? We're having dinner at his place today, right?"

"Yes." Fear was making a logjam of her throat. Jamie swallowed hard. "Sweetie, this is sort of a strange thing." She uttered a soft laugh. "I don't really believe it myself, but here's the deal. Remember the man who looked like Daddy? The one in your picture on your dresser?"

Sierra leaned up on her elbows, more interested than before. "My second daddy, the one with his own family."

"Right, well—" she pursed her lips, searching for the words— "that man is Clay's brother." She hesitated. "Isn't that strange?"

"Clay's brother is Mr. Michaels, the man we thought was Daddy?" Sierra sat all the way up now, her eyes wide.

"Yes." Jamie slumped. Clearly Sierra thought about Eric; otherwise she wouldn't have remembered his name. She clenched her fists. "I'm sorry, honey. I didn't know about this when I met Clay that day on the ferryboat. I just found out a little while ago."

"They're brothers?" Sierra looked toward the window, eyes distant.

"Yes." Jamie braced herself for what was ahead. Sierra might break down and cry, even be afraid to see the man again. Or maybe she would be confused, unwilling to go to the Thanksgiving dinner.

Instead Sierra turned her eyes back to Jamie and clapped her hands. "So I get to see Clay *and* Mr. Michaels, all in one day?"

Once again Jamie couldn't draw a breath. She was too intent on her daughter, waiting for the bad reaction she'd been dreading. "You're . . . you're not upset?"

"No." Sierra's eyes danced. "Remember, Mommy? I told you I wanted to see him again, the man I thought was my daddy." She grinned. "Now I get to." Her feet slid over the edge of the bed and she hopped onto the floor. "It's going to be the bestest Thanksgiving Day ever."

"But he's not your daddy." Jamie searched her daughter's eyes. "You understand that, right?"

Sierra's smile faded. "Daddy died in the Twin Towers." She paused, thoughtful. "Mr. Michaels might look like him, but he isn't him. I know that."

Jamie exhaled. All that worry, all the dread, and of the two of them, her daughter had the best grip on the situation. Jamie felt herself relax, and almost at the same time she looked at the clock. "Yikes." She tousled Sierra's long golden hair. "We'd better get ready."

Anxiety played with Jamie's mind while she showered and did her hair, even into the final minutes before Clay arrived. But the moment she saw him, her fears faded. They hugged, and his eyes held the questions she'd been asking herself all morning.

"I'm fine." She grabbed her purse and Sierra's hand. "Let's go have Thanksgiving dinner." She grinned at her daughter. "Sierra says it's going to be the bestest one yet."

They left the room happy and laughing and looking forward to the day. Because no matter how strange or bizarre the situation was, no matter how uncomfortable she might feel in Eric's house, meeting his wife, watching him with his family, it didn't matter.

Her feelings for Clay Michaels were stronger.

Eric looked out the window for the fifth time in as many minutes. His heart thudded deep within him, the way it did every time he stopped moving. They would be there any minute, Clay and Jamie and Sierra.

He understood his pounding heart. It simply wouldn't believe it was possible. Clay went to New York City and met Jamie Bryan? The woman he'd learned to love in those terrible days after September 11? The woman he'd worked so hard to put out of his mind?

There had been no wavering in Clay's voice when he called. His feelings for Jamie were strong and certain. Yes, she'd struggled with the idea that the two of them were brothers. She hadn't planned on seeing him again, any more than he'd planned on seeing her. But apparently she'd reached some sort of resolution in her mind, because she had flown to Los Angeles with Sierra, and now—at any time— she would be there.

Jamie Bryan. Walking into his world.

The last time they were together they'd had an emotional intimacy that was typically reserved for married couples. And why not? For more than two months they both believed they were married.

And what about Sierra?

It had killed him to tell her good-bye. He remembered it still, his last morning with her, curling her hair and holding back tears as she chattered about her little friend. Katy, wasn't it? And how nice it was that Mommy was going to church with them. And he had told her that next week maybe Mommy should curl her hair, that Mommy might do an even better job than him.

Eric pushed the memories away and stared out the window, searching for Clay's Jeep.

They'd told Josh the facts, that his uncle Clay had met up with the woman Eric had lived with. They'd told their son about Eric's time in New York before. But the blank look on Josh's face the other day told Eric that at eleven years old, his son still didn't quite understand. He seemed content that his parents were happy; nothing else mattered.

Josh was upstairs getting ready now; same with Laura.

A car pulled onto their street, but it was too small to be Clay's. Eric had to watch for them, had to see them pull up. Because unless he saw it for himself, he wouldn't believe it. Jamie Bryan? About to walk through his door? Not just Jamie, but Sierra. Sweet little Sierra, the little girl who captured his heart from the moment he woke up in a New York hospital with amnesia.

She would be . . . how old? Seven, at least.

The memories stirred in his soul, lifting and falling and taking wind like the last remains of autumn's fallen leaves.

Had it been three years since that final good-bye? He could see it all, feel the emotions from that day. The way he'd hugged Sierra in the entryway of her home, hours before his flight back to Los Angeles. He and Jamie had agreed to keep up the facade, pretending he was her daddy. She was too young to understand anything different. And so, in keeping with the act, he bid her good-bye the way he might've any other time. He played with her curls and at her request he promised to give her a horsie ride that night when he returned.

Only he never returned. Because by then he'd figured out who he was and where he belonged. Two hours later he stood in LaGuardia Airport telling Jamie good-bye, hugging her, holding her. Thanking her for helping him find his way back. They held hands until the last minute, when Laura appeared in the distance with a stream of passengers.

What he'd told Clay several weeks earlier had been right on. His physical healing, and the transformation in his life, had been only part of the miracle. The other part was that he'd been able to leave Jamie.

He felt someone behind him and he turned. "Laura."

Her expression was pained. "Do you have to stand there waiting like that?" Her voice was soft, defeated. "She'll be here soon enough."

"Hey." He pulled away from the window and faced her. A quiet warmth filled his tone. "Laura . . . don't be like that. This isn't my fault."

"It isn't anyone's fault. That's just it." She hugged herself tight. "Fault doesn't change how I feel."

He ran his knuckle along her brow. "How do you feel?"

"Scared." Her answer was quick, pointed. "Sometimes scared to death."

"Ah, Laura . . ." His heart went out to her. Of course she was anxious. The whole situation was too strange to believe. He brushed a piece of her blonde hair off her face and touched his lips to hers. "Clay met a woman and fell in love. The woman happened to be Jamie Bryan. It has nothing to do with you and me, okay? Don't be afraid."

"I'm trying not to, Eric." She looked straight to his heart. "You lived with her for three months. I keep thinking . . ." She hesitated and lifted her hands. "I don't know. I keep thinking you must've been in love with her." Defeat colored her eyes again. "I picture you spending that much time with another woman and I can't help but wonder what it was like. Not just the physical stuff, but the emotional connection."

He ached for the pain in her eyes. This was the road they never traveled, the one that took him back in time to Jamie Bryan. He'd been honest with her from the beginning, but once he'd shared the details, he locked them away in a place he never intended to go again. Over the years, when she expressed doubts about that time in his life, he quickly dismissed them.

But now . . .

"Laura." He took gentle hold of her shoulders. "I kept nothing from you. Yes . . ." He swallowed, praying she would believe him. Grateful it was the truth. "We kissed a few times, but nothing more. Neither of us wanted to be intimate unless I remembered."

"But you must've loved her, Eric. Or at least felt like you loved her."

This was the hard part. What was love, really? Eric leaned against the windowpane. "I thought I was her husband; I allowed myself to *believe* I loved her." He hung his head and rubbed the muscles in his neck. When he looked up he exhaled hard. "I thought it was the right thing, Laura. Whatever it was, God used it for good. But you know how I feel. I left Jamie planning to never look back."

She held his eyes for a long time. Then she nodded, her expression still troubled, but less doubtful. "Okay." She leaned up and kissed his cheek. "Maybe it's a bad case of morning sickness." She blew a wisp of hair off her forehead. "Anyway, Josh is still in the shower. I have to finish my makeup." She bit her lip. "I don't want to be out here when they pull up."

He waited until she was gone, then he turned around and looked out the window. If only the memories weren't so vivid. How many times after they knew the truth about his blood type, and before he realized who he was, had she looked in his eyes and told him what she was feeling.

That sometimes she hoped he would stay forever and never find his way back.

He drew in a sharp breath and sat on the edge of the windowsill.

After he left her, it was all he could do to put her out of his mind. God had given him the best way. He prayed for her. It wasn't something he talked about with anyone but God, but it was the least he could do. The least and the most.

Daily, hourly sometimes, he prayed that Jamie and Sierra would survive the loss of first Jake, and then him, his presence in their lives. That Jamie would grow strong in her new faith and lean on Christ when she wasn't sure she could make it through another day. And that ultimately, one day—if her heart allowed it—she might find someone else to love.

That was the most amazing part. All those prayers, all that time when he asked God to take care of Jamie, he still could hardly let himself believe this was the answer he'd prayed about. His own brother? A chill passed over his arms. *God . . . Your ways are so far beyond ours. Get us through this day, please. Let it be okay with everyone. For Clay's sake . . . and Jamie's.*

Be still . . . and know that I am God.

What? Eric stood up. He leaned against the window frame and closed his eyes. The response was so quick, so clear. Often when he prayed, he had a sense, a knowing that the Lord wanted him to do one thing or another. But this time . . .

The answer had been audible. Maybe not in the way most people might hear it. But no question someplace in his soul Eric had *heard* the words. *Be still and know that I am God.* It was a verse he'd learned first from Jake Bryan's Bible. During his days of amnesia, it had taught Eric he couldn't rush God, couldn't force himself to remember. Rather, he was to be still and let God do the work.

Now God was calling him to that again. Be still and wait; and know that whatever happened that day, God was in control.

His mouth was dry, his heart heavy with the weight of his memories. He went to the kitchen, put the kettle on, and grabbed a mug. A cup of coffee would help clear the cobwebs. After a few minutes the water came to a boil, and just as he poured his cup, he heard a knock at the door and the sound of it opening.

"Eric?" Clay's happy voice didn't sound forced, but it wasn't quite natural either.

No wonder. Clay couldn't help but feel the strain of the situation, same as the rest of them. "Coming." He left his coffee on the counter and headed for the front door.

Clay was just walking through the door. "Jamie's getting something from the car." He stepped inside.

Behind him came Sierra. A taller, older version of Sierra.

She saw him and there was a flicker of recognition. "Hi, Mr. Michaels." Her chin stayed tucked close to her chest, her eyes shy and nervous.

Eric's throat was thick. Too thick to speak. She was different now, not the same sprite she'd been as a four-year-old. This Sierra was more mature, touched by sorrow. He held out his arms. "Hi, Sierra."

With slow, uncertain steps she came and hugged him. Then she looked into his eyes and smiled. "My mom told me about when you lived with us." Her eyes softened and in them was a hint of the Sierra he'd so easily loved as a daughter. "I understand now."

"Sierra understands a lot." Clay stood a few feet away, his eyes damp.

At the sound of Clay's voice, Sierra lit up, skipped across the room, and took Clay's hand. Suddenly she was just a taller version of the girl Eric had known. "We have to tell him about Wrinkles and the jester hat, okay?"

Eric blinked. What was this? Sierra barely remembered him, but Clay . . . clearly she was taken with him. A strange sort of pain seared Eric's heart, but only for an instant. This was what he had prayed for. It was right. The little Sierra, the one he gave butterfly kisses to, was gone forever. She had never belonged to him in the first place, but to her father, Jake Bryan.

And by the way things looked, this new Sierra belonged to Clay.

Footsteps sounded in the doorway, and Eric felt his heart stand still. Jamie walked in, looking exactly as he remembered her, and her eyes found his. In her hands was a thick bouquet of orange and yellow flowers. She hesitated. "These are for you and Laura." Her voice was thick.

He remembered enough to know she was on the verge of tears. His eyes looked deep into hers, to the places they'd shared together. "Thanks." There was a sound from upstairs. "Laura'll be down in a minute."

"Good. I'm anxious to meet her."

Eric shifted his weight. He wasn't sure what to do, whether to go to her the way he wanted to, tell her he was so glad she'd survived the past few years. Or whether to keep his distance.

In the end she made the first move. She set the flowers down near the door and erased the years between them in a single heart-beat. Her arms came around his neck and he held her. It was not a hug borne of passion, but of pain. A hug that allowed them to say everything they couldn't voice, everything that only the two of them would ever understand. And for a handful of seconds, they were the only two in the room.

When he took a step back, her eyes were bright with tears. But she uttered a sound that was mostly laugh. "Can you believe this?" She laughed again and wiped at her eyes.

"No." He cleared his throat, trying to push his words past his emotions. "I knew I wouldn't believe it until you walked through the door."

"Me neither." She took his hands, squeezed them once and let go. "It's amazing."

"It is." And that's when he noticed it. There was something different about her. Something in her easy smile, a depth in her eyes. Then it hit him.

She was at peace.

In their short time together, he'd never seen her like this. First, because she was so determined to help him remember that he was Jake; next, because of the doubts that eventually crept in; and finally because she had to help him find his real identity. Even in the end, when she'd found faith in Christ and strength enough to let him go, even when she told him good-bye at LaGuardia, she wasn't at peace. Not like she was now.

He returned her smile. As strange as things were, this . . . this meeting again was going to be okay. He could feel it in his soul.

The moment changed. Memories faded and yesterday melted away. Eric took another step back and felt himself being brought back to the present. The entire exchange with Jamie had taken no more than a few seconds, and now he turned his attention to Clay. "Hey, brother. Glad you're here." He shook Clay's hand and grinned. "You know Laura's turkeys."

"Okay, I heard my name." Laura was at the top of the stairs, with Josh behind her. Her voice sounded as bright and sunny as she looked. Gone were the doubts and fears from her eyes. In their place was the confidence Eric loved. Confidence and cheerfulness and an underlying determination that she would not play victim that day.

She took the stairs with a spring in her step, hugged Clay, and then smiled first at Sierra, then at Jamie. "I'm Laura." She put her hand on Jamie's shoulder. "I'm glad you could come."

Whatever Laura had done upstairs must've involved more than makeup and mirrors. For this sort of transformation, she probably spent most of the time on her knees. Eric's love for her swelled. *You go, Laura. Thata girl.*

Jamie picked up the flowers and handed them to her. "These are for you." She gave Laura a warm smile. "Thanks ... for making us feel welcome."

"Well—" she returned the smile, utterly genuine—"I imagine God brought us together to be friends."

"Yes." Jamie's eyes were wet again. "I think so too."

Laura turned to Josh. "This is Josh, he's eleven."

"Hi." Jamie shook his hand. "You have a nice home here." She smiled at Clay and reached for Sierra's hand. "This is my daughter, Sierra."

Laura put her hands on her knees and stooped down. "Sierra. What a pretty name." She angled her head. "I'm glad you're here."

Sierra returned to her place by Clay. "Thank you."

From where he stood, Eric watched the whole thing, beaming. He looked around the room at Clay and Sierra, Jamie and Laura and Josh and suddenly Laura looked at him, a look that lingered. Her eyes sparkled and in her smile he saw something. It wasn't an act. Laura was okay. Despite all the worry she was going to be fine.

In fact, they all were.

TWENTY-SIX

He was still the mirror image of Jake.

From the moment she walked through Eric Michaels's door, that was what surprised Jamie most of all. She had expected him to look different, as if maybe now that his injuries were completely healed, now that his burns had faded from his face and arms, he would have his own look.

An Eric Michaels look.

But the resemblance between him and Jake was uncanny, amazing. Same face and build, same dark hair and blue eyes. When she walked through the door and saw him, it was all she could do to keep from gasping. She had wanted to run to Clay, take his hand, and lean on him for support, but she had to deal with the man standing before her.

Seeing Eric was like seeing a ghost.

Within her, though, she felt God at work, felt Him leading her through the moment, giving her perspective, and reminding her of the truth. Eric wasn't Jake. That truth came quick and served as a lead rope while she blindly walked through those first few minutes.

It wasn't until she met Laura that the swirling emotions in her heart settled. Laura was wonderful. Kind and upbeat, content with the situation in a way that was surprising. Jamie had wondered several times how difficult it must've been for her, how strange she would've felt if the tables were turned. If Jake had disappeared for three months only to resurface a victim of amnesia and having lived with another woman all that time.

But Laura seemed at ease, warm and welcoming. She was pretty, fair skinned with blonde hair and sparkling eyes. Their son, Josh, was a mix between his mother and father. He had her coloring and wider cheekbones rather than Eric's chiseled face. But what struck Jamie the most about him was his easy smile, his comfortable expression. If this boy had been neglected by Eric before September 11, it was impossible to tell now. He was obviously a happy, well-adjusted child. For some reason, that struck a chord of hope in Jamie.

Because in a very clear way, Josh Michaels's life was different because of what God did through Jake. The words in Jake's journal, and the power of the highlighted sections in Jake's Bible, had changed Eric. In the process, they'd changed Josh too.

It was part of Jake's legacy, really. Seeing that in person was far more powerful than she'd ever imagined.

Despite the dozens of thoughts and memories and observations fighting for position in Jamie's mind, she felt comfortable at the Michaels' home. The morning flew by, and Jamie found the most comfortable place—the spot next to Clay. Clay, not Eric, had captured her heart. She knew that now. Otherwise she never would've been able to sit at a table opposite the man who had lived with her and played the role of her husband, a man who so easily could've been Jake, and want nothing more than to savor every minute with Clay.

"I can't believe this is November." Jamie leaned just enough so that her arm occasionally brushed against Clay's. "It feels like summer."

"Sometimes I wish we had seasons." Laura gripped the arms of her chair and angled her face toward the sun. "But I don't wish it for long." She held her hands out with palms up as if she were weighing something. "Let's see . . . eight degrees on Thanksgiving Day or eighty degrees . . . piles of snow and ice or green grass and sunscreen." She grinned at Jamie. "I'll take Southern California."

Eric was inside peeling potatoes. Jamie, Clay, and Laura sat around the backyard patio table, watching the kids toss a Frisbee. Sierra hadn't played with one before, and more than once the plastic disc hit her in the head, but not hard enough to hurt her.

"Clay, guess what?" Sierra giggled in their direction. "I think I need the jester hat. You know why?"

"Why?" Clay leaned forward, his eyes dancing the way they did whenever he and Sierra teased each other. There was no denying how much he cared for her.

"'Cause then the Frisbee would hit the hat instead of my head."

Clay chuckled. "Or maybe a helmet might help." He stood and jogged out to Sierra's side. "Here, let me show you how to catch it." With his hand up in front of his face, he nodded to Josh. "Okay, bucko, show me what you got!"

Grinning, Josh flung it four times as hard as before. "Take that!"

The phone rang, and Eric must've answered it in the house. He came to the door, opened the screen, and handed it to Laura. "It's Gina." His eyes caught Jamie's for a minute, and he gave her a hesitant smile, checking, maybe, to see if she and Laura were still hitting it off.

Jamie gave him a knowing look. Yes, she was fine. Laura was easy to be around. Eric looked out at the yard. "Way to throw it, Josh. Uncle Clay won't last; he wears down easy." Eric winked at his brother. "Hey, Clay, if he wears you out come join me in the kitchen." Then he turned, shut the door, and disappeared into the house.

Jamie sat back in her chair. Laura's conversation seemed deep, as if maybe the Gina woman, whoever she was, had troubling news. Clay was caught up in what had now become Frisbee golf. Jamie stood and stretched, then went to the edge of the patio and called out to Clay. "I'm going to make some tea. Want some?"

"No, thanks." He grinned at her. "Tell Eric I'm beating his son."

She laughed and raised her eyebrows in Laura's direction. *Tea?* she mouthed the word.

Laura covered the phone again. "No, thanks." Her words were barely a whisper. "My friend's son is in the hospital." She frowned. "Sorry about this."

Jamie gestured that it didn't matter; Laura could take as long as she liked. Then she went inside and when the kitchen came into view she stopped. Eric was working over the pot of potatoes, and from the back . . .

She gritted her teeth and kept walking. He wasn't Jake. She drew a quick breath. "Clay says to tell you he's beating your son."

Eric turned around. "Is that right?" He nodded to the pot, his eyes brimming with laughter. "I'm almost done, and then we'll see who wins at Frisbee golf."

She took the teakettle from the stove, careful not to brush against him or get in his way. "Want some tea?" She filled it with water, brought it back, and set it on the burner next to the potatoes.

"No, thanks." He was peeling the last one, cutting it into chunks, and dropping it into the pot. He turned the burner on to the highest level and put the lid on; then he did the same for the adjacent burner, the one with the teakettle.

They were suddenly out of busy things to do.

She leaned against the kitchen island and he stood opposite her, a few feet away. "You doing okay?"

Just like that he could still speak to the deepest part of her. "Yes." Her eyes held his and for a moment neither of them spoke. "Thanks for not pretending."

"Not pretending?" He narrowed his eyes, seeing straight to her soul.

"That we were strangers, that we never . . ."

"Never had that time together?" His tone was soft, understanding.

"Yes." She looked at the floor and then back up at him. "Thanks for that."

He bit his lip, as though considering whether to say whatever was on his mind or not. "Wanna see something?"

"Okay." She'd hoped they'd have this, time alone to acknowledge the past and let it find its proper place.

She followed him to a small room off the entryway. "This is my office." He held open the door and let her go in first. The place was spacious with shelves and cupboards and a countertop that lined one wall. "I do most of my work from home now."

"Good for you, Eric." A sad smile tugged at the corners of her lips. "Jake taught you that."

"He did." Eric crossed the room and opened a cupboard at the far end, then looked back at her. "Come here."

She came closer, and he pulled something off the top shelf that made her heart skitter into a strange rhythm. It was the book she'd made him, the one she'd given him at LaGuardia the day they said good-bye. The cover—faded and weathered from use—read, "In Case You Ever Forget." Inside were photocopies of key entries from Jake's journal, special sections of highlighted Scripture that Eric came to love during his time with her and Sierra.

Tears blurred her eyes. With trembling hands she took the book from Eric. "You still have it."

He looked over her shoulder at it. "I read it all the time."

She sniffed and turned, lifting her eyes to him. "You still have his mannerisms, his way of helping out and laughing at himself." A single tear slid onto her cheek and she struggled to find her voice. She stroked her hand along the cover of the handmade book. Then she handed it back to him. "I . . . I understand things better now."

He put the book back, closed the cupboard, and rested against the wall. "About us?"

"Mmmhmm." She dabbed at her cheek and blinked back the tears that stood in line. "God brought us together so we'd both find Him." She searched his eyes. He understood what she was saying; she still knew him well enough to see that. "You were never supposed to replace Jake."

"No." He went to her then and hugged her, letting her know he still cared. Regardless of how right he'd been to go home to Laura, in some way that involved their souls, he still cared about her. "I was never him."

"Exactly." She drew back first and crossed her arms. She'd imagined this conversation with Eric, and always she pictured her heart breaking. Instead, all she felt were deep peace and hope because the truth about Eric's identity was clearer now than it ever had been. She led the way back to the office door. "Your wife is lovely. You seem very happy. Josh too."

He fell in step beside her and a glow lit up his eyes. "We are. In fact—" he hesitated—"Laura's pregnant. Just a couple months."

Jamie wasn't sure what to feel. She was excited for Eric and his family, thrilled for them. But oh, how she would've liked that for herself and Jake—another child. Something she would never have. She found her smile. "Congratulations."

"We haven't told Clay yet. Laura wanted to announce it tonight."

It was yet another bit of Jake's legacy, that Eric would come home from New York ready to love his wife and son, able to rebuild what he'd lost over the years to the point that now they were expecting another child. Jamie felt her own desire to have another child easing. Instead her heart sang for Eric and Laura. "I won't say a word."

"I know what you're thinking; that it's because of what I learned from Jake. What God let me learn. You're right, Jamie." He glanced toward the cupboard one more time as they left the room. "What God taught me because of Jake will stay with me forever." He stopped and looked at her again. "Always. God's plan in all this is . . ." He chuckled and raked his fingers through his hair. "Well, it's more than I can understand." He paused. "Even now, with you and Clay."

"Yes." She felt her cheeks get hot. The way she cared about Eric's brother was getting stronger every day. And now, alone with Eric, she could hardly wait to get back to Clay. She bit the inside of her lip. "He's . . . he's wonderful."

"He's more than that." Eric stuck his hands in his pockets and gave her a pointed look, his eyebrows raised. "He's in love with you. I've been watching. I've never seen my brother like he is with you."

Butterflies scattered in Jamie's stomach. "Really?" She felt like a high school girl being told that the guy she had a crush on liked her too. The corners of her mouth lifted. "Me too, Eric. I can't believe how fast I'm falling."

"I know; I see it." He looked deep at her one last time, seeing to the places he'd known back when she was at the lowest point in her life. "I prayed for this, Jamie. That you'd find someone one day." He chuckled. "Who would've thought it would be my very own brother?"

"I know." Jamie let her head fall back against the hallway wall. "I read something in Jake's Bible, something I hadn't caught before."

"What?"

"It was in Deuteronomy. It talks about God setting before His people life and death, blessings and destruction." She paused. "Then it says to choose life." Her eyes were dry now. "Jake wrote something beside it. A note to me. He told me, 'Jamie, as often as you have the chance, choose life.'"

"And that's what you're doing with Clay." Eric reached out and touched her shoulder. "You couldn't find a nicer guy than my brother."

"I know." She meant it. With her whole heart.

Eric led the way from the room, and when they reached the kitchen, he turned and grinned at her. "I guess that means there's only one question left." He chuckled. "How do you feel about California?"

They both laughed as they returned to the kitchen. The kettle was boiling, and they slipped into easy conversation about the gravy and stuffing and the timing of pulling together a Thanksgiving dinner. It felt wonderful, talking this way with Eric, building something new with him, something casual and current. Something they could share without constantly revisiting the past.

Dinner was far more pleasant than Jamie had ever imagined. The tension was gone, and in its place was something new. A friendship that seemed to be setting a stage for the future. Jamie sat between Sierra and Clay, savoring the friendly banter between the two brothers. Clay was like Eric in many ways, but he was his own person, a man whose faith ran deep and true, clearly strengthened by the passing of time.

As for Eric, sitting across from him now at the table, Jamie saw that something was different about his eyes. He looked so much like Jake, she'd missed it at first, but now that she had time to watch him, to study him while he interacted with Clay and Laura and the rest of them, she could see it clearly.

He didn't have Jake's eyes.

Oh, they looked like Jake's at a glance. But deep within them were memories and emotions that were Eric's alone. Memories he hadn't had when he was living with her in Staten Island. She took a bite of fruit salad and felt herself relax even more.

"This is good turkey, Mrs. Michaels." Sierra beamed at Laura. "Maybe the bestest ever."

"Thank you, Sierra." Laura cast a quick smile at Eric. "I had help with it."

Jamie let her eyes rest on her daughter. Sierra was in her element. She was a people person, someone who loved being around big families. No wonder she was ready to have a second daddy, as she called it. The past three years had been little more than a healing time, a time to say good-bye to Jake and figure out a way to face the future without him.

Watching her, Jamie was convinced. Sierra, too, was ready to choose life.

They went around the table then, telling what they were thankful for. Josh was thankful for his family; Sierra, for her new friends;

and Laura, for the chance to be together. Clay looked at Jamie when he gave his answer. "I'm thankful for God's gift of new life." Under the table, he took hold of her fingers for a few seconds. "Not just once, but every day."

Eric looked around the room at each of them and gave a slow nod. "I'm thankful for answered prayers."

It was Jamie's turn. She massaged her throat, working out the lumps that had sprung up in the last minute or so. Then she looked at Clay and said, "I'm thankful God allows us the chance to choose life."

"On that note—" Eric leaned close to Laura, his eyes on hers— "we have an announcement to make."

Laura looked at Josh and then Clay. "We're going to have a baby!" Her face glowed.

"Seriously?" Clay was on his feet.

"Seriously." Eric laughed. "I know. I can't believe it myself."

Clay walked around the table and gave Eric a hearty hug, slapping him hard on the back. "I'm so happy for you." He held on for a few seconds and then he hugged Laura. "Congratulations." On the way back to his seat he gave Josh a light punch in the arm. "You're going to be a big brother, eh, Josh?"

"I guess." He flashed a lopsided grin at his parents. "I just found out this morning. It's kinda hard to believe."

Jamie leaned forward. "Congratulations, guys. That's wonderful."

Sierra wanted to know if Laura was having a girl baby or a boy baby, and Laura tried to explain that it was too soon to tell.

The conversation took wing, shifting from the idea of a little one running around the house to Josh's basketball abilities to Sierra's make-believe dress-up games and the meaning of the jester hat.

When they hit a lull, Eric held up his finger. "Wait!" He wiped his mouth with a napkin and uttered a quiet laugh. Then he looked at Laura. "Can I tell them about your run-in with the law?"

"What?" Clay's eyes got wide. "Laura Michaels had a run-in with the law? I've got to hear this."

"Sort of." Laura gave Jamie a weak smile, and then lifted her shoulders in Eric's direction. "Ah, go ahead and tell it."

Eric was immediately in his element, explaining how Laura had to go to the mall before Josh's basketball game, and on the way home she was in a big hurry. "Apparently she'd missed the on-ramp for the freeway and tried to make a sweeping U-turn across six lanes of traffic." He laughed and patted her hand. "But she still didn't have a bead on the on-ramp, so she straightened out and wound up in oncoming traffic. That's when she heard the siren."

"I was scared to death." She looked at Jamie for sympathy. "They changed that whole intersection. It's impossible to figure out which lane gets on to the freeway."

Jaime nodded, trying to look earnest, but wanting to laugh out loud.

"So then—" Eric winked at his wife—"when the officer pulls up behind her, she parks with her two right tires way up on the curb."

Laura raised her brow, her eyes dancing. "I wanted to stay out of traffic."

"So the officer comes up to the window, taps on it, and tells her, 'Ma'am, I have several concerns.'"

"Yes," Laura nodded. "That's right. Several."

Everyone was laughing now. Eric waited until he caught his breath to continue. "The officer was so flustered he didn't know what to do." Eric anchored his elbows on the table, his laughter getting the better of him. "So they call for backup and give her a sobriety test. My Laura, standing there near the Thousand Oaks Mall exit to the Ventura Freeway, getting a sobriety test." He grabbed at his sides, still laughing. "'The amazing thing is,' the officer told her, 'you really haven't been drinking.'"

The kids were smiling at each other and shrugging their shoulders. Josh was busy helping Sierra butter her dinner roll.

Clay stopped laughing long enough to turn to Laura. "So what'd they get you for?"

She shrugged. "Nothing. Isn't that great?" She smiled at them, triumphant. "After I passed the test, he told me to buy a map and be more careful."

"Glad it wasn't me." Clay leaned back in his chair and took a long breath. His eyes were damp from laughing so hard. "I would've ticketed you for sure."

"Why?" Laura was indignant. "For parking on the curb?"

"Nope." Clay exhaled long and loud. "For impersonating a drunk driver."

The laughter continued throughout the meal, but even as they chatted, Jamie kept glancing at Clay, sensing his nearness to her and thinking about Eric's question, the one that had been on her own heart for the last week or so. Especially during the days when she and Clay had been apart. It was a question that might have to be answered one of these days, so as they finished dinner and cut into dessert, as they continued talking over coffee and finally as Clay helped them gather their things and head for the car, Jamie let it play again and again in her mind.

How *did* she feel about California?

TWENTY-SEVEN

Clay did everything he could to make the minutes last, but on Sunday afternoon he drove Jamie and Sierra back to the Burbank Airport. The trip had been better than either of them had hoped, and even Sierra was sad to leave. They had decided that he would help them in with their luggage and say a quick good-bye.

Their real good-byes were said the night before, in the hallway outside Jamie's hotel room. They'd gone to Disneyland that day, and Sierra had fallen asleep on the way home. Clay carried her up and set her on the nearest bed, and then he and Jamie snuck into the hallway.

For a while they did nothing but look at each other. Clay broke the silence first. "I'm trying to imagine how I'll get through a week without you." They were both leaning against the same wall, a few feet from each other. Clay reached out and took her hand. "What're we going to do?"

Jamie ran her thumb along the side of his hand, her eyes never leaving his. "I could cancel our flight." Her tone was light, half teasing.

"Forever?" He looked back at her hotel door. "Maybe live here for a year or so?"

"Right." She gave him a sad smile. "I had a wonderful time, Clay."

"Me too." He took a step closer. They hadn't kissed once since Jamie had been in California, and Clay was almost glad. She needed to sort through her feelings, figure out how to act around Eric— and how she felt about Clay outside of the routine they'd found on the East Coast.

But now that everything had worked out, now that she was comfortable around Eric, and after a day of holding hands through Disneyland, Clay didn't want to wait another minute. He closed the gap between them and took her into his arms, hugging her the way he'd known he wouldn't get to at the airport. "Jamie," he whispered her name near the side of her face. "I'll miss you so much."

She drew back first, searching his eyes. "When will I see you again?"

"I don't know." He brought his hand up along her cheek and worked his fingers into her hair. "I'll come for Christmas, maybe, how about that?"

Her eyes lit up. "Really, Clay?"

"Yes." He kissed first one cheek, then her other, never breaking eye contact. "If I can wait that long."

"Clay . . ." She hugged him closer, clinging to his shoulders as if she were desperate to find a way to keep from leaving him. She pressed her cheek against his and suddenly, with an intensity that had been building since she stepped off the plane the day before Thanksgiving, the mood between them changed.

Their lips met, and they kissed. Slowly at first, and then with an intensity that seemed to take both of them by surprise. "Jamie . . ." He was breathless. "If we spend much more time like this, I know I won't last a month."

"Maybe that's a good thing. That way you'll come to New York sooner." She framed his face with her hands and kissed him in a way that left no doubts about her feelings. When she pulled away, she looked straight to his soul. "God brought us together, don't you think so?"

"Yes." He stroked her hair, memorizing the look in her eyes.

"Then why does it feel like everything's going to change after tomorrow?"

He brought his lips to hers once more. "We'll be three thousand miles apart, but nothing's going to change. Nothing." His breathing was shaky, his body on fire for the way she made him feel. "Christmas is a month away, okay?"

"Okay."

They kissed one last time and then said good-bye.

Clay had been restless all night, dreading the airport scene. He kept telling himself the same thing he'd told her. Christmas was only a month away. But now, as he turned his Jeep into the airport parking lot, December 25 felt like a lifetime away. The three of them were quiet as they walked into the concourse and Jamie checked her bags with the attendant.

Boarding passes in hand, they found a place near a concession stand where they were out of the flow of traffic. Sierra took the lead. "Bye, Clay." She hugged his waist and gave him a teary smile. "Thanks for a fun time." She glanced at Jamie, and then crooked her finger in his direction. "C'mere. I wanna tell you a secret."

"Okay." He bent down so she could whisper whatever she wanted to say. "What's the secret?"

She cupped her hands over her mouth and pressed them on either side of his ear. "I wish you were my second daddy, Clay. Wouldn't that be great?" She leaned back, her eyes dancing. Then she came in close again. "But don't tell Mommy, 'cause she told me telling you that might make you confused."

Clay's heart soared, but he checked his reaction. Grinning at Jamie, he whispered back at Sierra. "Can I tell you a secret?"

Sierra nodded.

"I wish I were your second daddy too."

Sierra jumped back, her eyes big. "Really?" This time her voice was almost too loud. She clapped her hands and did a little circle dance. Then she hugged him again and her excitement faded as quick as if someone had thrown a bucket of water on her. She crooked her finger at him again, and once more he bent close to her. Her words were slow and sad. "Yeah, only you can't be my second daddy because we don't live in the same place."

He looked at Jamie and she gave him an understanding smile. They had time; if Sierra needed this private conversation with him, he had Jamie's approval. He cupped his hands over her ear and whispered back to her. "Let's pray about that. And maybe one day there won't be so much space between us, okay?"

Sierra took a step back. Her expression was still sad, but a smile played on the corners of her lips. "Okay, Clay." She hugged him one last time. "Good-bye."

He ran his hand along the back of her head. "Good-bye, Sierra."

She pointed to a drinking fountain a few feet away. "Can I get a sip, Mommy?"

"Sure, sweetie." Jamie looked at Clay. "I guess this is good-bye."

"No." Clay came to her, hugging her, and giving her a brief kiss. "It's only see ya later."

Tears formed a shiny layer over her eyes and she nodded. Sierra returned and stood at her side. "See ya later, Clay."

He watched them go. They went through security and waved one last time before heading down the hallway toward their gate. Only when he got back to his car did he realize how badly he was going to miss her, how much he wanted her in his life. Because that's when he noticed something that hadn't happened to him as far back as he could remember.

His cheeks were wet.

TWENTY-EIGHT

The weeks of December took forever to fall off the calendar.

Jamie continued volunteering at St. Paul's, but only once a week. Twice she worked a shift with Aaron Hisel, but their friendship wasn't what it had once been. At the end of the second shift, he approached her in the break room upstairs and stuffed his hands in his pockets.

"There's someone else, right?" His tone wasn't angry or defensive, but matter-of-fact. "I saw you with him once at the café."

Jamie thought about denying it, but it was impossible. He was right, and more so every day. She ran her tongue along her lower lip and prayed for the right words. "Yes, Aaron. There is."

He looked at the floor near his work boots and gave a slow nod. "I thought so." His eyes found hers again and he shrugged. "I guess it never would've worked anyway. The whole faith thing, you know? We never would've agreed about it." He paused. "I've thought about it, Jamie. I can't believe in God. I'm not ready, not even for you."

Her heart sank. "I'm sorry, Aaron." She touched his shoulder. "I can only tell you what I've told other people here, people who can't get past September 11." She hesitated. "God believes in you, even if you don't believe in Him. He'll keep calling to you the way He's been calling to all of us since the beginning of time. Since Adam and Eve hid from Him in the garden." She let her hand fall to her side. "One of these days, I know you'll hear Him, and then you'll understand. Without Him, nothing makes sense. Nothing at all."

His lips lifted in a crooked smile. "Maybe." He took a step back. His eyes told her he was uncomfortable, ready to end the conversation. "If that ever happens, you'll be the first to know."

"I'll be praying."

She hadn't seen him again after that. The days continued to pass slowly, until even Sierra seemed irritable.

"How many days, Mom?" she asked over dinner one night.

"Twelve. He'll be here in twelve days."

She set her fork down and frowned. "That's too long. Can't we call him and tell him to come sooner?"

"He works, Sierra. He's in training."

"But he could do training here, right, Mommy?"

The conversations were the same every night, and once in a while Jamie let Sierra have a turn on the phone when Clay called. When Jamie took over again, she and Clay talked about their days. Later, when Sierra was in bed, they talked about their feelings, about where things were headed and how they could solve the problem of the distance between them.

Jamie was still thinking about California, but she couldn't fathom leaving Staten Island. She'd grown up there. It was where she'd played with Jake as a child, where she'd gone to high school and buried her parents after their car accident. It was where she'd gotten married.

Clay wasn't opposed to moving, but his detective training had just begun. He needed to put in at least a year to finish and get grounded in the job before looking at another department. Once in a while they would agree that maybe the timing was wrong, maybe they were supposed to be good friends, an encouragement to each other and nothing more.

But as soon as she'd imagine that possibility, she'd lay in bed, sick at the thought of being apart from Clay. She could pack her bags tomorrow, couldn't she? So what if she'd lived all her life on the East Coast? That only meant she was ready for change, right? She would move to the moon to be with Clay, wouldn't she?

The options were confusing, and since the answers didn't come easy, she and Clay did their best to stay away from the hard questions.

Finally it was eight days before Christmas. Sierra was in bed, and Jamie was on the phone with Clay, telling him about Sierra, how neither of them could wait until he arrived. His flight was due in on Thursday, December 23.

"I have an idea." Clay sounded more upbeat than usual. "Tomorrow's Saturday. Take Sierra into Manhattan. You haven't done that yet, right?"

"Not yet." Jamie flopped onto her bed and considered the idea. "We haven't had time, really, with Sierra in school."

"And all the hours on the phone." Clay chuckled.

Jamie rolled onto her back and stared at the ceiling. "Manhattan, huh?"

"Yes. Do it, Jamie. Spend the day there; you'll both have a good time."

By the end of the phone call, Jamie agreed with Clay. A day in Manhattan, shopping on Fifth Avenue and taking in the Christmas lights, would do both her and Sierra good. When she told Sierra the next morning, her daughter jumped up and down. "What a great idea, Mommy. We'll wear our red gloves and pretty scarves and buy presents for Katy and Mrs. Henning and Clay and everyone we know!"

They set off after breakfast. Snow had fallen a few days before, so the scene was like something from a storybook. Crowded streets, bustling with shoppers looking for the perfect gift before time ran out. They bought Sue Henning a sweater at Bergdorf's and at FAO Schwartz they found Katy a stuffed Nala—like the one Clay had brought for Sierra.

For Clay, Sierra picked out a pair of woolly socks, so his feet wouldn't get cold when he was riding around in his police car. Jamie bought him a new Bible—something he'd talked about one of the days they were together in Los Angeles. The store was able to engrave his name on it while Jamie and Sierra had lunch together. She found a few other items before leaving the bookstore.

They were on their way out when Jamie looked at her watch. "Well, sweetie, I think it's time to head back."

Sierra looked alarmed. "But, Mommy, we haven't been in all the stores yet."

"Honey, we wouldn't have time for all the stores if we stayed here two days straight."

"I know but . . ." Sierra licked her lips. "What time is it?"

Jamie stared at her daughter. Usually by now Sierra would be tired, more than ready to go home. "It's three o'clock."

Immediately, Sierra took her hand. "Please, Mommy . . . please can we stay longer? What about that big store down there with the Christmas tree on top, please?"

"Sierra . . ." Jamie's feet hurt. She wanted to play the parent card and call it a day. But maybe Sierra was getting old enough that a day in the city couldn't last long enough. Maybe it was a sign that she was growing up. She bit her lip and searched Sierra's face. "It'll be dark soon."

Sierra jumped up and down. "That's right! That's why I want to stay; so I can see the lights!"

A chill wind passed over them and Jamie pulled her coat tighter. She made a silly face at Sierra and took her hand. "All right, missy. One more store, but that's it. Then we have to go."

It was four-thirty by the time they boarded the ferry and headed back to Staten Island. Jamie expected Sierra to be drained, but she was bouncing around the mostly empty ferryboat like a baby chimp.

"How long till we get back?" She did a skip number three feet in either direction of Jamie. "Come on, Mommy, how long?"

Jamie tried to get a bead on her daughter, but she wouldn't stand still long enough. "Sierra, what's gotten into you?"

"Happiness, Mommy. Happiness got in me today."

Jamie blinked at her daughter. She could hardly argue with that problem. "Shouldn't your happiness be toning down a little?" Jamie had packages stacked around her. Whatever Sierra lacked in exhaustion, she made up for it. The crowds and lights and Christmas music for hours on end had left her ready for bed.

"You didn't answer me, Mommy. How long till we get back?" Sierra twirled twice and did an impromptu tap number. "I want to take tap dancing lessons, is that okay? Katy said she's taking tap in third grade, so I wanna take them too, okay?" She tapped out a little rhythm again.

"Sierra!" Jamie's voice was half laugh, half exasperation. "Stand still for just a minute."

Sierra stopped moving. She stared at Jamie, breathless and at attention. "Yes, Mommy. Sorry."

"Okay." Jamie breathed out, tired just from watching her daughter. "I'll answer your first question first. We'll be back home in twenty minutes; second question, yes. I'll consider tap dancing lessons."

Sierra skipped around in a circle. "Goodie! Yes, it's the bestest day. I'm definitely happy, aren't you, Mommy?"

Jamie was about to order Sierra to stop again, but she couldn't. Suddenly looking at Sierra was like looking at the picture of herself. She'd been motionless for long enough, unable to hear the music of life let alone find the rhythm of it. But now she was dancing again. Just like Sierra. Jamie leaned back and smiled at her daughter.

Sierra was merely choosing life.

Fifteen minutes later they were off the ferryboat and in their car, headed home. It was dark by now, but that didn't stop Sierra. She grew more animated and talkative the closer they got to home. Jamie had long since given up the idea of curbing her enthusiasm. Instead she chuckled to herself and let Sierra carry on, bopping from a request for red hair bands to a curiosity about whether Wrinkles should get dress-up clothes in his stocking this year.

She talked all the way home, until they pulled in the driveway. Then, like a switch had been flipped, she fell silent. It wasn't until they stepped out of the car and headed up toward the front door that Jamie stopped short and gasped.

In the light from the street lamp, she saw . . .

It couldn't be. He wouldn't have come early and surprised her, would he? He stood up and her doubts vanished. She dropped her packages and ran to him.

"Clay!"

"I guess I got my dates mixed up." He grinned and took her into his arms. "Mmmm." He whispered into her ear. "I missed you."

"I can't believe you're here." Tears stung her eyes. It was the best surprise she'd had in years. Three years, to be exact. She drew back and raised her eyebrows at Sierra. "Did you know something about this, missy?"

Sierra giggled and clapped her hands. "I didn't say anything, Clay. I kept the secret."

Clay pulled back enough to give Sierra a high five. "Way to go!" He winked at her, the wink Jamie had come to love. "I knew I could trust you."

"You could, Clay. You could trust me a whole lot because I didn't even say anything about—"

Clay put his hand over her mouth and gave her a gentle pull back to the porch step.

Jamie stood a few feet away. Sierra and Clay were so good together. She put her hands on her hip. "Okay, what's up?"

Sierra pinched her lips into a straight line and did the zipping motion across them. She tried to speak, but with her words trapped in her mouth, it sounded like gibberish.

Clay put his arm around Sierra and whispered something to her. Then he took something from his coat pocket, something Jamie couldn't make out. A present of some kind, maybe. He nodded at Sierra, and she did the same.

It must've been a signal, because she jumped up and ran to Jamie. "Mommy! Come on." Sierra grabbed her hand and led her over to Clay. "It's time."

Jamie's heart was thudding hard inside her chest. What was this? Clay and Sierra had obviously planned this moment. She held her breath. It couldn't be what she was thinking, the thing she couldn't put into words even in her head.

Not this soon, God. I'm not ready.

Daughter, I am with you. I am with you.

The answer came quick and certain, echoing through her heart and reminding her to exhale. It was okay; God was with her. He was with her and whatever was coming, He was in control. She steadied her legs. "Okay." She forced a short laugh. "How come I'm the only one who doesn't know what's going on?" She stood in front of Clay now, trying to get his attention. The thing he'd taken out of his pocket was hidden under his arms.

Beside her Sierra giggled. She tugged on Jamie's arm. "Quiet, Mommy. Clay wants to ask us something."

Then, as if it were happening in slow motion, Clay pulled a small velvet box from his lap. He stood and came close enough that Jamie could smell his cologne, savor the way it mixed with the fresh soap smell he always had.

She looked at him, searched his eyes. "Clay?" It couldn't be happening, could it? Was she ready? Could she ever be ready?

Sierra bounced up on her toes a few times, but she had her mouth zipped again.

Jamie's head began to spin. She was just barely able to keep focused on Clay and the thing he was doing now. He was getting down on one knee in the crusty snow, his eyes shining, his gaze never leaving hers. And he was opening the box . . . and there inside was a brilliant white gold solitaire diamond ring.

"Jamie . . ." Clay searched her eyes, her face. He took the ring from the box, slipping the box back in his pocket. "The more I think about life, the more I'm convinced of one thing." He swallowed and shifted his position so that his other knee was in the snow now. "When you know what to do, and you know it's the most right thing in the world, then you should do it. Whether it's forgiving someone or loving someone." He stood and took a step toward her, his face intense, serious. "Or asking someone to marry you."

Sierra made a slight squeal.

Jamie heard herself suck in a quick breath, and her fingers came to her mouth. She expected to reel hard one way and then the other, fall to her hands and knees, maybe even faint. It was too soon, right? Wasn't that how she'd been feeling seconds ago?

But now . . . as she looked from the ring to Clay, she felt strangely centered. The spinning stopped and everything faded except the words he was saying.

"Life's a fragile thing." His expression sobered. "September 11 taught us that." His words were a gentle caress. "For those of us who remain—all of us touched by that day—we need to find strength and hope in Christ, and to do the thing He asks us to do. Choose life."

"Clay . . ." She felt like a person lost in the forest for weeks on end, a person who was only now seeing clear of the trees. In a single instant, everything she'd fretted about slipped behind her. Now all she saw ahead was a vista wide open and inviting. And if she walked toward it, she'd find a new life, a new home for her and Sierra.

She could see it all.

"Marry me, Jamie." A smile lifted his lips and with his free hand, he framed her face. "Come be my wife in California and start life over again. Trust me that I'll cherish you as long as I live, and that

I'll do everything I can to keep God at the center of us." He winked at Sierra. "All of us." He held the ring out to Jamie. "Say yes. Please, Jamie."

She circled her arms around his neck and felt the tears come. "Yes, Clay." The sound she made was half laugh, half cry. He was right; so what if they hadn't known each other for years? They weren't kids out of college, needing to figure each other out. They were adults who belonged together from the moment they first met; adults with faith at the center of everything, and a connection that rarely came around twice in a lifetime.

He drew back a few inches. Surprise and uncertainty fighting for position in his eyes. "You really will?"

Her head dipped back and she laughed out loud this time. She glanced at Sierra and pulled her into the embrace. Then she looked at Clay again. "Yes, I'll marry you."

"And we can move to California, right, Mommy? Because I think it would be the bestest thing to live with Clay *and* be near Disneyland."

They all laughed, and Jamie realized she had an answer for that question too. One that didn't feel painful or frightening or rushed because no matter how often she told herself she wasn't ready, she'd been thinking about it a long time. She locked eyes with Clay and grinned. Good thing his arms were around her, otherwise she would've floated away.

"Well?" The uncertainty was gone from his expression.

"Yes." Jamie said it once and the second time she practically shouted it. "Yes!" She tightened her grip on both Clay and Sierra. "I'll marry you, Clay, and I'll move right *into* Disneyland if you want." Her voice softened and a chill passed down her spine at God's provision, His perfect timing. "Sierra and I will be wherever you are, Clay. From now on."

The certainty in her heart was stronger than cement. It was sweet and sure and mingled with the sorrow of good-bye, because after today she would never again live in a memorial. In a little while, she would never again work in one. Her past—beautiful as it was—would simply be her past.

Her yesterdays belonged to Jake Bryan, where they would always belong.

But because of God's goodness, because He had led her to choose life, her future had a home that was calling to her. And not just her, but Sierra. A future suddenly bright and full and colored with happy expectations. A home together.

And maybe, one day, a home blessed with another child.

She would no longer be Jamie Bryan, except in her distant memories. Because her tomorrows would take her to a place where she had a new name, a name she was breathless to take on—Jamie Michaels.

The most amazing feeling flooded her. *Jamie Michaels.* The sound of it rang across the quiet places of her heart. Clay's touch on her hand made her turn. Through eyes blurred with happy tears, she leaned closer and kissed him. A kiss of joyful excitement over a future that was even now just beginning.

TWENTY-NINE

Sierra was almost finished packing.

Mommy had given her a big suitcase for her clothes and special things. Special things didn't go on the moving truck; they went with her on the airplane. Sierra got jumbles in her tummy whenever she thought of the moving truck, because it was coming in two days and then some mover guys would come into the house and take everything into the back of the truck.

Even their van!

But the jumbles and rumblies were extra moving around now that the truck was coming so soon. Because that meant they had to finish packing and do the thing Sierra didn't really want to do. Tell Katy and Mrs. Henning good-bye.

She'd already told her class friends good-bye. James jumped up and down and gave her a little punch in the arm when she told him she was getting a second daddy too. Just like he got a second daddy. Her teacher said the class would miss her, but she would have a wonderful life in California.

Sierra sat on her bed next to Wrinkles and studied her open suitcase.

It was true. She couldn't wait to get to California. They were going to live in something called a 'partment for a little while. Until summertime. That's when Mommy and Clay were getting married, and after that Sierra could call Clay the thing she wanted to call him.

Daddy.

A sad feeling came into her heart. But not her first daddy, because nothing could ever erase her first daddy's face from her heart. Clay would be her second daddy; just as nice and wonderful as her first daddy, but different.

She was running out of room in her suitcase, and she knew why. The helmet took up half the space. It was her first daddy's helmet, the one he wore when he was fighting fires. The one he was wearing when the Twin Towers fell down. She dropped to her knees next to the suitcase and patted the top of the helmet. It was big and strong looking, the way her first daddy had always looked.

The helmet made her remember some special times with that daddy. Times when he gave her horsie rides and curled her hair and did butterfly kisses and took her to church and sang songs with her. She looked around her room. Sometimes when she wanted to remember him she only had to move her eyes so they would see a special place. Like the chair she and Daddy sat in or the place on her bedroom floor where they used to play horsie.

So what about when she didn't have this house anymore?

Stinging happened in her eyes and she blinked. Wrinkles jumped off the bed and curled up next to her on the floor.

"Wrinkles, you know what?" Sierra stirred her fingers in the soft hair at the top of her cat's head. "Maybe I don't really want to move."

The cat yawned very big and did a few slow blinks. Probably he wasn't getting enough sleep.

Sierra looked at the place on the floor a little ways away, where she and Daddy used to play. At the same time, two hot little tears splashed down her cheeks. Then she looked at the helmet in her suitcase. And suddenly in her heart an idea started.

If she looked hard enough at her daddy's firefighter helmet, she could see him. She had always been able to see him. So maybe she didn't need her very own house to remember him. Maybe she could remember him even in a 'partment. And something else too.

Mommy said her first daddy would always be in her heart. Because in her heart she would always be that little girl with long yellow curlies walking into church, holding her daddy's hand.

And he would always be her hero.

She put her hand on the helmet and looked hard at it. Her first daddy wouldn't want her to stay in the old house if it meant not having Clay. Because Clay was very big and strong, just like Daddy was. And plus he liked *Lion King* just like her, and he even liked to play dress-up.

In California they would have other family too. Clay's family. And that meant she would get to see Mr. Michaels. Mommy said Mr. Michaels would be her uncle after they got married, and Josh— the nice boy who played Frisbee with her—would be her cousin.

So that was pretty nice. And after school was over and Mommy and Clay got married, they would all live in a house with a swimming pool! A real in-the-ground swimming pool!

She patted Wrinkles on the head. "We can get a little boat for you, Wrinkles. And you can go sailing while I swim, okay?"

Wrinkles closed his eyes, because he needed his rest. Mommy said he wouldn't sleep much in the plane because he had to be in a big box down with the luggage. Sierra hadn't told Wrinkles about that yet. Some things were better if they were surprises, actually. Plus also, Wrinkles might not want to go if he knew he was flying to California with the luggage.

Once more she looked at the helmet, and this time she picked it up and held it to her heart. She kissed the top of the helmet and then held it a little higher and gave it butterfly kisses, first with one set of eyelashes and then the other.

When she was done, she set the helmet back in her suitcase and a smile came to her face. Because she could still see him, her first daddy. Tall and nice and laughing, standing right beside her. And deep inside she could hear God telling her some good news. Yes, her daddy would always be there, the same way he was now. Whether they lived in Staten Island or California, he would be there.

Forever and ever and ever.

Jamie stood in the doorway and stared into her empty house.

The movers had come and were already headed west. She and Sierra had stayed one last night, and at four o'clock they would fly nonstop to Los Angeles. Now they had all day to say their good-byes. The old house was first on the list.

"Okay, Sierra." Jamie glanced at her daughter, sitting on the front porch steps sticking her finger through the holes in Wrinkles's air carrier box. The For Sale sign was fifteen yards away, sticking out of the snow. "Come say good-bye to your house."

Sierra looked up. "I already did, Mommy. After the movers left yesterday." She bit her lip. "Can I stay out here with Wrinkles?"

Jamie gave her a sad smile. "Okay." She looked back through the front door. "I'll hurry."

She started upstairs with Sierra's room, the same room she and her sister had slept in as little girls. She welcomed the torrent of memories, little moments that formed the skeleton of her entire life. It was a small room with a single window. Nothing remarkable, except the fact that it had been hers since she was born.

Now it would belong to someone else. "Good-bye, little room." She stepped out and closed the door.

The next room would be hardest of all. Her bedroom. The place where her parents had slept so many years ago; the place where she and Jake had shared their love for nearly a decade.

Jamie worked the muscles in her jaw and squinted, blinded by the brightness of the past. This was why she needed to move, why she couldn't welcome Clay into her East Coast world. Because in this house, her memories were so alive they fairly breathed. She would take them with her, of course. They were woven into the fabric of who she was. But if she was to have new life, she would need new surroundings.

She closed her eyes, stepped back, and closed that door.

The rest of the house was easier, though the memories of all that had happened there—family dinners, birthday parties, movie nights, and a thousand other memories—were not. She floated through the rooms, hating the emptiness, allowing the image of those warm old walls to burn a forever impression in her mind.

Soon she was back at the front door, taking one last look. She breathed in slow—she would even miss the smell of it, the old wood and windows.

It smelled like home. The way home had always smelled.

Jamie had known this day would involve tears, and it was no surprise that they kicked into action now. She hesitated. *God . . . bless whoever comes here next, whoever lives here and loves here and laughs here the way we did. Bless them that they might feel Your Spirit and know You are in this place.*

Then, her eyes blurred, she stepped back, closed the door, and locked it.

Sierra looked up at her and immediately she understood. "Mommy, it's okay." She stood and gave her a hug around her waist. "California will be good too."

"I know it will." Jamie sniffed. She gave Sierra a sad smile and looked deep into her eyes. "Crying is okay, you know why?"

"Why?" Sierra's eyes were damp too. The day was bound to be hard for both of them.

"Because if you cry a lot when you say good-bye, it means you loved a lot." She stooped down and kissed Sierra's nose. "Do you understand that?"

"Yes, Mommy." Sierra lowered her brow, very serious. "Then today will be a lot of crying. Because I loved living here and being friends with Katy Henning a very lot."

At that moment, the Hennings' car pulled up. Sue was picking them up and taking them to lunch. After that, Jamie and Sierra would board the ferry to Manhattan, and from there catch a cab to the airport.

Sue climbed out of her pickup truck, and the moment their eyes met, Jamie saw she wasn't the only one affected. Sue was crying too. She crossed the yard, her eyes on Jamie the entire time. Sierra ran to the car to see Katy and little Larry, both buckled into the backseat.

"I'll miss you so much." Sue hugged her, expressing the sorrow Jamie knew had been building for both of them since she accepted Clay's proposal. Sue stepped back and dragged her hand across her cheeks. "I'm sorry; you don't need this. It's just ..." Her features twisted as she gave a sideways nod of her head. "You're like a sister to me, Jamie. After all we've been through. The guys ... our faith—" Two short sobs interrupted her. "I can't ... imagine life without you."

"Oh, Sue." Jamie held her again. "I'll visit. I promise I will." She took her friend's shoulders and leaned back enough to see her eyes. "And you will too. Okay? This spring you fly out, and we'll take the kids to Disneyland, okay?"

Sue nodded, but still the tears poured down her face. She stared at Jamie's house for several seconds and then grabbed a suitcase with each hand. When the car was loaded and they drove off, the conversation lightened up. They spent the morning at the Henning house, talking about old times, remembering the friendship between Larry and Jake, how fun they were together, how well they embraced life right until the end.

They shared lunch together and cried again when Sue dropped them off at the ferry. Less, this time, because of their own sorrow than the sadness of seeing their daughters say good-bye.

Sierra hugged Katy tight. "Don't forget me, Katy. Best friends forever, okay?"

"Best friends forever." Katy ran to Sue's side and buried her face in her mother's jacket.

Both girls were crying too hard to say more than that. Jamie gave one last wave to Sue, and a look that told her this wasn't the end. That a friendship like theirs, forged out of the very best moments and the most horrifically painful ones, would not end simply because of a move.

Sue and her children turned then and headed back for their car; Jamie did the same, pulling their suitcases while Sierra clutched Wrinkles's carrier. Just before they boarded the ferry, Sierra stopped, stooped down, and spread her hand out on the ground.

"What're you doing, honey?" Jamie felt her tears drying in the winter wind. She pulled up and watched her daughter.

"Saying good-bye." Sierra stood and picked up Wrinkles again. "Good-bye to Staten Island."

The ferry ride felt faster than usual, and they found a cab without any wait. Jamie directed the driver to St. Paul's, promising to pay him extra if he'd wait while she and Sierra ran inside.

She'd had her last shift two weeks earlier, but it wouldn't be right to pass by the area without a final farewell. Someday she'd come to St. Paul's again, but once the new buildings were built—the ones that would stand where the Twin Towers had stood—the atmosphere at the chapel would change.

Items that formed the memorial inside the little church would be moved to the official memorial, the one planned for somewhere in the new construction. And St. Paul's would return to being only a nice little chapel in the middle of Manhattan's financial district. A landmark, yes, but not the mission it had been in the years after September 11.

Jamie wasn't sure she wanted to see St. Paul's that way.

Neither did most of the other volunteers, those who helped remove the pile of debris and those who served and offered their time. She was part of a community of people who would never enter St. Paul's without seeing the place lined with posters and pictures and letters, without seeing photographs of the dead and pews full of vacant-eyed firefighters, covered in soot and weary from the grim task of working the pile.

This . . . this final good-bye, was the last time the chapel would look the way she would always remember it.

She led Sierra by the hand, jogged lightly across the street, up the steps, and inside. The place was quiet, as usual. She turned to the first table, the one on the left of the front door, and immediately found Jake's picture.

Sierra stayed close at her side. "That's Daddy!"

"Yes." Jamie had always figured she would know when it was right to bring Sierra. But they'd run out of time, so right or not, this was the moment. "Remember when I would do my volunteer work?"

"Yes." Sierra looked at her, eyes wide.

"Well—" Jamie shifted her eyes back to Jake's picture—"this is where I would come."

"Oh." Sierra looked at the picture again too. Then she caught a quick breath and pointed. "That's my letter to Daddy!"

"Yep." Jamie put her arm around Sierra's shoulders and hugged her. "It'll stay with his picture for always."

Sierra thought about that for a minute. "I like that."

One of the other volunteers approached her then, an older woman who had connected often with Jamie. She knew why Jamie was there and she introduced herself to Sierra. "Want some cookies upstairs? I baked them this morning."

Sierra looked at Jamie. "Can I?"

"Yes." Jamie cast the woman a grateful look. "But only for a minute. The cab's waiting."

Sierra went off with the woman. Once she was gone, Jamie turned and found Jake's picture again. Sweet Jake, the man who had prayed for her and cherished her and written words that guided her way still. The man who had led her to God.

She looked deep into his eyes. So much of their time together she had worried about him, that he would lose his life fighting fires. What a waste of time. If she had it to do all over again, she would choose to love Jake, even knowing their time together would be short.

The lessons he'd taught her would live on, as would the memory of his love. Yes, the page was turning. She could feel it in her heart, feel the way St. Paul's didn't quite have the same hold on her as it once had. She didn't need a memorial to remember Jake, to honor him.

She would do that with her life.

The volunteer returned with Sierra, and Jamie hugged the woman. "Tell the others good-bye, okay?"

"I will." She pulled an envelope from her pocket. "Aaron Hisel told me to give this to you. He heard you were moving."

Jamie's heart sank. Aaron had been important in her life for a time, one of the reasons she'd been able to process the pain of losing Jake. She would miss him, even though their time together had ended long before she decided to marry Clay.

"Did . . . did he say anything?"

The woman smiled. "He wanted you to hear it from him."

Sierra nodded. She slipped the envelope in her coat pocket, said another quick good-bye, and led Sierra back outside. She walked to the corner and for a moment she stared at the empty sky, the place where the buildings had stood.

It would be good to get away from that part of the skyline, good to know she could drive to the market without catching a glimpse of the emptiness. Jake went into those towers because it was the right thing to do. She had no doubt that even until the last few seconds, he and Larry were helping people, probably praying with them and telling them about Jesus.

She didn't need St. Paul's or Ground Zero to remind her of that.

"That's where the Twin Towers were, right, Mommy?" Sierra squinted up, shading her eyes so she could see despite the glare from the snow and white cloudy sky.

"Yes." Even now she hated the past tense, hated how it reminded her that such an awful thing really had happened. "That's where they were."

Sierra looked at her and squeezed her hand a little tighter. "But that's not where Daddy is now. Daddy's in heaven." Her eyes were dry now, the trauma of good-bye already fading. She touched her fingers to her chest. "And his picture is right here." She angled her head, her eyes curious. "Do you think Daddy's happy that we're moving to California and marrying Clay?"

Jamie looked at her feet for a minute and then up at the empty skyline again. Jake's smile, the memory of it, flashed in her mind as big and bright as heaven itself. "Yes, Sierra. I think he's very happy."

The plane was halfway to Los Angeles when Jamie remembered Aaron's letter. Sierra was sleeping in the seat beside her, so she was careful not to wake her. She pulled out the envelope, opened it, and slid out the letter.

> *Dear Jamie,*
> *I won't make this long, but I promised you I'd tell you if something changed. Well, something did.*

Jamie closed her eyes, her heart doing a double beat. What was this? Aaron couldn't be talking about the one thing they never agreed on, could he? She blinked and found her place.

> *One of the new guys at the station had a baby with a heart problem. The guy asked every one of us who believed to pray. You know me; I told him I couldn't pray because I didn't believe. But that night I asked God to show me He was real, let me know if I was wrong about the whole faith thing.*
> *And guess what happened?*
> *The new guy comes up to me the next day and says, "You don't have to believe in God, Hisel, He believes in you."*
> *The exact words you told me. And I don't know, I got chills and something happened inside me. Like I knew right then that God was real, and He was there. I'm not saying I have it all figured out or any of it figured out, really. But the new guy's talking to me. He's buying me a Bible.*
> *I guess I just wanted you to know so you could keep praying for me. I already know Jake's praying. I'm happy for you, Jamie. Take care of yourself.*

Aaron

Jamie blinked back tears and read the letter again. Then she closed her eyes and let her head fall against the seat back. *God ... You're so good, so faithful. I knew You'd get Aaron's attention, and now You have. You work all things out in Your timing.*

The hum of the jet soothed her, helped clear her mind.

She opened her eyes and looked out the window. Down below were clusters of lights, places where families gathered, sharing notes from a day of work or school. The way she and Clay and Sierra would be soon.

Joy rose up within her and warmed her heart. There was really nothing more to be sad about. She pictured Clay's face, the way he would look when they got off the plane and walked into his world once and for all. Thoughts of the future filled her head. It would be so good to see him and hold him and plan a wedding with him, so much fun unpacking her things and watching Sierra and Clay and Wrinkles play dress-up together.

Choose life. Jake's voice sounded in her soul once more, ringing with sincerity and faith, the way it had always done back when he was alive, when he was hers. *Choose life, Jamie. Choose life.*

She smiled at the sleeping form of their daughter. *I am, Jake. I'm choosing life.*

The jet engines hummed low in the background. She looked out the window, every mountain or field they passed taking them a little closer to California. Closer to Clay. A warm certainty settled in her chest, convincing her of what she'd known all along. With all its trials and tragedies, all its brokenhearted confusion, life was still the greatest choice of all. God-given life. That was her choice.

Now and always.

A Note from Karen

Those of you who read *One Tuesday Morning* know that telling Jamie Bryan's story was something I had to do. That first book came to me almost complete on the afternoon of September 11, 2001, and it stayed in my heart until I wrote it for you.

It was the same way with this sequel.

Beyond Tuesday Morning is really the rest of the story, the way the rest of the story might play out for all those touched or changed by tragedy. Like Jamie, all of us will have the chance to choose life. For some of you, that might mean making a recommitment to a dying marriage or looking for ways to encourage your husband or wife.

Choosing life might mean taking time to play with your children. So often we get caught up in the business of raising a family—making vacation plans, buying a house, getting a job, doing housework, fixing up the yard—that we miss the point. Making time with your children and the people you love is definitely a way to choose life.

But the way that is illustrated in this book is vitally important.

I've heard it said that all of us are either leaving a trial, heading into one, or smack in the middle of one. Trials can vary from issues at work to the death of a loved one. In Jamie's case, she was willing to spend her life memorializing the years she'd had with Jake.

But ultimately it was God's Word, combined with words written by Jake, that helped her choose life.

Grief and sorrow are important stages, seasons that we must go through. To some extent we will never be fully rid of either—not when we're dealing with the loss of someone we loved. I hear from hundreds of you every week—mostly letters of encouragement and offers of prayer, for which I will forever be grateful. But once in a while you tell me of tragic events in your families or communities.

When I hear about a car accident or illness or loss, I always pray. I pray for hope and healing wherever possible.

And I pray for life.

Life is God's gift to us. With every sweet breath, we confirm the fact that God has us here for a reason, that He has a plan for our lives. I truly believe that the more we surrender our lives to Him, the more we trust Him with the days He gives us, the better off we'll be. There is such peaceful freedom, such uninhibited joy, in knowing that God Almighty is the reason we woke up today. If we have tomorrow, it's because He has more for us to do.

In that light, it's almost impossible to spend a day bemoaning our situation, unwilling to rejoice. Grief stays with us, but it need not stay *on* us. I think of the apostle Paul, chained in a Roman prison, rats nibbling at his knees. What was he doing? Singing ... telling the jailors about Jesus ... and writing letters to his friends back home, encouraging them to glorify God with their lives.

If you or someone you love is in a difficult situation, I pray this book has given you hope. But I also pray it sends you looking for the purpose God has for your life. Allow the possibility that whatever you're going through, this too shall pass. Not without pain, not without tears, but with possibility and trust in God.

Things are good on the home front. Kelsey is fifteen and in high school and has just finished cheering for the freshmen football team. Tyler, twelve, is being homeschooled so he can have more time for the arts he's so passionate about. He is very involved in Christian Youth Theater and will audition for all three of the musicals this year. Sean, Josh, EJ, and Austin have just completed a wonderful season of soccer. With Christmas behind us, we're settling in for a productive winter/spring season. We still do devotions every morning, and I am thrilled to see each of the kids gradually making decisions for Christ that are motivated by their own love for God, their own choices for life.

If you're a believer in Jesus Christ, I pray this book encourages you to keep on fighting the good fight. If you're not, then this may be the chance in a lifetime, the chance to call on Jesus as your Savior, to get to a Bible-believing church and find out about a relationship with the true God of the universe. Trusting Jesus for life is the very first step to choosing life. *Abundant* life. John 10:10 says that the thief comes to kill, steal, and destroy, but Jesus has come to give us life, life to the fullest measure.

Don't waste another day with the thief; rather make the choice to spend your life, from this day on, with the Giver of life. One of my favorite sections of Scripture is Hebrews 12, which encourages us to never give up, but to "run with perseverance the race marked out for us." The race of life. That's what God called Jamie Bryan to do.

It's what He calls each of us to do.

Until next time, I pray God keeps His mighty arms around you, that you feel the presence of His loving touch, His gentle hug, even on the darkest nights. May He bless you and yours and grant you life. Always life.

In His light and love,
Karen Kingsbury

P.S. My website, www.KarenKingsbury.com, has become a big part of my ministry. You can leave a prayer request, pray for other readers with specific needs, and meet prayer partners at the Prayer Ministry link. You can get involved in discussions about my books at the Reader Forum link, and you can see how God is using these books to affect the lives of other readers at the Guest Book link.

You can contact me at the website or at my email address: rtnbykk@aol.com. As always, I love hearing from you and look forward to your letters.

Book Club or Study Guide Questions

1. Why did Jamie volunteer at St. Paul's?

2. What good did she bring to others by volunteering?

3. What good did God bring about in her because of her volunteering?

4. Why did she feel she was supposed to be interested in Fire Captain Aaron Hisel?

5. What warning signs did she have that this might not be the right relationship for her?

6. What could Jamie have learned from Sierra about moving on with her life?

7. What lessons did Jamie learn from Jake in this season of change?

8. Has God ever clearly set before you the choice of life or death? Explain.

9. What did you choose and how did it work out?

10. Jamie spent most of her earlier years living in fear. How did that tendency creep back into her life in this story?

11. How did Jamie finally get over her fears? What were the steps she took?

12. Has there ever been a time when fear stopped you from doing something you wanted to do? Share it.

13. Were you able to get past that fear at a later time? If so, how?

14. Part of choosing life is having the courage to say the things you need to say—whether it is an admission of love or an apology to a parent or child or sibling or friend. What role did Joe Reynolds play in helping Jamie embrace life?

15. If today was your last day, how would you choose life? How would you embrace it? Make a plan to do some of those things every day to the glory of God.

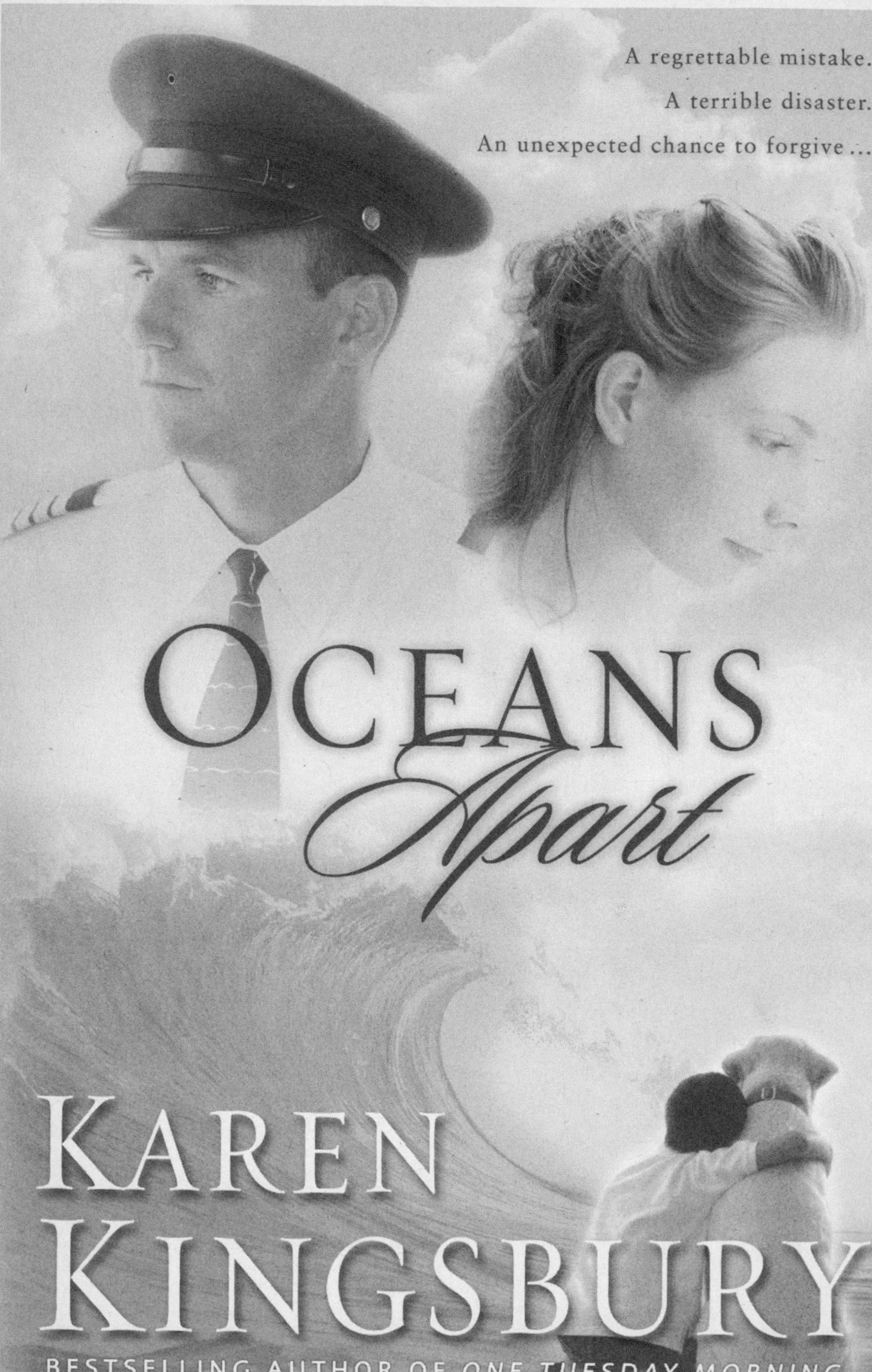
A regrettable mistake.
A terrible disaster.
An unexpected chance to forgive…
OCEANS
Apart
KAREN
KINGSBURY
BESTSELLING AUTHOR OF ONE TUESDAY MORNING

Read an Excerpt from Karen Kingsbury's Bestselling *Oceans Apart*

ONE

Fear was an owl that rarely lighted on the branches of Kiahna Siefert's heart.

Especially in the light of day.

But it was nine o'clock on the sunniest morning of spring, and Kiahna couldn't shake the feeling—the strange gnawing in her soul, the way the skin around her neck and chest felt two sizes too small.

What is it, God . . . what are You trying to tell me?

No answer echoed back at her, so Kiahna kept busy. The passenger briefing was nearly finished, and the pilots were in their seats. She anchored herself against the service wall and found her smile, the one she used every time she flew.

Flight 45, Honolulu to Tokyo, was a nine-hour flight. With a layover in Tokyo, the roundtrip gave Kiahna eighteen flight hours. Five times a month she made the two-day turnaround, and after a decade with the airline, her pay was better than any she could get anywhere else. Out the door at seven and, with the time change, home before dinner the next day. Kiahna had earned the route after ten years with the airline, and it was perfect for one reason.

It allowed her most days to be home with Max.

"Movie today?" The man was a light traveler, briefcase and a carry-on, a regular in first class. Whatever his worn leather bag held, it took him to Japan at least once a month.

"Yes, sir. Mel Gibson's latest."

"Good." He smiled and kept moving. "Gets me over the ocean quicker."

One by one the passengers filed in, same as always. But still she couldn't shake the feeling.

It took fourteen minutes to seat the cabin, and Kiahna worked the routine. The flight was nearly full, which meant the usual readjusting to make people and bags fit comfortably in the cramped quarters. She greeted passengers, sorted out seat assignments for confused travelers, and poured a drink tray for first class.

A family with four children was seated over the wing, and already their baby was crying. Kiahna found a package of crackers and coloring books for the couple's older children. With every motion she tried to sort out her feelings.

"Kiahna?"

She jumped and turned to face her partner. Stephanie was working the back part of the cabin. "We're waiting."

The announcement. She'd completely forgotten. A quick breath. "They're all in?"

"For two minutes now."

Kiahna snapped the drink tray into place on the small service counter and edged past the other woman. The announcement was hers that morning; she should have remembered. She took hold of the microphone and began the routine.

"Welcome aboard Flight 45. We're expecting a full cabin this morning, so if you have two carry-ons with you today, please store one of them in the space beneath the seat in front of you." She paused, her mouth still open.

What came next? There was more to say, something about oxygen and masks, but the words scrambled in her mind and refused to come. She stood unmoving, her heart slamming against her chest.

"Here"—Steph took hold of the microphone—"I've got it."

Kiahna's arms shook as she backed away, up against the closed front cabin door. What was wrong with her? She'd given that announcement a thousand times; she could be in a coma and say it.

Steph finished, and the copilot came on. "Flight attendants, prepare for takeoff."

They pushed their jump seats down and buckled in. Usually this was Kiahna's favorite part. A few minutes of power and thrust while the airplane barreled down the runway and lifted into the air, minutes where she wasn't needed by anyone for anything, when she could think about the day and all that lay ahead.

This time, though, was different.

All Kiahna could think about was the part of her day that lay behind, the part with Max.

At seven years old, Max was both brilliant and beautiful, a wonder boy streaking through her life like a comet at breakneck speeds. He wore red tennis shoes, and his best friend was his yellow Labrador retriever, Buddy. At school, Max had a reputation for being the fastest—and sometimes the silliest—boy on the playground. And his mouth ran faster than his legs. Kiahna liked to hold court with Max on dozens of adult topics. The death penalty—Max was against it; more money for public schools—he was for it. Max was fiercely patriotic, and at school he sometimes organized red, white, and blue days in honor of the U.S. troops in the Middle East.

But this morning he'd been quiet.

"When do you finish working?" They lived in a two-bedroom apartment, and he slipped into her room while she was still pressing her standard-issue airline navy blazer.

Kiahna studied him. "Dinnertime tomorrow, same as always."

"No, not that way." He hopped up on her bed and sat crosslegged. "When will you stay home in the daytime? Like Devon's mom or Kody's mom?"

"Max." She turned from the ironing board and leveled her gaze at him. "You know I can't do that."

"Why?" He anchored his elbows on his knees.

"Because"—she came a few steps closer and sat on the edge of the bed—"those moms have husbands who work."

"So why can't we have a husband?"

"C'mon, Max." She cocked her head and brushed her finger against the tip of his nose. "We've been through this, sport."

Buddy padded into the room and sank in a heap near Max's feet. "Yeah, but . . ." Max brought his fists together and rested his chin on them. His green eyes caught a ray of morning light. "Forever?"

"For now." She crooked her arm around his neck, pulled him close, and kissed the top of his head. His dark hair felt soft and damp against her cheek, still fresh from his morning shower. "Until something better comes along."

"Like a husband?" Max lifted his face to hers. He was teasing, but beyond the sparkles in his eyes was a river of hope, a hope that ebbed and flowed, but never went away.

Kiahna smiled. She tousled the hair at the back of his head and returned to the ironing board. Max knew better than to push. A husband had never been in the picture. Not a husband and not a daddy. Kiahna couldn't trust a man with her own heart, let alone her son's. Besides, it wasn't God's plan for her to have a husband. At least that's the way she'd always felt.

Max slid onto the floor and looped his arms around Buddy's neck. The dog rewarded him with a solid swipe of his tongue across Max's cheek. "Buddy understands."

"Yes." Kiahna smiled. "Buddy always does."

A soft bell sounded, and Kiahna sucked in a quick breath. They were at ten thousand feet—time to prepare the beverage cart and make the first pass through the cabin. Steph approached her from the other side of the aisle.

"You okay?" She had one hand on her hip, her eyebrows lowered into a *V*. "What was the trip about the announcement? Never seen you freeze like that."

Kiahna stood and smoothed out the wrinkles in her navy cotton skirt. "I don't know." She gave her partner a smile. The feeling, the strange restlessness, had plagued her ever since her talk with Max. "Busy morning, I guess."

"Yeah, well"—she rolled her eyes—"you wanna talk busy? It's four o'clock, and Ron . . . you know Ron, right?"

"He moved in last month?"

"Right." Steph grabbed a piece of gum from her skirt pocket, slipped the wrapper off in a single move, and popped it into her mouth. "Anyway, he gets this call at four this morning, and it's the—"

A sudden jolt rocked the aircraft so hard Steph fell to her knees. Gasps sounded throughout the cabin, and somewhere near the wing one of the children began to cry. Kiahna fell back against the service counter and reached for a handful of soda cans that had fallen to the floor.

"What the . . ." Steph was struggling to her feet when the plane tilted hard in the other direction. The motion knocked her back to the floor. In the tenth row, a handful of screams and shouts rang out from a group of college kids, journalism students heading back home from a convention.

Turbulence.

Kiahna grabbed hold of the nearest wall and felt the blood drain from her face. The air was always choppy over the islands, especially in spring. She was about to help Steph to her feet when the copilot leaned out from the cockpit.

"We're going back." The man's upper lip was twitching. His whispered words came fast. "Something's wrong with the tail." He swallowed hard. "The whole bloody aircraft wants to nosedive."

Nosedive? Kiahna stared at him. This wasn't happening, not this morning. Not when every fiber in her being had warned her something wasn't right. The copilot was gone again, and Kiahna shifted her gaze to Steph. The girl was a New Yorker, twenty-two, twenty-three tops. She was cocky and brash and had a quick tongue, but now her face was gray-white. "What … what do we do?"

Kiahna reached for her partner's hand and helped her to her feet. "We work the cabin. I've done an emergency before." Her voice sounded familiar, but only remotely so. "We stay calm and everything will work out fine."

"But what if we—"

"No *what-ifs*." She took the lead and headed down the aisle. "We have to work."

They weren't through first class when a strange popping sound shook the plane and propelled it downward. *It's the descent*, Kiahna said to herself. And then again for the benefit of the passengers. "We're making our descent. Cover your heads and assume a forward roll position."

Kiahna didn't dare turn around, couldn't bear to meet Steph's questioning eyes. The truth had to be written across her face: the sharp angle of the aircraft didn't feel like a normal descent pattern.

It felt like a nosedive.

Panic worked its way through the rows in a sort of sickening wave. "Jesus, help us!" a lady shouted from row eight. She had an arm around each of her children.

"Someone *do* something!" The scream came from an area near the back of the plane, and it set off a chain reaction of loud words and frantic cries for help. No one had any doubt they were in trouble.

Still Kiahna moved forward. At each row she demonstrated the crash-landing position. Hands clasped at the back of the neck, body tucked as far forward as possible. "Assume the emergency position," she said over and over again. "Assume the emergency position."

"What happening?" An Oriental man grabbed her arm; his eyes locked on hers. "What, lady? What?"

Kiahna jerked herself free as the nose of the plane dropped again. The aircraft was almost entirely vertical.

The captain's voice—tense, but steady—filled the cabin. "Prepare for an emergency landing. I repeat, prepare for an emergency landing!"

Babies were wailing now; parents grabbed their children to keep them from falling toward the front of the plane.

"Lord, have mercy on us," a woman screamed.

The voices mingled and became a single noise, a backdrop that grew louder and then faded as Kiahna caught a glimpse of the ocean out one of the windows. In that instant time froze.

Kiahna was back at home again.

⁓

"Come on, Max. Get your backpack. We're running late!"

Max rounded the corner, Buddy at his side. "I can't find it."

"Check the coat closet."

He darted across the kitchen and toward the front door. She heard him yank the closet open. "Here it is!"

"Grab it; let's go."

The whole scene took a fraction of a second to flash across her mind, all of it routine, mundane. No subtle nuances or hesitations, nothing to indicate that this morning could be their last. Nothing but the strange pit in her stomach.

She closed her eyes . . . where was Max right now? He stayed with Ramey Aialea mornings until the school bus came, and again in the afternoon and through the night when she had a layover. The woman would see him off to school the next day and take care of him for an hour or so when school got out. Ramey was in her late sixties, a weathered grandmother in poor health who took in Max as a way of staying young. She lived just a block away and felt like family to Kiahna.

Max had been with Ramey since he was born.

That morning, as happened so often, Kiahna and Max had piled into Kiahna's old Audi and made time to Ramey's first-floor unit.

Ramey and Kiahna both lived in the same modest residential section of the island, the place where apartments filled every available square inch, leaving room for only an occasional palm tree. The place where the island's food servers and hotel maids and resort staff lived.

The apartments weren't much, really. But Kiahna's complex had a fairly clean pool and a patch of gravel with a swing set. More amenities than some. That, and paradise every day of the year. It wasn't a bad place to raise a boy. A native to Honolulu, Kiahna wouldn't have lived anywhere else.

By the time she and Max arrived at Ramey's apartment, Kiahna's strange feeling had set in. She didn't want to waste time making idle talk with her old friend. Instead she stepped out of the car and met Max near the front bumper. "Have a great day, sport."

He squinted into the sun. "Do you have to go?"

"Yes." She pecked him on the cheek. "We'll play Scrabble tomorrow night, okay?"

"It's too sunny for Scrabble."

"Okay, then basketball? Give and go, all right?" Kiahna rested her hands on her knees and kept her face at his level.

"Really?" Max's eyes held a hint of doubt. "Give and go?"

She winked at him. "As long as it's light out."

Max bit his lip. "Japan's a long way from here."

"Yes." Kiahna angled her face. Why was he talking like this? She'd flown since before he was born. "But not so bad when you go all the time."

"Yeah." He lifted one shoulder and let his gaze fall to the ground. "Sorry about this morning."

"For what?" She fell back on her heels.

"The husband stuff." He lifted his eyes to hers. "I just get sad when you're so far away all day." A few seconds passed. "What if I break my arm? Who'll help me?"

"Ramey, silly."

"She's my 'mergency contact." He pushed the toe of his tennis shoe against her leather loafers. "But I mean the hug part and the singing part. Who'd do that?"

Kiahna hesitated only a moment. This was the part of being a single mom that always made her throat swell—the idea that she couldn't be all things to Max, not while she had a full-time job.

"Well"—she framed his small face with her fingers—"*I* would."

"You'd be somewhere over the ocean." He wasn't arguing with her, only making a point. Sharing a fear she hadn't known he'd had until now.

"Even if we're oceans apart I'll always be right here." She lowered one hand and let her fingers rest on the spot just above his heart. "You know that, right, sport? Remember our song?"

A breath that was more sad than frustrated slipped from him. In a rush of arms and hands and fingers he threw himself into her embrace.

Her voice was a whisper, and she breathed it against his face as she stroked the back of his head. "Come on, sport, right?"

"Right." The word was a defeated huff, but it would have to do.

"Taco Bell tomorrow?"

"Sure."

"You can do better than that." She straightened and made a silly face, hoping she could coax a smile from him before she left. She did an exaggerated pout and mimicked him. "*Sure . . .*"

The hint of a grin broke Max's expression, and before he could stop himself, a giggle followed. "Okay, fine. Taco Bell!" He burst out the word and laughed at his own humor. "Better?"

"Much." She stooped down and kissed his cheek again. "Keep your chin up." When her face was still at his level, she looked straight through to his soul. "I love you, Max. See you tomorrow."

⌒

A faint whistling sound was coming from outside the airplane, and it snapped Kiahna from her memories. They were headed straight for the Pacific Ocean, the pilots unable to pull out of the dive. They had half a minute at best, and Kiahna was using all her strength to keep from tumbling down the aisle and slamming into the cockpit doors.

The news would have to come from Ramey ... the news and the details that would follow. She'd written out her last wishes seven years ago, days after Max's birth. And there was the letter, of course. A different one every year on Max's birthday. But even with all her preparations, she never thought it would come to this.

Don't forget what I told you, sport ... I'm with you ... always with you ... as close as your heart.

For an instant she turned her thoughts toward God. She had loved the Lord all her life, loved Him even when she didn't always understand Him. If this was the end, then she would be with Him in a matter of minutes. *God ... give us a miracle ... or give one to Max. Please, God.*

The screaming and crying around her grew louder, then in the final moments it faded. Kiahna made a desperate attempt to right herself, to stand up so she could calm the craziness in the cabin.

They could still make it, couldn't they? The aircraft could straighten out before impact and settle safely on the surface of the ocean. The Coast Guard would be called out and they'd inflate the emergency slides and rafts. Everything would be okay and she'd tell Max all about it that night. Each seat cushion was a flotation device, right? Wasn't that what they told people every day on this flight?

I love you, Max ... don't forget me.

Her mind jumbled, and then cleared just as quickly, until finally two thoughts remained. As the plane made impact with the water, as the fuselage splintered apart and ocean water gushed into the cabin, it was those two thoughts that became her last.

The thought of Max, and what would become of him after today.

One Tuesday Morning

Karen Kingsbury

I'm a firefighter, God, so I know I've been in some tough places before. But this . . . this not knowing the people I love . . . this is the hardest thing I can imagine.

The last thing Jake Bryan knew was the roar of the World Trade Center collapsing on top of him and his fellow firefighters. The man in the hospital bed remembers nothing. Not rushing with his teammates up the stairway of the south tower to help trapped victims. Not being blasted from the building. And not the woman sitting by his bedside who says she is his wife.

Jamie Bryan will do anything to help her beloved husband regain his memory, and with it their storybook family life with their small daughter, Sierra. But that means helping Jake rediscover the one thing Jamie has never shared with him: his deep faith in God.

Jake's fondest prayer for his wife is about to have an impact beyond anything he could possibly have conceived. *One Tuesday Morning* is a love story like none you have ever read: tender, poignant, commemorating the tragedy and heroism of September 11 and portraying the far-reaching power of God's faithfulness and a good man's love.

Softcover: 0-310-24752-7
Unabridged Audio Pages® CD: 0-310-25402-7

Pick up a copy today at your favorite bookstore!

ZONDERVAN™

GRAND RAPIDS, MICHIGAN 49530 USA

WWW.ZONDERVAN.COM

A Riveting Story of Secret Sin and the Healing Power of Forgiveness

Oceans Apart

Karen Kingsbury

Airline pilot Connor Evans and his wife, Michele, seem to be the perfect couple living what looks like a perfect life. Then a plane goes down in the Pacific Ocean. One of the casualties is Kiahna Siefert, a flight attendant Connor knew well. Too well. Kiahna's will is very clear: before her seven-year-old son, Max, can be turned over to the state, his father must be contacted; the father he's never met, the father who doesn't know he exists: Connor Evans.

Now will the presence of one lonely child and the truth he represents destroy Connor's family? Or is it possible that healing and hope might come in the shape of a seven-year-old boy?

Softcover: 0-310-24749-7

Unabridged Audio Pages® CD: 0-310-25403-5

Pick up a copy today at your favorite bookstore!

ZONDERVAN™

GRAND RAPIDS, MICHIGAN 49530 USA

WWW.ZONDERVAN.COM

We want to hear from you. Please send your comments about this book to us in care of zreview@zondervan.com. Thank you.

GRAND RAPIDS, MICHIGAN 49530 USA

WWW.ZONDERVAN.COM